A CAMPER'S GUIDE TO OREGON & WASHINGTON

A GUIDE TO THE REGION'S IMPROVED CAMPGROUNDS

A CAMPER'S GUIDE TO OREGON & WASHINGTON

A GUIDE TO THE REGION'S IMPROVED CAMPGROUNDS

By KiKi Canniff

Illustrations by Janora Bayot

Ki² Enterprises
P.O. Box 13322
Portland, OR 97213

Library of Congress Cataloging-in-Publication Data

Canniff, KiKi
A camper's guide to Oregon & Washington: a guide to the
region's improved campgrounds / by KiKi Canniff; illustrations
by Janora Bayot.   p.   cm.
Rev. ed. of: A camper's guide to Oregon & Washington. ©1988.
Includes index.
ISBN 0-941361-02-0 $12.95
1. Camp sites, facilities, etc. -- Oregon -- Directories. 2. Camp
sites, facilities, etc. -- Washington (State) -- Directories.
I. Title. II. Title: Camper's guide to Oregon and Washington.
GV191.42.07C36   1991
647'.94795 09--dc20   91-3138 CIP

ISBN #0-941361-02-0

Ki² Enterprises
P.O. Box 13322
Portland, Oregon 97213

TABLE OF CONTENTS

INTRODUCTION

This is the only guide to Oregon and Washington campgrounds written by a Northwest resident. **A Camper's Guide to Oregon & Washington**'s improved campgrounds was first published in 1988; this is the second edition.

Together, Oregon and Washington have more than 2,000 individual campgrounds. Those listed in this book are the "improved" campgrounds; those that have improved facilities and charge a fee for overnight use. You will find those campgrounds that do not charge a fee detailed in **Free Campgrounds of Washington & Oregon**. Free campgrounds generally offer very minimal facilities.

Improved campgrounds in Oregon and Washington offer a variety of facilities. You will find full utility hookups, swimming pools, hot tubs, game rooms, showers, laundry facilities, boat rental, charter fishing and more at some; while others provide little more than picnic tables, fire pits and primitive toilet facilities. The price of an overnight stay ranges from less than $1.00 to more than $20.00. Each type of campground affords a different type of experience. This book was designed to help you locate the type of camping experience you desire.

In order to provide the best information, Ki2 books do not carry advertisements. All campgrounds receive the same treatment; no matter what their advertising budget. I have attempted to include all the improved campgrounds located in Oregon and Washington but if you come across any I've missed, please let me know. I will try to add them to future editions. I have made every effort to insure that the information provided is accurate. However, time brings changes so if you visit a listed campground and find the facilities differ please let me know. Updated information may be sent to me at Ki[2] Enterprises, P.O. Box 13322, Portland, Oregon 97213.

Happy camping!
KiKi Canniff
Author

HOW TO USE THIS BOOK

Start by reading the opening chapter. It will give you information about the variety of elevations, terrains, scenery and climates campers can enjoy in Oregon and Washington along with tips on avoiding rain. It also explains who the major campground operators are and what facilities you can expect to find at their campsites.

Each state's campground listings opens with a map. This will help you to locate the general area you plan to visit. These maps were not intended for navigation; you can get a full-size highway map free from either state's tourism office. The grid coordinates are also printed beside each city's listing to help you to find other cities within the area you plan to visit.

Campgrounds are then listed alphabetically by city. Each individual listing begins with the campground name followed by that of its operating agency. Next, you will find a brief, but complete, listing of facilities. The type of toilet is listed only when it differs from the normal facilities offered by that agency. At the end of the facilities line you will find one, two, or three dollar signs; $ tells you it is less than $5, $$ means $5 to $10, and $$$ more than $10. The final information consists of simply stated directions. FSR has been substituted for Forest Service Road and CR for County Road.

For your convenience, an alphabetical listing of all the campgrounds in this book can be found in the campground index at the back of the book. This can be used to quickly find campgrounds you know by name.

CAMPING IN OREGON & WASHINGTON

Camping in Oregon and Washington offers an opportunity to enjoy the real Northwest experience, getting in touch with nature. This enchanting corner has it all. Picturesque ocean beaches, rugged mountain ranges, lush old growth forests, world renowned fishing, crystal clear high mountain lakes, sun drenched desert landscapes, snow capped peaks, an array of geological wonders, restful small towns and bustling big cities can all be found.

This is a land where getting close to nature is always within reach. The Northwest's outstanding physical features and wildlife are what attracted the first settlers; and although civilization has brought many changes to the area, much of the landscape remains uncluttered.

Throughout the Pacific Northwest large parcels of land have been set aside as public lands and wilderness areas so that you, and future generations, might enjoy the same experience that enticed those early pioneers and explorers. This preserved much of the area's early history .

There are many similarities in these two states. The Cascade Mountain Range divides them both from north to south. The western sides of both states offer summers where beautiful sunny weather comes mixed with rain. It's this same rainfall however, that gives this part of the states the lush green beauty that brings visitors from all over the world. The drier, eastern half of the two states is hot and dry all summer long. Summer temperatures on both sides of the mountains are often over 90°, while higher elevations can see nighttime temperatures below 40°.

Archaeological digs have unearthed proof that people have lived in this area for more than 9,000 years. Other discoveries have documented prehistoric plant and animal life as well as flooding by a great inland sea. Volcanos and ice age glaciers have sculpted much of this land's present terrain. Settled in the 1800s, Indians roamed this land freely until about 100 years ago. Their culture is still very visible. They knew how to hide from the rain and bad weather, and many of the most popular campgrounds and recreational areas exist in areas where they once had their winter camps.

CAMPING IN OREGON

In Oregon practically all of the Pacific Ocean's beaches are public land. The variety of these coastal playgrounds include spots where the mountains reach the shore, beaches that range from sparkling white sands to agate strewn or black sand beaches, tidal pools and secluded coves.

The southern Oregon coast harbors the state's "banana belt", the wild Rogue River and one of the world's largest coastal dune areas. The northern coast has historic lighthouses, wildlife refuges, estuaries, Indian shell mounds, spouting horns, whale watching and a number of interesting seaside towns.

When fog blankets the Oregon coast you can often escape its clutches with a short drive eastward, into the mountains. There you will encounter rushing streams, forested lands, wildlife and quiet towns. Campgrounds are plentiful both near the beach and in the mountains.

Oregon's I-5 corridor is the most often used route for travelers in a hurry. Yet just off its asphalt expanse a myriad of experiences beckon. Along the corridor you'll encounter heavily forested mountain passes, scenic valleys, historic towns, thriving cities, spectacular views and access routes to a half dozen National Forests. Most of the state's dozens of covered bridges are within a short drive as well. Wildlife is abundant and history, if you know where to look, is easy to view.

The southern portion of the I-5 corridor harbors Crater Lake National Park, Oregon Caves National Monument, the mind boggling Oregon Vortex, historic Jacksonville, and many great fishing streams. In the northern portion you'll discover pristine wilderness areas, 11,235' Mt. Hood, the scenic Columbia River Gorge, the first incorporated city west of the Rocky Mountains, the state's capitol city and its largest city. Even the biggest towns have rugged campgrounds within an hours drive and RV parks are everywhere.

The eastern side of the Cascade Mountain Range and central Oregon offer plenty of sunshine. The sheer height of these mountains snags most rain clouds causing them to dump their rain before they can ascend. This creates a desert environment where campers can retreat when the western side is too wet for their plans.

The largest collection of volcanic remains in the continental United States can be found in the southern half of central Oregon. Ice caves, lava cast forests, obsidian flows, lava fissures, lava cracks, and beautiful Newberry Crater are all fun to visit. The John Day Fossil Beds, Smith Rock's mountain climbers, sun bleached ghost towns, plus the Deschutes, Metolius, Crooked and Columbia Rivers entice you north.

Cross Oregon to its very eastern edge and you'll find yet another experience waiting. It is here, in the very northeast corner, that you'll encounter what residents refer to as the Little Switzerland of America. Hell's Canyon, the world's deepest canyon, guards its eastern border. Two National Forests occupy much of this land and a number of recreation areas and wilderness lands protect its use. The southeast corner shelters a 30 mile long, 4 mile wide, lava flow filled with obsidian, agate and petrified wood plus Leslie Gulch Canyon. Lake Owyhee and lots of great rockhounding areas can also be found there.

CAMPING IN WASHINGTON
A camping outing in Washington has plenty of rewards too. The northern portion of its Pacific Ocean coastline hides America's last unspoiled wilderness beach. Together, Olympic National Park and Olympic National Forest protect most of the area's best natural features. This section's rain forests, old growth trees, wildlife refuges, whale watching viewpoints, hiking trails, pristine lakes and unique plants are all worth investigating.

Along the southern Washington coast you'll encounter the world's longest driveable beach, historic Forts Columbia and Canby, sheltered bays, aging lighthouses, colorful cranberry bogs, charter fishing boats, and lots of great beachcombing areas.

A trip along Washington's I-5 corridor will give you access to many of the state's better known attractions. These include Mt. St. Helens, where you can view and visit an active volcano; Mt. Rainier National Park, which protects the 14,410' Mt. Rainier; Hood Canal; Puget Sound; the spectacular San Juan Islands; and the western beginnings for the famed Cascade Loop.

History is easy to enjoy at Port Townsend, Coupeville, Snohomish, and Fort Lewis to name just a few sites. The I-5 corridor and its surrounding land also harbors both Washington's capitol city Olympia, and Seattle, the state's largest. At 55-65 mph it all goes by in a quick blur but anyone taking the time to leave the freeway will find lots to see and plenty of great camping areas.

Heading east over the Cascade Mountain Range, toward central Washington, you'll find a slightly drier climate. Less rain falls east of the mountains since clouds heavy with moisture must empty before making the ascent. These mountains do not run due north and south, so you'll find some of the cities in this section actually sit on the western slopes.

The full glory of northern Washington's Cascade Loop unfolds here. Most of the land it passes by is protected by National Forests and Parks. Along the way you'll have the chance to visit pristine wilderness areas, a bald eagle sanctuary, recreational lakes, a multitude of hiking trails and two unique villages. A visit to Winthrop is like a trip to the old west; Leavenworth is situated high in the Cascades and resembles a Bavarian village.

As you leave the Cascade Mountains, heading east, you will find a dry, desert climate. Recreation here generally centers around lakes and rivers. Moses Lake, Lake Conconully, Roosevelt Lake and the Columbia River are four good spots. Geological wonders like Dry Falls and Ginkgo Petrified Forest provide a look at prehistoric

Washington. More recent historical attractions include Indian rock paintings, ghost towns, small town museums and displays.

Washington's most eastern portion holds the state's largest limestone cave, the reconstructed 1880 Fort Spokane, Indian caves, and the tragic remains of Whitman Mission. Water oriented camping is popular here too and much activity is centered along the Snake, Columbia and Pend Oreille Rivers. Spokane is this region's largest city and offers a wide range of recreational opportunities.

CAMPGROUND OPERATORS
National Park Service
The National Park Service provides campground facilities at Washington's Mount Rainier, Olympic and North Cascades National Parks, as well as Oregon's Crater Lake National Park. National Parks were established at these locations to regulate land use toward the conservation of wildlife, scenery, natural and historic objects for the enjoyment of future generations.

Fees are charged for entrance to most National Park areas. Although camping permits are not required for the campgrounds listed in this book, anyone who wants to backpack and/or camp in the less traveled portions of these lands must obtain a Backcountry Use Permit. These permits help to regulate visitor use and are cost free. Handicapped visitors and those over the age of 62 should inquire about Golden Eagle and Golden Age Passports.

Mount Rainier National Park protects a 14,410' mountain that harbors more glaciers than any other single mountain in the continental United States. Sunrise, the highest point in the park open to automobiles is at 6,400'. To get higher, you'll need to hike some of the park's 305 miles of trails. These range from sort family hikes to one 95 mile route that completely circles the mountain.

This land is inhabited by bears, mountain goats, deer, elk, mountain lions, beavers, marmots, rabbits and raccoons. Waterfalls, ice caves, wildflowers, undisturbed wildernesses and crisp mountain lakes add to its beauty. Lower elevation campgrounds are open from late May thru October, higher elevation camps do not open until late June and close in late September.

Improved camps offer piped water, flush toilets, picnic tables, fireplaces, garbage pickup and have a 14 day limit. Nighttime temperatures drop to 40° throughout the summer and many trails are not completely free of snow until mid-July. Call (206)569-2211 or write Mt. Rainier National Park, Tahoma Woods - Star Route, Ashford, WA 98304 for more information.

The Olympic National Park protects two distinct areas on Washington's Olympic Peninsula. The first, a 57 mile stretch of wild Pacific Ocean coastline, contains a unique coastal rain forest. Hiking in this area will reveal foaming sea stacks, undisturbed tidepools and perhaps a glimpse of harbor seals, river otters or migrating gray whales. The second area is nearly surrounded by the Olympic National Forest and covers a magnificent region of glacier-clad peaks, alpine meadows, cascading streams and virgin forests.

An average annual rainfall of 140" creates lush vegetation and enormous trees. No firearms are allowed in the Olympic National Park and no pets or motorized vehicles are allowed on the trails. Most trails are open to pack and saddle horses. Park campgrounds offer picnic tables, fireplaces, piped water and toilet facilities.

A 25 mile drive around scenic Lake Quinault, three temperate rain forests, abundant wildlife and the view from atop Hurricane Ridge provide visitors with plenty of things to see. An entry fee is charged at some sites during the summer. Visitor centers can be found at Port Angeles, Lake Crescent and the Hoh Rain Forest; park headquarters are located at 600 East Park Avenue, Port Angeles, WA 98362 or call (206)452-0330.

North Cascades National Park encompasses 1,053 square miles of alpine scenery. You can explore deep glaciated canyons, frozen glaciers, stark jagged peaks, ice cold mountain lakes and streams, or perhaps see a mountain goat, deer, wolverine, cougar or moose. Four district units; North, South, Ross Lake and Lake Chelan National Recreation Areas are included within the park.

Year round ranger stations are operated at Marblemount, Stehekin, Chelan and during the summer at Concrete too. The only road into this area is the Cascade River Road which extends from Marblemount to below Cascade Pass. The best weather occurs between mid-June and late-September, although summer storms are not uncommon. Snow is off all but the higher trails by July, and you'll generally find less rain on the eastern side of the mountains. For further information write North Cascades National Park, Marblemount, WA 98267 or call (206)873-4590.

Oregon's Crater Lake National Park is situated on the crest of the Cascade Mountain Range, 80 miles northeast of Medford. This spot was once the site of a 12,000' volcano, Mount Mazama,. It was destroyed nearly 7,000 years ago by successive flows of molten rock. Centuries of rain water and melting snows have filled its caldera with water creating the United States' deepest lake. Additional volcanic activity later caused Wizard Island to appear in its crystal clear pool.

At its greatest depth Crater Lake reaches nearly 2,000', making it the seventh deepest lake in the world. Eagles, deer, bears, coyote, porcupine, bobcat, elk, fox and cougar frequent the area. Trails access the land allowing panoramic vistas, wildflower filled meadows and crisp mountain air to unfold to the hardy hiker. For further information call (503)594-2211 or write Crater Lake National Park, P.O. Box 7, Crater Lake, OR 97604.

Coulee Dam National Recreation Area
The Coulee Dam National Recreation Area consists of Roosevelt Lake and a 660 mile long narrow strip of land adjacent to the lake shore. Roosevelt Lake was created by the construction of Grand Coulee Dam, the largest and most important dam on the Columbia River. The lake's western shore offers very little shade and is generally

warm and sunny; the north portion tends to be forested and cooler.

The lake is at its maximum level by early July and remains that way thru Labor Day. Water skiing is popular, sailing is excellent and fish abundant. Summertime temperatures range from a daytime high of 75-100° to a nighttime low of 50-60°. Deer, coyotes, marmots, porcupine and an occasional bear are spotted.

Recent archaeological excavations have unearthed evidence that people have lived in this area for more than 9,000 years. Fort Spokane, a reconstructed 1880s army post, relates the more recent past belonging to America's colorful frontier period. Additional information may be obtained by visiting park headquarters in Coulee Dam or by writing to P.O. Box 37, Coulee Dam, WA 99116.

National Forest Service
There are nineteen National Forests in Oregon and Washington. No matter where you go, you're always within a few hours drive of at least one National Forest, sometimes two or three. This public land provides recreational land for camping, hiking, picnics, boating, fishing, swimming, mountain climbing, skiing and more.

A quick visit to any National Forest ranger station will provide you with current information on area trails, weather, special attractions and avoiding crowds. Although there are no entrance fees for National Forests most improved campgrounds charge a fee. Lower elevation campgrounds are open year round and high country camps from about mid-June thru August, depending upon weather. Improved campgrounds generally offer designated spaces, drinking water, road access, toilet facilities, and firepits. Many campgrounds are accessible to the physically challenged. Group campsites are available in some areas. Boat ramps, picnic areas and visitor centers are free.

Maps of each National Forest showing roads, trails, camps and natural areas are available for a small cost. For further information contact the Pacific Northwest Regional Headquarters, 319 SW Pine Street (P.O. Box 3623), Portland, OR 97208, (503)326-2877. They can also supply details on their participation in the National Park Golden Eagle/Age Passport and how to obtain camp stamps.

Oregon's National Forests include Deschutes, Fremont, Malheur, Mt. Hood, Ochoco, Rogue River, Siskiyou, Siuslaw, Umatilla, Umpqua, Wallowa-Whitman, Willamette and Winema. Washington's are Colville, Gifford Pinchot, Mt. Baker-Snoqualmie, Okanogan, Olympic and Wenatchee. These lands encompass some of the region's best recreational areas. Many also protect and regulate roadless wilderness lands where backpackers can enjoy a pristine wilderness adventure.

Visitors to wilderness areas must obtain a permit for overnight trips; some overused areas also require permits for all day journeys. A stop at the local ranger station will get you full details on these free permits and information that will allow you to avoid crowded areas and travel as a minimum impact visitor.

Bureau of Land Management
The Bureau of Land Management (BLM) manages 15.7 million acres in Oregon. Recreational lands are scattered throughout the state with district offices located in Salem, Eugene, Roseburg, Coos Bay, Medford, Lakeview, Prineville, Burns, Baker and Vale. Several white water rivers flow through this land, including the Deschutes, John Day, Grande Ronde, Owyhee and Rogue Rivers. Areas for off-road vehicles are also provided. The gathering for personal use of rocks, minerals, gemstones, berries, nuts and flowers is okay. Permits are required for large collections. Historic and related artifacts must be left undisturbed.

Unless posted otherwise, the maximum stay in BLM campgrounds is 14 days. Facilities generally include drinking water, picnic tables, toilets, firepits and recreational opportunities. National Park Golden Eagle/Age Passport holders receive a discount on fees. The region's BLM headquarters are located at 1300 NE 44th Avenue (P.O. Box 2965), Portland, OR 97208, (503)231-6274.

Oregon State Parks
Oregon State Parks manages most of the state's Pacific Ocean beaches; some as day-use areas and others as campgrounds. Other state park campgrounds are situated along rivers and lakes, or near natural attractions. A few are open year round; others from mid-April to late October. Most have flush toilets, showers, picnic tables and firepits; many have full utility hookups.

During the summer, a campsite with full utilities is $14.00, those with electrical hookups are $13.00, tent sites $10.00, primitive sites $8.00, overnight moorage $5.00 per night and hiker/biker campgrounds $2.00 per person. Group campsites are $30.00 with advance reservation required.

Reservations are also taken by mail for 13 high use camps in Brookings, Coos Bay, Culver, Detroit, Florence, Hammond, Joseph, Lincoln City, Newport, Prineville, Tillamook and Waldport. For further information, and reservation applications, write Oregon State Parks, 525 Trade Street SE, Salem, OR 97310 or call (503)238-7488. The summertime toll free number within Oregon is (800)452-5687.

Washington State Parks
Nearly 100 Washington State Parks offer camping. Most provide flush toilets, hot showers, picnic tables, firepits, garbage service, running water, utility hookups, and have a 10 day maximum stay. Parks featuring picnic areas offer tables, piped water, fireplaces/stoves and shelters; some also have kitchens. Sites with interpretive displays focus on historical or geological events.

Many of these campgrounds are open year round; others from April 1 thru September 30. Most parks offer facilities which meet barrier-free guidelines for accessibility. The fee for standard campsites is $7.00, an additional $2.50 is charged for utility hookups. Campers from states where an out of state surcharge is levied are required to pay the same surcharge. Primitive campsites, those which cannot accommodate a motorized vehicle, range from $3.00 to $4.50 a night. Summer boat camping at one of the many moorage areas will cost you $4.00 to $6.00 per night depending on the length of your craft. Horses are permitted only in designated areas and pets must be leashed at all times.

For further information write the Washington State Parks & Recreation Commission, 7150 Cleanwater Lane - KY11, Olympia, WA 98504-5711, or call (206)753-2027.

Private Campground Operators
Private campgrounds, along with a couple of campgrounds operated by agencies like the Corp of Engineers, Pacific Power and some counties, provide the balance of improved campgrounds.

Private campgrounds sometimes offer the most deluxe facilities. Swimming pools, hot tubs, saunas, game rooms, full utility hookups, cable tv and laundry facilities are among the amenities offered. Most provide accommodations for RVs and some do not permit tents. Rates for individual sites range from $5.00 to more than $20.00 depending upon location and facilities. These campgrounds are operated by individuals, families and businesses. Most take reservations and phone numbers have been provided within the listings.

GETTING THE MOST OUT OF YOUR CAMPING EXPERIENCE
Planning ahead is the best way to avoid hassles. Those new to the area will want to start by contacting each state's tourism office. Besides general and camping information, ask about receiving a calendar of annual events, map and specific information on attractions geared toward your interests (fishing, hiking, history, etc.). In Washington you can call (206)586-2088 or 586-2102. For information on Oregon call (800)233-3306 from within the state or (800)547-7842 from outside the state.

Next, check with your local bookstore for some good regional guidebooks; those that pertain only to the northwest corner. Something published within the area, or written by someone who lives there, will generally show you more. These can be especially helpful when you're looking for information on a specific type of attraction or worthwhile sites that most visitors overlook. Upon comparison, you will generally find that a book which tries to cover more than a couple of states in one volume includes far less specific information than something devoted strictly to the area. Books that do not carry advertising or charge businesses for their listings are also more likely to give you an unbiased look at available attractions.

With all of this information in hand, you're ready to plan your trip. Keep your schedule flexible, this will allow you to escape an extended bout of wet weather by fleeing to the drier side of the mountains. You'll find plenty of campgrounds on either side. Start by listing your "must see" spots. Hitting these sights first will help you to remain flexible. Then, if the weather changes, you can check your list and head elsewhere.

Campers who live here year round always pack for a variety of weather conditions and so should you. Having warm clothes along will make gray skies seem sunny because it won't slow you down. You may actually find that the cooler weather makes hiking and other strenuous activities less so. Wet weather is also great for visiting museums and other inside attractions.

WHERE TO FIND OREGON'S IMPROVED CAMPGROUNDS

OREGON MAP

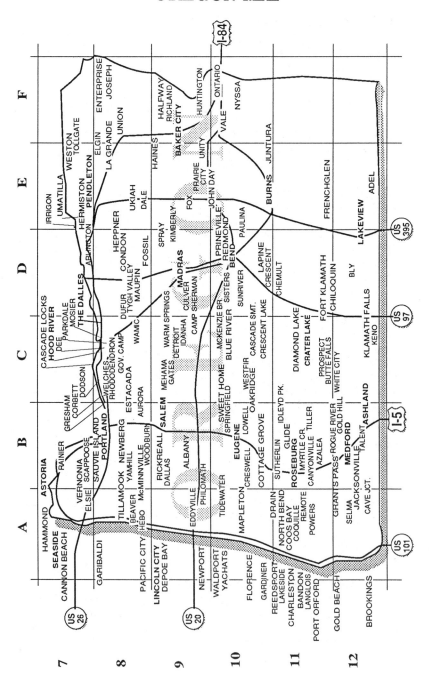

ADEL (E-12)

ADEL STORE & RV PARK (Private)
7 trailer sites w/hookups for water/electricity/sewer, no tents, reservations - (503)947-3850, groceries, nearby fishing, $-$$$. In Adel. Located in Adel at store.

ALBANY (B-9)

ALBANY TRAILER PARK (Private)
22 trailer sites w/hookups for water/electricity/sewer, trailers to 35', no tents, reservations - (503)928-8532, showers, laundry, groceries, $$$.
East of Albany. Take I-5 south to Viewcrest exit #237, east to Century Drive, follow this 3.0 miles to trailer park.

BABE THE BLUE OX RV PARK (Private)
100 trailer sites w/hookups for water/electricity/sewer, reservations - (503)926-2886, showers, laundry, groceries, $$$.
In Albany. Leave I-5 on exit #233 and head east to Price Road. Campground is located at 4000 Blue Ox Drive.

CORVALLIS-ALBANY KOA (Private)
53 campsites, 26 w/hookups for water/electricity/sewer, 14 pull-thru sites w/hookups for electricity, plus 13 tent sites, reservations - (503)967-8521, showers, groceries, tv, laundry, playground, mini golf, heated pool, $$-$$$.
Southwest of Albany. Take exit #228 off I-5 and drive 5.0 miles west on State 34 to Oakville Road, follow this south to campground.

SUNNYSIDE PARK (Linn County)
138 campsites, 62 w/hookups for water/electricity, information - (503)967-3917, picnic shelter, showers, lake, boat launch, hiking, fishing, swimming, $$-$$$.
Southeast of Albany. Take US 20 east 27.0 miles to Quartzville Drive. Campground is located on Foster Lake.

ARLINGTON (D-7)

TERRACE HEIGHTS MOTOR HOME PARK (Private)
10 trailer sites w/hookups for water/electricity/sewer, reservations - (503)454-2757, showers, laundry, cable tv, $$$.
In Arlington. Leave I-84 at Arlington exit #137, take Main Street .5 mile south to motor home park.

ASHLAND (B-12)

CAMPERS COVE (Private)
25 trailer units w/hookups for water/electricity/sewer, reservations - (503)482-1201, showers, ice, lake, swimming, fishing, boat launch, hiking, elev. 5000', $$$.
Southeast of Ashland. I-5 south to State 66, east 18.0 miles to Hyatt Lake Road, northeast 3.0 miles to Hyatt Prairie Road, north 1.5 miles to campground.

EMIGRANT CAMPGROUND (Jackson County)
40 campsites, reservation information - (503)776-7001, showers, laundry, trailer waste disposal, lake, fishing, boat launch, boat rental, swimming, playground, hiking, $$.
Southeast of Ashland. I-5 south to State 66, east 5.0 miles to campground.

GLENYAN KOA (Private)
68 campsites, 11 w/hookups for water/electricity/sewer, 35 w/hookups for water/electricity, plus 22 w/hookups for water only, reservations - (503)482-4138, showers, laundry, groceries, trailer waste disposal, swimming pool, pond, fishing, playground, $$$.
Southeast of Ashland. I-5 south to State 66, east 3.5 miles to campground.

GRIZZLY CAMPGROUND (Jackson County)
36 campsites, trailers to 25', lake, fishing, boat launch, hiking, elev. 4500', $.
East of Ashland. I-5 south to State 66, after 1.0 mile follow Dead Indian Road 20.0 miles east, Hyatt Prairie Road 2.0 miles south to campground.

HOWARD PRAIRIE LAKE RESORT (Private)
300 campsites, 60 w/hookups for water/electricity/sewer, 90 w/hookups for water/electricity, plus 150 tent units, information - (503)482-1979, showers, laundry, groceries, trailer waste disposal, lake, swimming, fishing, boat launch, boat rental, hiking, wheelchair access, elev. 4500', $$.
East of Ashland. I-5 south to State 66, after 1.0 mile follow Dead Indian Road 20.0 miles east, Hyatt Prairie Road 3.5 miles south to campground.

HYATT LAKE (BLM)
25 units, trailers okay, picnic area w/shelter, drinking water, boat launch, boating, hiking, fishing, swimming, nature study, elev. 5000', $-$$.
Southeast of Ashland. State 66 east 16.0 miles, then take East Hyatt Lake Road 4.0 miles north to campground.

HYATT LAKE RESORT (Private)
25 campsites, trailers okay, no hookups, reservations - (503)482-3331, showers, wheelchair access, ice, trailer waste disposal, lake, fishing, boat launch & rental, playground, restaurant, gasoline, hiking, $$.
Southeast of Ashland. I-5 to State 66, east 18.0 miles to Hyatt Lake Road, northeast 3.0 miles to Hyatt Prairie Road, north 1.0 mile.

JACKSON HOT SPRING (Private)
52 campsites, 14 w/hookups for water/electricity/sewer, 13 w/hookups for water/electricity, plus 25 tent units, information - (503)482-3776, showers, laundry, ice, mineral water swimming pool & baths, $$-$$$.
North of Ashland. I-5 to exit #19, South Valley View Road .5 mile southwest to campground.

LILY GLEN CAMPGROUND (Jackson County)
15 campsites, some group sites, reservation information - (503)776-7001, lake, fishing, hiking, $.
East of Ashland. I-5 south to State 66, after 1.0 mile follow Dead Indian Road 21.0 miles east.

SUGAR PINE (Jackson County)
11 group campsites, reservations - (503)776-7001, lake, swimming, fishing, boat launch, hiking, elev. 4500', $$$.
East of Ashland. I-5 south to State 66, after 1.0 mile follow Dead Indian Road 20.0 miles east, Hyatt Prairie Road 2.0 miles south to campground.

WILLOW POINT CAMPGROUND (Jackson County)
30 campsites, reservation information - (503)776-7001, lake, swimming, fishing, boat launch, hiking, elev. 5000', $$.
East of Ashland. I-5 south to State 66, after 1.0 mile follow Dead Indian Road 20.0 miles east, Hyatt Prairie Road 5.0 miles south to campground.

ASTORIA (A-7)

ASTORIA KOA (Private)
100 campsites w/hookups for water/electricity/sewer, reservations - (503)861-2606, showers, laundry, groceries, swimming pool, spa, satellite tv, playground, $$-$$$.
West of Astoria. Located approximately 10.0 miles west of Astoria, across from Fort Stevens.

FORT STEVENS (Oregon State Park)

605 campsites, 213 w/hookups for water/electricity/sewer, 130 w/hookups for electricity, plus 262 tent units, mail reservations available, maximum site 69', group campsites, wheelchair access, picnic area, historical museum, self-guided walking tour, remains of Civil War era fort, showers, trailer waste disposal, boat launch, swimming, fishing, ocean beach access, beachcombing bicycle trail, hiking trails, $-$$$.
West of Astoria. Campground is located 10.0 miles west of Astoria, off US 101, near Warrenton.

KAMPERS WEST KAMPGROUND RV PARK (Private)

200 campsites, 100 w/hookups for water/electricity/cable tv, plus 100 tent units, reservation information - (503)861-1814, showers, laundry, ice, trailer waste disposal, river, fishing, $$.
West of Astoria. Campground is located 10.0 miles west of Astoria, off US 101. Follow the Warrenton/Fort Stevens signs, campground is located at 1140 NW Warrenton Drive.

AURORA (B-8)

ISEBERG PARK RV (Private)

84 campsites w/hookups for water/electricity/sewer, tents okay, reservations - (503)678-2646, showers, laundry, groceries, trailer waste disposal, rec room, miniature golf, hiking, $$$.
West of Aurora. Leave I-5 at exit #278 and look for signs.

AZALEA (B-11)

MEADOW WOOD RV RESORT & CAMPGROUND (Private)

63 trailer sites w/hookups for water/electricity, reservation information - (503)832-2959, showers, laundry, groceries, trailer waste disposal, swimming pool, playground, $$$.
Southwest of Azalea. I-5 south 9.0 miles to exit #86, Frontage Road 4.0 miles south to 862 Autumn Lane, Glendale.

BAKER CITY (E-9)

LARIAT MOTEL & RV PARK (Private)

21 campsites w/hookups for water/electricity/sewer/cable tv, showers, laundry, nearby fishing, $$.
In Baker City. Located at 880 Elm Street.

MOUNTAIN VIEW HOLIDAY TRAV-L-PARK (Private)
60 campsites, 52 w/hookups for water/electricity/sewer, plus 8 tent units, reservations - (503)523-4824, showers, laundry, trailer waste disposal, swimming pool, playground, cable tv, groceries, $$-$$$.
In Baker City. Leave I-84 on exit #304 and travel west .5 mile on Campbell, 1.0 mile north on Cedar, and 1.0 mile west on Hughes Lane to campground.

UNION CREEK CAMPGROUND (Private)
58 campsites, 24 w/hookups for water/electricity, plus 34 w/hookups for electricity, trailers to 22', group sites, piped water, flush toilets, trailer waste disposal, wheelchair access, boat gasoline, ice, boat launch, boating, swimming, fishing, water skiing, hiking, adjacent to Phillips Reservoir, bicycling, boat rentals, elev. 4100', $$-$$$.
Southwest of Baker City. State 7 south 20.0 miles.

BANDON (A-11)

BLUE JAY CAMPGROUND (Private)
40 campsites, 2 w/hookups for water/electricity/sewer, 2 w/hookups for water/electricity, 16 w/hookups for electricity, plus 20 tent units, reservation information - (503)347-3258, showers $$-$$$.
South of Bandon. US 101 south 4.0 miles, Scenic Beach Loop Drive .5 mile west to campground.

BULLARDS BEACH (Oregon State Park)
192 campsites, 92 w/hookups for water/electricity/sewer, plus 100 w/hookups for electricity, maximum site 64', picnic area, wheelchair access, showers, trailer waste disposal, boat launch, fishing, horse trails & camp facilities, ocean access, beachcombing, 1896 Coquille Lighthouse, $$-$$$.
North of Bandon. US 101 north 1.0 mile to campground.

DRIFTWOOD SHORES RV PARK (Private)
40 trailer sites w/hookups for water/electricity/sewer, reservation information - (503)347-4122, showers, laundry, groceries, trailer waste disposal, $$-$$$.
In Bandon. Located 1 block west of US 101 junction with State 42 at 935 E. 2nd Street.

BEAVER (A-8)

CAMPER COVE (Private)
17 campsites, 12 w/hookups for water/electricity/sewer, plus 5 tent units, trailers to 35', reservation information - (503)398-5334, showers, laundry, trailer waste disposal, river, trout fishing, meeting hall, hiking, $$-$$$.
North of Beaver. US 101 north 2.5 miles.

BEND (D-10)

BEND KOA (Private)
100 campsites, 50 w/hookups for water/electricity/sewer/cable tv, plus 50 w/hookups for water/electricity, tents okay, reservations - (503)382-7728, showers, laundry, groceries, gas, propane, pond, fishing, playground, $$$.
North of Bend. US 97 north 2.0 miles.

CRANE PRAIRIE RESORT (Private)
38 campsites w/hookups for water/electricity/sewer, tents okay, reservation information -(503)382-2787, boat & motor rentals, boat ramp, tackle shop, small store, boat gas, guide service, trout fishing, on Crane Prairie Reservoir, $$-$$$.
Southwest of Bend. Take Cascades Highway to Crane Prairie Reservoir and campground.

CROWN VILLA RV PARK (Private)
126 trailer sites, 106 w/hookups for water/electricity/sewer/cable tv, plus 20 w/hookups for electricity, no tents, reservations - (503)388-1131, showers, laundry, ice, trailer waste disposal, pond, bicycle rentals, playground, wheelchair access, nearby golf, $$$.
Southeast of Bend. US 97 south just past city limits, 2.0 miles southeast on Brosterhaus Road.

ELK LAKE (Deschutes National Forest)
22 units, trailers to 22', picnic area, piped water, lake - speed limits, boating, swimming, fishing, elev 4900', $$.
Southwest of Bend. State 46 southwest 20.0 miles, CR 46 south 11.5 miles to campground.

LITTLE FAWN (Deschutes National Forest)
28 units, 5 group sites, reservations required - (503)388-5664, trailers to 22', on Elk Lake - speed limits, boat launch, boating, swimming, fishing, elev. 4900', $$.
Southwest of Bend. State 46 southwest 20.0 miles, CR 46 south 11.3 miles, FSR 4625 southeast 2.1 miles to campground.

JOHN'S RV PARK (Private)
30 campsites w/hookups for water/electricity/sewer/cable tv, no tents, reservation information - (503)382-6206, showers, laundry, $$-$$$.
At Bend. US 97 south, located near city limits 2.5 miles south of junction with US 20.

POINT (Deschutes National Forest)
9 units, trailers to 22', piped water, on Elk Lake - speed limits, boating, swimming, fishing, elev. 4900', $$.
Southwest of Bend. State 46 southwest 20.0 miles, CR 46 south 13.0 miles to campground.

QUINN MEADOW HORSE CAMP (Deschutes National Forest)
26 units, reservations required - (503)388-5664, trailers to 18', well, stream, fishing, hiking & horse trails, elev. 5100', $.
Southwest of Bend. State 46 southwest 20.0 miles, CR 46 south 10.0 miles, FRS 450 .3 mile southeast.

TUMALO (Oregon State Park)
88 campsites, 20 w/hookups for water/electricity/sewer, plus 68 tent units, maximum site 44', group campsites, showers, fishing, hiking trails, $$-$$$.
Northwest of Bend. US 20 northwest 5.0 miles to campground.

BLUE RIVER (C-10)

DELTA (Willamette National Forest)
39 units, trailers to 22', picnic area, well, river, wheelchair access, fishing, old growth nature trail, elev. 1200', $$-$$$.
East of Blue River. State 126 east 3.5 miles, FSR 19 south .3 mile, FSR 194 west .7 mile.

FRENCH PETE (Willamette National Forest)
17 units, trailers to 18', well, river, wheelchair access, boating, swimming, fishing, water skiing, hiking, elev. 2000', $$-$$$.
Southeast of Blue River. State 126 east 3.5 miles, FSR 19 south 11.0 miles.

FRISSELL CROSSING (Willamette National Forest)
12 units, trailers to 18', well, river, fishing, hiking, elev. 2600', $-$$.
Southeast of Blue River. State 126 east 3.5 miles, FSR 19 south 23.0 miles.

HORSE CREEK (Willamette National Forest)
42 units, trailers to 22', group sites - reservations required (503)854-3366, well, fishing, elev. 1400', $$-$$$.
Southeast of Blue River. State 126 east .2 mile, CR 161 southeast 5.1 miles.

LAZY DAZE MOTOR HOME PARK (Private)
23 trailer sites w/hookups for water/electricity/sewer/cable tv, reservations - (503)822-3889, showers, laundry, river, fishing, $$.
East of Blue River. State 126 east 1.5 miles.

MONA (Willamette National Forest)
23 units, trailers to 22', piped water, river, flush toilets, wheelchair access, boat launch, boating, swimming, fishing, water skiing, elev. 1400', $$-$$$.
Northeast of Blue River. State 126 east 2.0 miles, FSR 15 northeast 3.9 miles, FSR 15120 south .3 mile.

PATIO RV PARK (Private)
66 trailers sites, 44 w/hookups for water/electricity/sewer/cable tv, plus 22 w/hookups for water/electricity/cable tv, no tents, reservations - (503)822-3596, showers, laundry, trailer waste disposal, river, fishing, playfield, hiking, $$$.
East of Blue River. State 126 east 6.0 miles, McKenzie River Drive east 2.5 miles to park.

SLIDE CREEK (Willamette National Forest)
16 units, trailers okay, picnic area, lake, boating, swimming, fishing, water skiing, elev. 1700', $$-$$$.
Southeast of Blue River. State 126 east 3.5 miles, FSR 19 south 11.6 miles, FSR 195 north 1.5 miles.

BLY (D-12)

GERBER RESERVOIR (BLM)
50 units, trailers okay, picnic area, drinking water, fishing, hiking, swimming, boat launch, boating, $.
Southwest of Bly. Take Gerber Road approximately 19.0 miles southwest to west side of reservoir and campground.

BROOKINGS (A-12)

CHETCO RV PARK (Private)
120 trailer sites w/hookups for water/electricity/sewer/cable tv, 80 are pull-thru sites, reservation information - (503)469-3863, showers, laundry, ice, trailer waste disposal, $$$.

South of Brookings. US 101 south 1.0 mile past the Chetco River Bridge.

DRIFTWOOD RV PARK (Private)
108 campsites, 100 w/hookups for water/electricity/sewer/cable tv, plus 8 w/hookups for water/electricity/cable tv, reservations - (503)469-3213, showers, laundry, ocean access, fishing, boat launch, $$-$$$.
South of Brookings. US 101 south over Chetco River Bridge, Lower Harbor Road west .7 mile.

HARRIS BEACH (Oregon State Park)
151 campsites, 34 w/hookups for water/electricity/sewer, 51 w/hookups for electricity, plus 66 tent units, group campsites, mail reservations available, maximum site 50', picnic area, wheelchair access, showers, trailer waste disposal, fishing, ocean access, beachcombing, hiking trails, $$-$$$.
North of Brookings. US 101 north 2.0 miles to campground.

LITTLE REDWOOD (Siskiyou National Forest)
12 units, trailers to 18', picnic area, piped water, river, boating, swimming, fishing, elev. 100', $.
Northeast of Brookings. US 101 south .5 mile, CR 784 northeast 7.5 miles, FSR 376 northeast 6.0 miles.

LOEB (Oregon State Park)
53 campsites w/hookups for electricity, maximum site 50', picnic area, fishing, swimming, $$$.
Northeast of Brookings. Leave US 101 at Brookings on Chetco River Road, follow this 10.0 miles northeast.

LUDLUM PLACE (Siskiyou National Forest)
1 group site, reservations advised - (503)469-2196, trailers to 32', river, swimming, fishing, elev. 200', $$.
East of Brookings. US 101 southeast 5.7 miles, CR 896 northeast 6.3 miles, FSR 3907 east 1.0 miles, FSR 4029 north 1.5 miles.

PORT OF BROOKINGS BEACH FRONT RV (Port)
184 campsites, 48 w/hookups for water/electricity/sewer/cable tv, 56 w/hookups for water/electricity, plus 75 w/out hookups, reservation information - (800)441-0856, showers, laundry, trailer waste disposal, ocean access, river, swimming, fishing, boat launch, wheelchair access, $$-$$$.
In Brookings. US 101 south to Lower Harbor Road, located at Benham Lane and Lower Harbor Road.

PORTSIDE RV PARK (Private)
90 units w/hookups for water/electricity/sewer/cable tv, reservations - (503)469-6616, showers, laundry, rec room, propane, picnic area, $$-$$$.
South of Brookings. Located .3 mile south of Chetco River Bridge on Lower Harbor Road.

RIVER BEND PARK (Private)
91 trailer sites, 83 w/hookups for water/electricity/sewer/cable tv, plus 8 w/hookups for electricity/cable tv, reservations - (503)469-3356, showers, wheelchair access, laundry, rec room, river, fishing, boat ramp, $$-$$$.
Southeast of Brookings. US 101 south over Chetco River Bridge, Southbank Chetco River Road east 1.5 miles to park.

SEA BIRD RV PARK (Private)
60 trailer sites w/hookups for water/electricity/sewer, no tents, reservation information - (503)469-3512, showers, laundry, cable tv, wheelchair access, ocean fishing, trailer waste disposal, $$.
In Brookings. US 101 south over Chetco River Bridge, proceed 1 block to park.

SNUG HARBOR (Private)
26 campsites, 4 w/hookups for water/electricity/sewer, 15 w/hookups for water/electricity, plus 7 tent sites, reservation information - (503)469-3452, boat basin, ocean fishing, ocean access, $-$$.
In Brookings. Located on North Bank Road .7 mile from US 101.

WHALESHEAD RV PARK (Private)
71 trailer sites w/hookups for water/electricity/sewer, reservation information - (503)469-7446, showers, laundry, private beach access, beachcombing, hiking, $$$.
North of Brookings. Take US 101 north 7.0 miles, located at 19936 Whaleshead Road.

WINCHUCK (Siskiyou National Forest)
13 units, trailers to 18', picnic area, piped water, river, swimming, fishing, elev. 100', $.
East of Brookings. US 101 southeast 5.7 miles, CR 896 northeast 6.3 miles, FSR 3907 east 1.1 miles.

BURNS (E-10)

CHICKAHOMINY RECREATION SITE (BLM)
Campsites, picnic facilities, lake fishing, boating, boat ramp, elev. 4350', $.
West of Burns. US 20 west 34.0 miles to campground.

DELINTMENT LAKE (Ochoco National Forest)
24 units, trailers to 22', picnic area, boat launch, boating, fishing, elev. 5600', $.
Northwest of Burns. FSR 47 northwest 15.0 miles, FSR 41 northwest 25.0 miles, FSR 4365 west 3.0 miles, FSR 41 west 5.0 miles.

EMIGRANT (Ochoco National Forest)
6 units, trailers to 22', piped water, stream fishing, $.
Northwest of Burns. FSR 47 northwest 15.0 miles, FSR 41 northwest 20.0 miles.

FALLS (Ochoco National Forest)
5 units, trailers to 22', piped water, stream fishing, $.
Northwest of Burns. FSR 47 northwest 15.0 miles, FSR 41 northwest 18.0 miles.

SANDS TRAILER PARK (Private)
16 campsites, 10 w/hookups for water/electricity/sewer, plus 6 tent units, reservation information - (503)573-7010, showers, nearby trout fishing, bird refuge, $$.
South of Burns. US 395/20 south 1.0 mile.

VILLAGE TRAILER PARK (Private)
41 campsites, 32 w/hookups for water/electricity/sewer, plus 9 tent units, reservation information - (503)573-7640, showers, laundry, river, playground, $$.
At Burns. US 395/20 northeast to Seneca Drive, located at 1273 Seneca Drive.

BUTTE FALLS (C-11)

FOURBIT FORD (Rogue River National Forest)
7 tent units, well, stream, fishing, elev. 3200', $.
East of Butte Falls. CR 30 southeast 9.3 miles, FSR 3065 northeast 1.2 miles.

PARKER MEADOWS (Rogue River National Forest)
8 tent units, well, picnic area, fishing, elev. 5000', $.
Northeast of Butte Falls. CR 30 southeast 10.0 miles, FSR 37 northeast 11.0 miles.

WHISKEY SPRINGS (Rogue River National Forest)
36 units, trailers to 18', picnic area, piped water, hiking, elev. 3200', $.
Southeast of Butte Falls. CR 30 southeast 9.3 miles, FSR 3065 east .3 mile.

WILLOW LAKE RESORT (Private)

75 campsites, 25 w/hookups for water/electricity/sewer, 20 w/hookups for water/electricity, plus 30 tent units, reservations - (503)865-3229, showers, groceries, restaurant & lounge, trailer waste disposal, lake, swimming, fishing, boat launch, boat rental, hiking, elev. 3000', $$.
Southeast of Butte Falls. Fish Lake Road 8.0 miles southeast, Willow Lake Road 2.0 miles southwest.

WILLOW PRAIRIE HORSE CAMP (Rogue River National Forest)

10 tent units, horse camp only, well, elev. 4400', $.
Southeast of Butte Falls. Leave Butte Falls heading southeast toward State 140, take FSR 3738 west 1.5 miles to campground.

CAMP SHERMAN (C-9)

ALLEN SPRINGS (Deschutes National Forest)

17 units, 1 group site, trailers to 22', piped water, river, fishing, hiking, elev. 2800', $$-$$$.
North of Camp Sherman. FSR 14 north 5.0 miles to campground.

ALLINGHAM (Deschutes National Forest)

6 units, 4 group sites, trailers to 22', piped water, river, fishing, hiking, elev. 2900', $$.
North of Camp Sherman. FSR 14 north 1.0 mile to campground.

BLACK BUTTE MOTEL & RV PARK (Private)

28 campsites, 19 w/hookups for water/electricity/sewer, plus 9 w/hookups for water/electricity, reservation information - (503)595-6514, showers, laundry, trailer waste disposal, river, fishing, playfield, playground, hiking, $$$.
At Camp Sherman. Located on Camp Sherman Road.

CAMP SHERMAN (Deschutes National Forest)

13 units, 2 group sites, trailers to 22', piped water, river, fishing, hiking, elev. 3000', $$.
North of Camp Sherman. FSR 14 north .2 mile to campground.

FOSTER'S COLD SPRINGS RESORT (Private)

32 trailer sites w/hookups for water/electricity/sewer, no tents, reservation information - (503)595-6271, river, trout flyfishing, hiking, elev. 3000', $$$.
North of Camp Sherman. Located on Camp Sherman Road, just north of town.

GORGE (Deschutes National Forest)
12 units, 6 group sites, trailers to 22', piped water, river, fishing, hiking, elev. 2900', $$.
North of Camp Sherman. FSR 14 north 2.0 miles to campground.

LOWER BRIDGE (Deschutes National Forest)
11 units, 1 group site, trailers to 22', piped water, river, fishing, hiking, elev. 2800', $$-$$$.
North of Camp Sherman. FSR 14 north 7.0 miles to campground.

METOLIUS RIVER RESORT (Private)
35 trailer sites w/hookups for water/electricity/sewer, no tents, reservation information - (503)595-6281, showers, ice, river, fishing, hiking, elev. 2900', $$$.
At Camp Sherman. Located on Camp Sherman Road.

PINE REST (Deschutes National Forest)
38 tent sites, piped water, river, fishing, hiking, elev. 2900', $$.
North of Camp Sherman, FSR 14 north 1.5 miles to campground.

PIONEER FORD (Deschutes National Forest)
18 units, trailers to 22', piped water, river, wheelchair access, fishing, hiking, elev. 2800', $$-$$$.
North of Camp Sherman. FSR 14 north 7.0 miles to campground.

SHEEP SPRINGS HORSE CAMP (Deschutes National Forest)
11 units, trailers to 18', well, horse facilities, elev. 3200', $$-$$$.
Northwest of Camp Sherman. FSR 12 west 7.0 miles, FSR 12400 north 1.5 miles, campground road .5 mile.

SMILING RIVER (Deschutes National Forest)
38 units, trailers to 22', piped water, river, fishing, hiking, elev. 2900', $$.
North of Camp Sherman. FSR 14 north 1.0 mile to campground.

CANNON BEACH (A-7)

BUD'S CAMPGROUND & RV PARK (Private)
32 sites, 24 w/hookups for water/electricity/sewer/cable tv, plus 8 tent sites, reservation information - (503)738-6855, showers, laundry, wheelchair access, groceries, ocean fishing, crabbing & clamming, $$$.
North of Cannon Beach. US 101 north 11.0 miles, just past Gearhart.

NEHALEM BAY (Oregon State Park)
291 campsites w/hookups for electricity, maximum site 60', wheelchair access, picnic area, showers, trailer waste disposal, boat launch, fishing, ocean access, beachcombing, bicycle trail, horse trails, $$-$$$.
South of Cannon Beach. US 101 south approximately 17.0 miles, campground is located 3.0 miles south of Manzanita junction.

NEHALEM BAY TRAILER PARK (Private)
40 trailer sites w/hookups for water/electricity/sewer/cable tv, no tents, reservation information - (503)368-5180, showers, laundry, ocean & river fishing, crabbing & clamming in bay, groceries, $$.
South of Cannon Beach. US 101 south 14.0 miles.

NEHALEM SHORES RV PARK (Private)
25 trailer sites w/hookups for water/electricity/sewer, reservation information - (503)368-6670, showers, laundry, ice, river, fishing, $$.
South of Cannon Beach. US 101 south 15.0 miles to Nehalem, 7th Street north .2 mile, North Fork Road .6 mile east to park.

OSWALD WEST (Oregon State Park)
36 primitive campsites, hike-in only, picnic area, hiking, fishing, situated in rain forest w/massive spruce & cedar trees, $$.
South of Cannon Beach. US 101 south 10.0 miles, take trail to campground.

RIVERSIDE LAKE RESORT (Private)
69 campsites, 20 w/hookups for water/electricity/sewer/cable tv, 19 w/hookups for water/electricity, plus 30 tent units, reservation information - (503)738-6779, showers, laundry, river, swimming, fishing, $$-$$$.
North of Cannon Beach. US 101 north 7.0 miles.

RV RESORT AT CANNON BEACH (Private)
100 trailer sites w/hookups for water/electricity/sewer, no tents, reservations - (503)436-2231, showers, laundry, cable tv, groceries, propane & gasoline, swimming pool, therapy pool, river, fishing, boat rental, game room, playfield, playground, hiking, wheelchair access, $$$.
At Cannon Beach. Located just off the Cannon Beach exit ramp; about .6 mile past milepost 29.

SADDLE MOUNTAIN (Oregon State Park)
9 primitive campsites, picnic area, hiking, $$.
Southeast of Cannon Beach. US 26 southeast, campground is 8.0 miles northeast of Necanicum junction.

SEA RANCH RESORT (Private)
71 campsites, 25 w/hookups for water/electricity/sewer, 13 w/hookups for electricity, plus 33 tent units, information - (503)436-1268, showers, trailer waste disposal, ocean access, swimming, fishing, hiking, summer horseback riding, fishing boat charters, $$-$$$.
North of Cannon Beach. Resort is located 6 blocks north of city center on old US 101.

CANYONVILLE (B-11)

CHARLES V. STANTON PARK (Douglas County)
40 campsites, 20 w/hookups for water/electricity/sewer, plus 20 tent units, showers, river, fishing, playground, pavilion, wheelchair access, $$.
North of Canyonville. I-5 northbound take exit #99; southbound exit #101. Campground is located 1.0 mile north of Canyonville.

SURPRISE VALLEY MOBIL VILLAGE (Private)
25 campsites, 15 w/hookups for water/electricity/sewer, 8 w/hookups for water/electricity, plus 2 tent sites, reservation information - (503)839-8181, laundry, $$$.
Northeast of Canyonville. I-5 to exit #102, Gazley Road 1.0 mile east.

CASCADE LOCKS (C-8)

BRIDGE OF THE GODS RV PARK (Private)
15 sites w/hookups for water/electricity/sewer, reservations - (503)374-8628, showers, laundry, tv hookup, nearby golf, fishing, $$-$$$.
In Cascade Locks. Located on US 30 just before you cross bridge.

CASCADE LOCKS KOA CAMPGROUND (Private)
81 campsites, 32 w/hookups for water/electricity/sewer, 40 w/hookups for water/electricity, plus 9 tent units, reservation information - (503)374-8668, showers, laundry, groceries, swimming pool, playground, trailer waste disposal, hiking, $$$.
East of Cascade Locks. At east end of town take Forest Lane 1.0 mile southeast to park.

CASCADE LOCKS MARINE PARK (Port of Cascade Locks)
38 campsites, information - (503)374-8619, showers, trailer waste disposal, river, fishing, boat launch, playground, wheelchair access, wind surfing area, historic site, $$.
In Cascade Locks. Located 3 blocks north of Cascade Locks exit off I-84.

EAGLE CREEK (Mt. Hood National Forest)
19 units, trailers to 22', piped water, flush toilets, wheelchair access, swimming, fishing, hiking, bicycling, elev. 200', $$.
West of Cascade Locks. I-84 west 4.5 miles, I-84 east 2.0 miles, FSR 240 southeast .1 mile.

HERMAN CREEK (Mt. Hood National Forest)
4 tent units, spring, fishing, geology, hiking, elev. 1000', $$.
West of Cascade Locks. US 30 to Herman Creek Road N22, 2.0 miles southeast of Columbia Gorge Work Station, follow this to campground.

OVERLOOK (Mt. Hood National Forest)
Group campsites, trailers to 22', reservations required - (503)695-2276, picnic area w/community kitchen, piped water, river, flush toilets, boating, swimming, fishing, bicycling, elev. 200', $$$.
West of Cascade Locks. I-84 west 4.5 miles, I-84 east 2.0 miles, FSR 243 north .3 mile.

WYETH (Mt. Hood National Forest)
3 units, trailers to 32', piped water, stream, flush toilets, wheelchair access, swimming, fishing, hiking, elev. 200', $$.
East of Cascade Locks. I-84 east 7.0 miles.

CASCADE SUMMIT (C-10)

PEBBLE BAY (Deschutes National Forest)
Campsites, on Odell Lake, boat-in only, swimming, fishing, water skiing, elev. 4800', $.
Southeast of Cascade Summit. On southwest end of Odell Lake.

CAVE JUNCTION (A-12)

CAVE CREEK (Siskiyou National Forest)
18 tent units, piped water, fishing, hiking, elev. 2900', $.
East of Cave Junction. State 46 east 16.0 miles, FSR 4032 south 1.0 mile. Located 4.0 miles northwest of Oregon Caves National Monument.

CAVES HIGHWAY (Private)
20 sites w/hookups for water/electricity/sewer, reservation information - (503)592-3338, showers, trailer waste disposal, $$-$$$.
Southeast of Cave Junction. Leave US 199 at south end of town and head east on State 46 for 1.0 mile to campground.

GRAYBACK (Siskiyou National Forest)
35 units, trailers to 22', picnic area, piped water, stream, flush toilets, swimming, fishing, elev. 1800', $.
East of Cave Junction. State 46 east 12.0 miles. Located 8.0 miles northwest of Oregon Caves National Monument. The road beyond Grayback Campground is narrow and winding; trailers and campers not recommended.

KERBY TRAILER PARK (Private)
14 campsites, 5 w/hookups for water/electricity/sewer, plus 9 w/hookups for water/electricity, reservation information - (503)592-2897, showers, laundry, trailer waste disposal, fishing, $$.
North of Cave Junction. US 199 north 2.8 miles.

SHADY ACRES RV PARK (Private)
29 campsites, 25 w/hookups for water/electricity/sewer, plus 4 tent units, reservation information - (503)592-3702, showers, trailer waste disposal, $$.
South of Cave Junction. US 199 south 1.0 mile.

TRAILS END CAMPGROUND (Private)
30 campsites, 7 w/hookups for water/electricity/sewer, plus 23 w/hookups for water/electricity, reservation information - (503)592-3354, showers, trailer waste disposal, river, swimming, $$-$$$.
South of Cave Junction. US 199 south 2.5 miles, Burch Drive southwest .1 mile to campground.

WOODLAND ECHOES FAMILY RESORT (Private)
17 sites w/hookups for water/electricity, reservations - (503)592-3406, pull-thru sites, tents okay, historical theme park, showers, swimming, fishing, $$.
East of Cave Junction. State 46 east 8.0 miles to campground.

CHARLESTON (A-11)

BASTENDORFF BEACH PARK (Coos County)
81 campsites, 56 w/hookups for water/electricity, plus 25 tent units, trailers to 70', showers, trailer waste disposal, picnic area, flush toilets, playground, horseshoes, ocean access, hiking, fishing, $$.
South of Charleston. Take Cape Arago Highway 2.0 miles south.

CHARLESTON MARINA & TRAVEL PARK (Port of Coos Bay)
112 campsites, 60 w/hookups for water/electricity/sewer, 32 w/hookups for water/electricity, plus 20 tent units, reservation information - (503)888-9512, showers, laundry, ice, propane, trailer waste disposal, ocean access, river, fishing, boat launch, playground. $-$$.
In Charleston. At west end of Charleston Bridge turn north on Boat Basin Drive, after 2 blocks turn east on Kingfisher Drive, park is 1 block.

HUCKLEBERRY HILL MOBILE HOME PARK (Private)
10 trailer sites w/hookups for water/electricity/sewer, reservation information - (503)888-3611, showers, laundry, trailer waste disposal, hiking, ocean fishing, crabbing & clamming in bay, $$.
In Charleston. Located .2 mile west of Charleston Bridge, on Cape Arago Highway.

SEA PORT RV PARK (Private)
26 sites w/hookups for water/electricity/sewer/cable tv, information - (503)888-3122, RVs to 40', laundry, close to ocean beaches, fishing, clamming, crabbing, $$-$$$.
In Charleston. At west end of Charleston Bridge turn north on Boat Basin Drive and follow to park.

CHEMULT (D-11)

DIGIT POINT (Winema National Forest)
64 units, trailers to 32', piped water, lake - speed limits, flush toilets, trailer waste disposal, boat launch, boating, swimming, fishing, hiking, mosquitoes, elev. 5600', $$.
West of Chemult. US 97 north 1.0 mile, FSR 9772 west 12.0 miles.

CHILOQUIN (D-11)

COLLIER (Oregon State Park)
68 campsites, 50 w/hookups for water/electricity/sewer, plus 18 tent units, maximum site 60', picnic area, wheelchair access, showers, trailer waste disposal, fishing, horse facilities, hiking trails, historic logging museum & pioneer cabins, $$-$$$.
North of Chiloquin. US 97 north to Collier State Park.

JACKSON F. KIMBALL (Oregon State Park)
6 primitive campsites, maximum site 45', no drinking water, fishing, $$.
North of Chiloquin. US 97 to State 232; campground is located 3.0 miles north of Fort Klamath.

NEPTUNE PARK RESORT (Private)

25 campsites, 8 w/hookups for water/electricity/sewer, 12 w/hookups for water/electricity, plus 5 tent units, reservation information - (503)783-2489, showers, groceries, gas & propane, lake, swimming, fishing, boat launch, boat rental, elev. 4200', $$-$$$.
West of Chiloquin. West 6.0 miles, Lakeside Road 3.0 miles south.

WALT'S COZY CAMP (Private)

34 campsites, 12 w/hookups for water/electricity/sewer, 2 w/hookups for water/electricity, plus 20 tent units, reservation information - (503)783-2537, showers, elev. 4200', $$.
Southwest of Chiloquin. Near milepost #248 on US 97.

WATER WHEEL CAMPGROUND (Private)

44 campsites, 10 w/hookups for water/electricity/sewer, 14 w/hookups for water/electricity, plus 20 tent units, reservation information - (503)783-2738, showers, laundry, groceries, propane, trailer waste disposal, river, swimming, fishing, boat launch, playground, elev. 4200', $$-$$$.
Southwest of Chiloquin. Campground is located on US 97 north .1 mile from junction of US 97 with State 62.

WILLIAMSON RIVER (Winema National Forest)

10 units, trailers to 32', piped water, fishing, elev. 4200', $.
North of Chiloquin. US 97 5.0 miles north, FSR 9730 northeast 1.0 mile. Campground is 1.0 mile from Collier State Park.

WILLIAMSON RIVER TRAILER PARK (Private)

18 trailer sites w/hookups for water/electricity/sewer, reservation information - (503)783-2834, showers, laundry, river frontage, trout fishing, swimming, boat launch, elev. 4100', $$.
Southwest of Chiloquin. US 97 south 9.0 miles to Modoc Point Road, northwest 5.0 miles to park.

CONDON (D-8)

CONDON MOBILE HOME & RV PARK (Private)

17 trailer sites w/hookups for water/electricity/sewer, reservation information - (503)384-5666, cable tv, showers, laundry, playground, near game reserve, $$.
In Condon. At west city limits on State 206.

COOS BAY (A-11)

DRIFTWOOD RV PARK (Private)
15 trailer sites w/hookups for water/electricity/sewer, reservation information - (503)888-6103, showers, cable tv, laundry, ocean access, fishing, crabbing & clamming, $$.
West of Coos Bay. US 101 to Cape Arago Highway, west 7.0 miles to park.

KELLEY'S RV PARK (Private)
38 trailer sites w/hookups for water/electricity/sewer, no tents, reservation information - (503)888-6531, showers, cable tv, laundry, trailer waste disposal, river, $$.
West of Coos Bay. US 101 to Cape Arago Highway, west 4.5 miles to park.

PLAINVIEW TRAILER PARK (Private)
34 trailer sites, 32 w/hookups for water/electricity/sewer/cable tv, plus 2 w/hookups for water/electricity/cable tv, reservation information - (503)888-5166, showers, laundry, ocean access, lake, fishing, $$-$$$
West of Coos Bay. US 101 to Cape Arago Highway, west 7.5 miles to park.

SAND BAR MOBILE & RV PARK (Private)
18 units w/hookups for water/electricity/sewer/cable tv, 7 pull-thrus, reservation information - (503)888-3179, laundry, near ocean, off highway, fishing, crabbing & clamming, $$-$$$.
West of Coos Bay. US 101 to Cape Arago Highway, west 5.5 miles to park.

SUNSET BAY (Oregon State Park)
137 campsites, 29 w/hookups for water/electricity/sewer, plus 108 tent units, group campsites, maximum site 47', mail reservations available, picnic area, wheelchair access, showers, swimming, fishing, beach access, beachcombing, hiking access to Oregon Coast Trail, $$-$$$.
Southwest of Coos Bay. Leave US 101 at Coos Bay heading west past Charleston to Sunset Bay.

COQUILLE (A-11)

LAVERNE PARK (Coos County)
85 campsites, 45 w/hookups for water/electricity, plus 40 tent sites, community kitchen, flush toilets, showers, fish ladder, playfield, playground, swimming, hiking, horseshoes, rockhounding, $$.
East of Coquille. Take Coquille/Fairview Road 15.0 miles.

CORBETT (C-8)

CROWN POINT RV PARK (Private)
15 trailer sites w/hookups for water/electricity/sewer, reservation information - (503)695-5207, showers, laundry, trailer waste disposal, $$$.
East of Corbett. Take Scenic Loop Highway .2 mile east of town to milepost #9 and campground.

COTTAGE GROVE (B-10)

BAKER BAY (Lane County)
48 campsites, 2 group campsites, reservation information - (503)942-7669, on Dorena Reservoir, showers, picnic area, trailer waste disposal, fishing, boat dock, boat launch, $$-$$$.
East of Cottage Grove. Take Dorena Reservoir Road 7.0 miles east to campground.

COTTAGE GROVE LAKE PRIMITIVE AREA (Corps)
34 campsites, lake, fishing, $.
South of Cottage Grove. London Road 3.5 miles south, Reservoir Road 1.0 mile east to campground.

PASS CREEK (Douglas County)
30 camp sites w/hookups for water/electricity/sewer, showers, stream, pond, playground, pavilion, wheelchair access, $$.
South of Cottage Grove. Leave I-5 at exit #163, campground is 10.0 miles south of Cottage Grove, in Curtin.

PINE MEADOWS (Corps)
93 campsites, showers, trailer waste disposal, lake, swimming, fishing, playground, $$.
South of Cottage Grove. London Road 3.5 miles south, Reservoir Road .5 mile east to campground.

SCHWARZ PARK/DORENA LAKE (Corps)
50 campsites, showers, trailer waste disposal, fishing, canoeing, wheelchair access, $$.
East of Cottage Grove. Take Dorena Lake exit #174 off I-5, Row River Road 5.0 miles east.

THE VILLAGE GREEN (Private)
42 trailer sites w/hookups for water/electricity/sewer, reservation information - (503)942-2491, swimming pool, spa, playground, laundry, nearby golf & bowling, $$$.
East of Cottage Grove. Take Dorena Lake exit #174 off I-5, Row River Road .1 mile east to 725 Row River Road.

CRATER LAKE NATIONAL PARK (C-11)

LOST CREEK (Crater Lake National Park)
16 tent units, information - (503)594-2211, elev. 6000', $$.
In Crater Lake National Park. Follow signs on Pinnacles Road.

MAZAMA (Crater Lake National Park)
200 campsites, information - (503)594-2211, showers, groceries, trailer waste disposal, lake, fishing, hiking, wheelchair access, elev. 6000', $$.
In Crater Lake National Park. Located east of Annie Spring entrance .5 mile.

CRESCENT (D-10)

CRESCENT CREEK (Deschutes National Forest)
10 units, trailers to 22', stream, fishing, elev. 4500', $.
West of Crescent. CR 61 west 8.2 miles. Campground is located on Crescent Creek.

EAST DAVIS LAKE (Deschutes National Forest)
33 units, trailers to 22', well, on Davis Lake - speed limits, boating, fishing, hiking, elev. 4000', $.
Northwest of Crescent. CR 61 west 9.0 miles, FSR 46 north 6.5 miles, FSR 855 west 1.5 miles. Located on south end of Davis Lake at mouth of Odell Creek.

SIMAX GROUP CAMP (Deschutes National Forest)
Group sites by reservation only - (503)433-2234, on Crescent Lake, boating, fishing, swimming, water skiing, elev. 4850', $.
West of Crescent. Take State 58 west of Crescent to Crescent Lake. Campground is 30.0 miles, on east end of lake.

WEST DAVIS LAKE (Deschutes National Forest)
25 units, trailers to 22', well, on Davis Lake - speed limits, boating, fishing, elev. 4400', $.
Northwest of Crescent. CR 61 west 9.0 miles, FSR 46 north 3.3 miles, FSR 4660 northwest 3.8 miles, FSR 4669 east 2.0 miles. Located on south end of Davis Lake at mouth of Odell Creek.

CRESCENT LAKE (C-10)

CRESCENT LAKE (Deschutes National Forest)
44 units, trailers to 22', picnic area, piped water, on Crescent Lake, boat launch, boating, swimming, fishing, elev. 4800', $$.

Southwest of Crescent Lake. FSR 60 southwest 2.7 miles to campground. Located at north end of Crescent Lake, across creek from resort.

ODELL CREEK (Deschutes National Forest)
22 units, trailers to 22', well, on Odell Lake, boating, swimming, fishing, elev. 4800', $.
Northwest of Crescent Lake. CR 61 to junction of State 58N, follow west 5.0 miles. Located on east end of Odell Lake, at head of Odell Creek.

PRINCESS CREEK (Deschutes National Forest)
46 units, trailers to 22', picnic area, piped water, on Odell Lake, boating, swimming, fishing, water skiing, elev. 4800', $$.
Northwest of Crescent Lake. State 58 northwest 9.0 miles to campground. Located on north shore of Odell Lake.

SPRING (Deschutes National Forest)
68 units, trailers to 22', picnic area, well, on Crescent Lake, boating, swimming, fishing, water skiing, elev. 4800', $$.
Southwest of Crescent Lake. CR 61 to junction with State 58, State 58 southeast 3.5 miles, FSR 60 another 9.0 miles to campground. Located on southwest side of Crescent Lake.

SUNSET COVE (Deschutes National Forest)
27 units, trailers to 22', picnic area, well, on Odell Lake, boat launch, boating, swimming, fishing, water skiing, elev. 4800', $$.
Northwest of Crescent Lake. CR 61 to junction with State 58, State 58 northwest 6.0 miles to campground. Located at northeast end of Odell Lake.

TRAPPER CREEK (Deschutes National Forest)
32 units, trailers to 22', piped water, on Odell Lake, boat launch, boating, swimming, fishing, water skiing, hiking, near Diamond Peak Wilderness, elev. 4800', $$.
Northwest of Crescent Lake. CR 61 to junction with State 58, State 58 northwest 6.9 miles, FSR 5810 southwest 1.8 miles to campground. Located at west end of Odell Lake.

WHITEFISH HORSE CAMP (Deschutes National Forest)
19 units, trailers okay, reservation only - (503)433-2234, stream, hiking, elev. 4800', $
West of Crescent Lake. FSR 60 west 6.7 miles to campground. Located at west end of Crescent Lake.

CRESWELL (B-10)

SHERWOOD FOREST KOA (Private)
150 campsites, 100 w/hookups for water/electricity/sewer, 25 w/hookups for water, plus 25 tent units, reservations - (503)895-4110, showers, laundry, groceries, trailer waste disposal, swimming pool, therapy pool, playground, $$-$$$.
At Creswell. Located .1 mile off I-5 on Creswell exit #182.

TAYLOR'S TRAVEL PARK (Private)
24 campsites, 17 w/hookups for water/electricity/sewer, plus 7 w/hookups for water/electricity, reservation information - (503)895-4715, showers, trailer waste disposal, playfield, playground, $$.
West of Creswell. Leave I-5 at exit #182 and head west to Highway 99S, go south 1.3 miles to Davisson Road then .4 mile south to campground.

CULVER (D-9)

PERRY SOUTH (Deschutes National Forest)
63 units, trailers to 22', well, on Metolius Arm of Lake Billy Chinook, flush toilets, wheelchair access, boat launch, boating, swimming, fishing, elev. 2000', $.
Northwest of Culver. State 97 north thru Redmond, turn at sign for Cove Palisades State Park, FSR 63 to FSR 64, 16.0 miles.

DALE (E-8)

MEADOWBROOK RV PARK (Private)
16 campsites, 2 w/hookups for water/electricity/sewer, plus 14 w/hookups for electricity, reservation information - (503)421-3104, showers, groceries, trailer waste disposal, stream, fishing, hiking, mini golf, gasoline, propane, diesel, elev. 4000', $-$$$.
South of Dale. US 395 south to milepost #71 and campground.

DALLAS (B-9)

HAWTHORNE ACRES MOBILE HOME COURT (Private)
4 trailer sites w/hookups for water/electricity/sewer, reservations - (503)623-6851, showers, laundry, tv hookup, nearby golf, fishing, $$-$$$.
North of Dallas. Take Kings Valley Highway north, court is on left.

DEE (C-8)

LADD CREEK (Mt. Hood National Forest)
2 tent units, stream, fishing, elev. 2000', $$.
Southwest of Dee. Take either US 26 or State 35 to Lolo Pass
Road and follow to campground. Located 15.0 miles southwest
of Dee.

DEPOE BAY (A-9)

FOGARTY CREEK RV PARK (Private)
53 trailer sites w/hookups for water/electricity/sewer, no tents,
reservation information - (503)764-2228, showers, cable tv, laun-
dry, trailer waste disposal, propane, $$$.
North of Depoe Bay. US 101 north 2.0 miles.

HOLIDAY RV PARK (Private)
110 trailer sites w/hookups for water/electricity/sewer, no tents,
reservation information - (503)765-2302, showers, laundry, groceries, indoor swimming pool, therapy pool, overlooks ocean,
fishing, $$$.
In Depoe Bay. Located 1.0 mile north of Depoe Bay city center on
US 101.

MARTIN'S TRAILER HARBOR (Private)
16 trailer sites w/hookups for water/electricity/sewer, no tents,
reservation information - (503)765-2601, showers, laundry, $$$.
In Depoe Bay. Leave US 101 2 blocks north of bridge on Collins
Street, campground is 2 blocks.

SEA & SAND RV PARK (Private)
95 campsites w/hookups for water/electricity/sewer/cable tv,
trailers to 35', reservation information - (503)764-2313,
wheelchair access, showers, laundry, trailer waste disposal,
ocean access, swimming, fishing, $$-$$$.
North of Depoe Bay. US 101 north 3.5 miles.

DETROIT (C-9)

B & B RV COURT (Private)
12 trailers sites w/hookups for water/electricity/sewer/tv, reservations - (503)854-3614, fishing, $$-$$$.
At Detroit. Take Breitenbush Road to junction with State 22.

BREITENBUSH (Willamette National Forest)
30 units, group sites, trailers to 18', piped water, wheelchair access, river, groceries, gasoline, fishing, elev. 2200', $$-$$$.
Northeast of Detroit. FSR RS46 northeast 9.8 miles. Campground is located 1 mile from Breitenbush Hot Springs Resort and 3 miles north of Breitenbush Gorge National Recreation Trail.

CLEATOR BEND (Willamette National Forest)
9 units, trailers to 18', river, fishing, elev. 2200', $.
Northeast of Detroit. FSR RS46 northeast 9.6 miles. Campground is located 1 mile from Breitenbush Hot Springs Resort and 3 miles north of Breitenbush Gorge National Recreation Trail.

DETROIT LAKE (Oregon State Park)
311 campsites, 107 w/hookups for water/electricity/sewer, 70 w/hookups for electricity, plus 134 tent units, maximum site 60', group sites, mail reservations available, picnic area, showers, boat launch, fishing, swimming, $$-$$$.
West of Detroit. State 22 west 2.0 miles to campground.

HOOVER (Willamette National Forest)
37 units, trailers to 22', piped water, on Detroit Lake, flush toilets, wheelchair access, boat launch, interpretive services, boating, swimming, fishing, water skiing, elev. 1600', $$-$$$.
Southeast of Detroit. State 22 southeast 2.9 miles, FSR 10 northwest .8 mile.

HOOVER GROUP CAMP (Willamette National Forest)
5 units, 1 group site, trailers to 18', reservations required - (503)854-3366, piped water, picnic shelter, playfield, boating, swimming, fishing, water skiing, elev. 1600', $$-$$$.
Southwest of Detroit. State 22 southwest 2.9 miles, FSR 10 northwest .8 mile.

HUMBUG (Willamette National Forest)
22 units, trailers to 22', piped water, river, fishing, hiking, elev. 1800', $$.
Northeast of Detroit. FSR RS46 northeast 4.8 miles. Located 5 miles from Detroit Lake on Breitenbush River.

KANE'S HIDEAWAY MARINA (Private)
19 sites w/hookups for water/electricity, reservations - (503)854-3362, showers, groceries, on Detroit Lake, fishing, boating, trailer waste disposal, $$-$$$.
At Detroit. From State 22 take a left on Clester Road and follow signs to marina.

MT. VIEW PARK RV & CAMPING (Private)
13 campsites, reservations - (503)854-3774, pull-thru sites, tents okay, showers, wheelchair access, tv hookup, on Detroit Lake, fishing, $$-$$$.
In Detroit. Located at 577 Mountain Avenue.

SOUTHSHORE (Willamette National Forest)
30 units, trailers to 22', picnic area, well, on Detroit Lake, wheelchair access, boat launch, boating, swimming, fishing, water skiing, elev. 1600', $$.
Southwest of Detroit. State 22 southeast 2.9 miles, FSR 10 west 4.1 miles.

DIAMOND LAKE (C-11)

BROKEN ARROW (Umpqua National Forest)
148 units, trailers to 35', reservations - (800)283-2267, picnic facilities, piped water, flush toilets, wheelchair access, trailer waste disposal, boat ramp, fishing, hiking, on south end of Diamond Lake - speed limits, $-$$.
On Diamond Lake. State 138 to FSR 4795, south 3.8 miles.

DIAMOND LAKE (Umpqua National Forest)
260 units, trailers to 30', picnic facilities, piped water, flush toilets, interpretive services, trailer waste disposal, on Diamond Lake - speed limits, boat launch, boating, swimming, fishing, hiking, bicycling, elev. 5200', $$.
At Diamond Lake. State 138 to FSR 4795, south 2.5 miles to campground.

DIAMOND LAKE RV PARK (Private)
160 campsites, 140 w/hookups for water/electricity/sewer, plus 20 w/hookups for water/electricity, reservation information - (503)793-3318, wheelchair access, showers, laundry, groceries, trailer waste disposal, lake, swimming, fishing, boat launch, hiking, elev. 5300', $$$.
Southwest of Diamond Lake. South to Diamond Lake South Shore Road, north 1.0 mile to park.

THIELSEN VIEW (Umpqua National Forest)
60 units, trailers to 30', piped water, picnic facilities, on west shore of Diamond Lake - speed limits, boat launch, boating, swimming, fishing, hiking, elev. 5200', $$.
On Diamond Lake. State 138 to FSR 4795, west 3.1 mile to campground.

DODSON (C-8)

FISHERY - COVERTS LANDING (Private)
15 campsites w/hookups for water, tents okay, reservations - (503)374-8577, showers, wheelchair access, trailer waste disposal, ice, gasoline, boat launch, boat moorage, fishing, $$.
At Dodson. Take exit #35 off I-84 at Dodson and follow signs to campground.

DRAIN (A-11)

ELKTON RV PARK (Private)
46 campsites, 11 w/hookups for water/electricity/sewer, 25 w/hookups for water/electricity, plus 10 tent units, reservation information - (503)548-2832, groceries, river, swimming, fishing, $$.
West of Drain. State 38 west 14.0 miles to Elkton, 2 blocks west of bridge turn on 2nd Street, park is 1 block.

DUFUR (D-8)

DUFUR CITY PARK (Private)
15 trailer sites w/hookups for water/electricity/sewer, reservations - (503)467-2349, showers, picnic area, swimming pool, play area, baseball field, trailer waste disposal, $$.
In Dufur. Located in town of Dufur.

EDDYVILLE (A-9)

BIG ELK (Siuslaw National Forest)
9 units, 1 group site, trailers to 18', piped water, stream, swimming, fishing, elev. 200', $.
Southeast of Eddyville. US 20 east 10.0 miles, CR 547 south 7.5 miles, CR 538 west 1.1 miles. Also accessible from Burnt Woods, take CR 547 southwest 9.0 miles to campground.

ELGIN (E-8)

MINAM (Oregon State Park)
12 primitive campsites, maximum site 71', picnic area, fishing, $$.
Northeast of Elgin. State 82 northeast 15.0 miles to campground.

ELSIE (A-7)

SPRUCE RUN (Clatsop County)
40 campsites, trailers to 25', stream, swimming, fishing, hiking, $$.
Southwest of Elsie. Located 5.2 miles south of US 26.

ENTERPRISE (F-8)

OUTPOST RV PARK (Private)
40 trailers sites w/hookups for water/electricity/sewer, reservation information - (503)426-4027, showers, elev. 3500', $$.
North of Enterprise. State 3 north .5 mile to park.

ESTACADA (B-8)

ARMSTRONG (Mt. Hood National Forest)
18 units, trailers to 32', well, on Clackamas River, wheelchair access, fishing, elev. 900', $$.
Southeast of Estacada. State 224 southeast 15.4 miles.

BARTON PARK (Clackamas County)
97 campsites w/hookups for water/electricity, reservation information - (503)650-3440, trailer waste disposal, river, swimming, fishing, boat launch, playground, $$.
Northwest of Estacada. State 224 northwest 9.0 miles, County Road .5 mile south to park.

BIG SLIDE LAKE (Mt. Hood National Forest)
2 tent sites, swimming, fishing, hike-in only, elev. 4300', $$.
Southeast of Estacada. State 224 southeast 26.7 miles, FSR S46 south 3.7 miles, FSR S63 south 5.4 miles, FSR S708 southwest 2.9 miles, FSR S708A 2.0 miles to Dickey Creek Trailhead, Trail #533 for 4.0 miles to campground. Also accessible via Trails #550 and 555.

CARTER BRIDGE (Mt. Hood National Forest)
11 units, trailers to 32', piped water, on Clackamas River, wheelchair access, trailer waste disposal, fishing, elev. 800', $$.
Southeast of Estacada. State 224 southeast 15.0 miles.

FISH CREEK (Mt. Hood National Forest)
21 units, trailers to 18', well, on Clackamas River, fishing, elev. 900', $$.
Southeast of Estacada. State 224 southeast 15.6 miles.

HARRIET LAKE (Mt. Hood National Forest)
13 units, trailers to 32', well, wheelchair access, boat launch, boating, fishing, elev. 2100', $$.
Southeast of Estacada. State 224 southeast 27.0 miles, FSR 57 east 6.5 miles, FSR 4630 west 1.2 miles.

HIDEAWAY LAKE (Mt. Hood National Forest)
9 units, trailers to 18', piped water, lake - no motors, boating, swimming, fishing, hiking, elev. 4500', $$.
Southeast of Estacada. State 224 southeast 27.0 miles, FSR 57 east 7.5 miles, FSR 58 north 3.0 miles, FSR 5830 northwest 5.3 miles.

INDIAN HENRY (Mt. Hood National Forest)
88 units, trailers to 22', piped water, on Clackamas River, flush toilets, wheelchair access, reservations advised for wheelchair accessible campsites - (503)630-6861, trailer waste disposal, interpretive services, fishing, hiking, elev. 1200', $$.
Southeast of Estacada. State 224 southeast 23.0 miles, FSR 53 southeast .5 mile.

KINGFISHER (Mt. Hood National Forest)
25 units, trailers to 18', well, on Hot Springs Fork of Collawash River, fishing, elev. 1600', $$.
Southeast of Estacada. State 224 southeast 26.5 miles, FSR 46 south 3.5 miles, FSR 63 south 3.0 miles, FSR 70 southwest 2.0 miles. Bagby Hot Springs Trailhead is 4.3 miles southwest of campground.

LAZY BEND (Mt. Hood National Forest)
19 units, trailers to 22', piped water, on Clackamas River, flush toilets, swimming, fishing, elev. 800', $$.
Southeast of Estacada. State 224 southeast 10.7 miles.

LOCKABY (Mt. Hood National Forest)
14 units, trailers to 32', well, on Clackamas River, fishing, elev. 900', $$.
Southeast of Estacada. State 224 southeast 15.3 miles.

MILO McIVER (Oregon State Park)
45 campsites w/hookups for electricity, maximum site 50', group campsites, group picnic area, wheelchair access, showers, trailer waste disposal, boat launch, fishing, horse & hiking trails, $$-$$$.
West of Estacada. Leave State 211 at Estacada; campground is 5.0 miles west.

PAUL DENNIS (Mt. Hood National Forest)
19 units, trailers to 18', lake - no motors, groceries, gasoline, ice, boat launch, boat rental, boating, swimming, fishing, hiking trails, elev. 5000', $$.
Southeast of Estacada. State 224 southeast 27.0 miles, FSR 46 south 21.8 miles, FSR 4690 southeast 8.2 miles, FSR 4200 south 6.3 miles.

PENINSULA (Mt. Hood National Forest)
38 units, trailers to 22', well, lake - no motors, wheelchair access includes trails and fishing, boat launch, boating, swimming, fishing, elev. 4900', $$.
Southeast of Estacada. State 224 southeast 27.0 miles, FSR 46 south 21.8 miles, FSR 4690 southeast 8.2 miles, FSR 4220 south 6.6 miles.

PROMONTORY (Clackamas County)
58 campsites, trailers to 20', reservation information - (503)650-3440, showers, groceries, lake, fishing, boat launch, boat rental, playground, hiking, $$.
Southeast of Estacada. State 224 southeast 7.0 mile.

RAINBOW (Mt. Hood National Forest)
15 units, trailers to 18', piped water, river, wheelchair access, swimming, fishing, hiking, elev. 1400', $$.
Southeast of Estacada. State 224 southeast 27.0 miles, FSR 46 south .1 mile.

RIPPLEBROOK (Mt. Hood National Forest)
14 units, trailers to 18', piped water, stream, wheelchair access, fishing, elev. 1500', $$.
Southeast of Estacada. State 224 southeast 26.5 miles.

RIVERSIDE (Mt. Hood National Forest)
16 units, trailers to 22', well, river, wheelchair access, fishing, hiking, elev. 1400', $$.
Southeast of Estacada. State 224 southeast 27.0 miles, FSR 46 south 2.7 miles.

ROARING RIVER (Mt. Hood National Forest)
11 units, trailers to 18', well, at junction of Roaring & Clackamas Rivers, fishing, hiking, elev. 1000', $$.
Southeast of Estacada. State 224 southeast 18.2 miles.

SKOOKUM LAKE (Mt. Hood National Forest)
2 tent units, fishing, elev. 4500', $$.
Southeast of Estacada. State 224 southeast 15.6 miles to Fish Creek, FSR S54 to FSR S505 for 16.4 miles to campground.

SUNSTRIP (Mt. Hood National Forest)
8 units, trailers to 18', well, on Clackamas River, trailer waste disposal, fishing, elev. 1000', $$.
Southeast of Estacada. State 224 southeast 18.6 miles.

EUGENE (B-10)

ECONOLODGE & RV PARK (Private)
68 campsites w/hookups for water/electricity/sewer, reservations - (503)484-2000, pull-thrus, showers, laundry, tv hookup, swimming, tennis, horseback riding, nearby golf, fishing, restaurant, $$-$$$.
North of Eugene. I-5 north 6.0 miles to exit #199. Park is at 33100 Van Duyn Road in Coburg.

EUGENE KOA (Private)
144 campsites, 56 w/hookups for water/electricity/sewer/cable tv, 44 w/hookups for water/electricity, plus 44 tent sites, reservation information - (503)343-4832, showers, laundry, groceries, trailer waste disposal, mini-golf, playground, $$-$$$.
North of Eugene. I-5 north 6.0 miles to exit #199, campground is .3 mile west.

EUGENE MOBILE VILLAGE (Private)
20 trailer sites, 4 w/hookups for water/electricity/sewer, plus 16 w/hookups for electricity, no tents, reservation information - (503)747-2257, showers, laundry, groceries, trailer waste disposal, playground, $$.
South of Eugene. I-5 south to exit #189, east over I-5, Frontage Road 1.0 mile north toward Springfield and park.

FERN RIDGE SHORES (Private)
37 units w/hookups for water/electricity, information - (503)935-2335, tents okay, pull-thrus, showers, laundry, trailer waste disposal, boat ramp & moorage, picnic facilities, ice, fishing, swimming, shade trees, pets okay, $$-$$$.
West of Eugene. State 126 west 7.3 miles to Ellmaker Road, follow to Jeans Road, campground is at 29652 Jeans Road.

SHAMROCK MOBILE HOME VILLAGE (Private)
81 trailer sites, 73 w/hookups for water/electricity/sewer, plus 8 w/hookups for water/electricity, no tents, reservation information - (503)747-7473, showers, laundry, trailer waste disposal, river, fishing, $$$.
South of Eugene. I-5 to exit #191, Glenwood Blvd. north .7 mile, Franklin Blvd. east/southeast 1.0 mile to campground.

FLORENCE (A-10)

ALDER LAKE (Siuslaw National Forest)
22 units, trailers to 32', piped water, flush toilets, lake - no motors, swimming, fishing, elev. 100', $$.
North of Florence. US 101 north 7.0 miles, FSR 792 west .2 mile.

BUCK LAKE MOBILE HOME & RV PARK (Private)
12 campsites w/hookups for water/electricity/sewer, reservations - (503)997-2840, showers, laundry, swimming, fishing, $$-$$$.
North of Florence. US 101 north 7.0 miles. Located 3 miles south of Sea Lion Caves.

CARL G. WASHBURNE (Oregon State Park)
66 campsites, 58 w/hookups for water/electricity/sewer, plus 8 tent units, maximum site 45', picnic area, showers, ocean access, beachcombing, hiking, fishing, swimming, wildlife, $$$.
North of Florence. US 101 north 14.0 miles.

CARTER LAKE WEST (Siuslaw National Forest)
22 units, trailers to 22', piped water, lake - speed limits, flush toilets, boat launch, boating, swimming, fishing, hiking, sand dunes, elev. 100', $$.
South of Florence. US 101 south 8.5 miles, FSR 1084 west .1 mile.

CUSHMAN RV & BOAT DOCK (Private)
10 campsites w/hookups for water/electricity/sewer, reservations - (503)997-2169, showers, laundry, groceries, gasoline, boat launch & marina, on Siuslaw River, fishing, $$$.
East of Florence. State 126 east 4.0 miles.

DARLINGS RESORT (Private)
15 campsites w/hookups for water/electricity/sewer, reservations - (503)997-2841, tents okay, showers, laundry, rec room, groceries, lake access, boating, fishing, motor & paddle boat rentals, $$.
South of Florence. US 101 south 5.0 miles to milepost #196 exit, Darling Loop to resort.

DRIFTWOOD II (Siuslaw National Forest)
100 units, trailers to 22', piped water, flush toilets, wheelchair access, fishing, hiking, ORV, elev. 100', $$.
South of Florence. US 101 south 7.0 miles, FSR 1078 west 1.4 miles.

DUNE LAKE (Siuslaw National Forest)
17 units, trailers to 22', picnic area, piped water, lake - no motors, flush toilets, swimming, fishing, hiking, elev. 100', $$.
North of Florence. US 101 north 7.0 miles, FSR 791 west .2 mile.

FISH MILL LODGES (Private)
11 units w/hookups for water/electricity/sewer, reservations - (503)997-2511, showers, trailer waste disposal, lake, boat rental, boat launch, tackle shop, $$.
South of Florence. US 101 south 6.0 miles.

HARBOR VISTA CAMPGROUND (Private)
26 campsites, 20 w/hookups for water/electricity, plus 6 tent sites, reservation information - (503)997-5987, showers, trailer waste disposal, playground, beach access, $$-$$$.
In Florence. US 101 to Heceta Beach Road, follow to junction with Harbor Vista Drive. Campground is at 87658 Harbor Vista Drive.

HECETA BEACH RV PARK (Private)
51 units, 20 w/hookups for water/electricity/sewer, 28 w/hookups for water/electricity, plus 3 tent sites, reservations - (503)997-7664, showers, laundry, trailer waste disposal, pull-thrus, nearby beaches & sand dunes, fishing, $$-$$$.
North of Florence. US 101 north 3.0 miles, left at Heceta Beach Road, follow signs to 04636 Heceta Beach Road.

JESSIE M. HONEYMAN (Oregon State Park)
382 campsites, 66 w/hookups for water/electricity/sewer, 75 w/hookups for electricity, plus 240 tent units, mail reservations available, maximum site 55', group campsites, picnic area, wheelchair access, showers, trailer waste disposal, boat launch, fishing, swimming, hiking trails, sand dunes, lakes, wild rhododendrons, $$-$$$.
South of Florence. US 101 south 3.0 miles.

LAGOON (SILTCOOS) (Siuslaw National Forest)
51 units, trailers to 22', piped water, river, flush toilets, swimming, fishing, hiking, ocean beach access, ORV, elev. 100', $$.
South of Florence. US 101 south 7.0 miles, FSR 1076 west 1.3 miles.

LAKE VIEW PARK (Private)
6 trailer sites w/hookups for water/electricity/sewer, trailers to 40', no tents, reservation information - (503)997-6688, showers, cable tv, laundry, lake, swimming, fishing, $$.
North of Florence. US 101 north 5.5 miles, Mercer Lake Road east 1.0 mile.

LAKE'S EDGE RV PARK (Private)

13 trailer sites w/hookups for water/electricity/sewer, no tents, trailers to 35', reservation information - (503)997-6056, showers, cable tv, laundry, groceries, lake & ocean fishing, boat launch, boat rental, hiking, $$$.

South of Florence. US 101 south 6.0 miles, Pacific Avenue east .5 mile, Laurel Street east .01 mile.

LAKESHORE TRAVEL PARK (Private)

12 trailer sites w/hookups for water/electricity/sewer, no tents, reservation information - (503)997-2741, showers, laundry, lake, swimming, fishing, $$.

South of Florence. US 101 south 4.5 miles, located near milepost #195.

LANE COUNTY HARBOR VISTA (Lane County Parks)

26 units w/hookups for water/electricity/sewer, showers, trailer waste disposal, picnic area, playground, $-$$.

North of Florence. US 101 north 3.0 miles, Rhododendron Drive to North Jetty Road and park.

PORT SIUSLAW RV PARK & MARINA (Port)

80 campsites, 33 w/hookups for water/electricity/sewer/cable tv, plus 45 w/hookups for water/electricity, reservation information - (503)997-3040, showers, laundry, trailer waste disposal, river frontage, crabbing off dock, fishing, boat launch, $$-$$$.

In Florence. At north end of bridge proceed north on US 101 3 blocks to Maple, go 2 blocks southeast to 1st Street, park is 3 blocks east.

RHODODENDRON TRAILER PARK (Private)

18 trailer sites w/hookups for water/electricity/sewer, reservation information - (503)997-2206, pull-thru sites, showers, laundry, cable tv, groceries, $$.

North of Florence. US 101 north 3.0 miles, located at Heceta Beach Junction.

SILTCOOS LAKE RESORT (Private)

12 campsites, 9 w/hookups for water/electricity/sewer, plus 3 w/hookups for water/electricity, trailers to 32', reservation information - (503)997-3741, showers, lake, swimming, fishing, boat launch, boat rental, playground, hiking, $$-$$$.

South of Florence. US 101 south 6.0 miles, Pacific Avenue .03 mile, located at corner of Pacific and Fir Streets.

SUTTON CREEK (Siuslaw National Forest)

91 units, 2 group sites, trailers to 22', piped water, flush toilets, fishing, hiking trail to ocean, elev. 100', $$.
North of Florence. US 101 north 6.0 miles, FSR 794 northwest 1.6 miles. Bicycles can take access route from US 101.

SUTTON CREEK GROUP CAMP (Siuslaw National Forest)

6 group sites, trailers to 22', reservations advised - (503)268-4473, piped water, flush toilets, fishing, hiking, elev. 100', $$.
North of Florence. US 101 north 6.0 miles, FSR 794 northwest 1.6 miles, FSR 793 northeast .3 mile. Pacific Ocean is 1 mile west.

TYEE (Siuslaw National Forest)

15 units, trailers to 22', piped water, boat launch, boating, swimming, fishing, elev. 100', $$.
South of Florence. US 101 south 6.0 miles, FSR 1068 southeast .1 mile. Campground is 1 mile from Siltcoos Lake.

WAXMYRTLE (SILTCOOS) (Siuslaw National Forest)

53 units, trailers to 22', piped water, river, flush toilets, access to Pacific Ocean & sand dunes, fishing, hiking, ORV, elev. 100', $$.
South of Florence. US 101 south 7.0 miles, FSR 1078 west 1.4 miles.

WAYSIDE RV & MOBILE PARK (Private)

22 trailer sites w/hookups for water/electricity/sewer/cable tv, no tents, reservation information - (503)997-6451, showers, laundry, trailer waste disposal, lounge, near ocean beaches, $$$.
North of Florence. US 101 north 1.7 miles.

WOAHINK LAKE RV RESORT (Private)

40 trailer sites w/hookups for water/electricity/sewer/cable tv, no tents, pets upon approval, reservation information - (503)997-6454, showers, laundry, game room, ice, lake, atv dune access, hiking, fishing, swimming, $$$.
South of Florence. US 101 south 4.5 miles.

FORT KLAMATH (D-11)

CRATER LAKE RV PARK (Private)

63 campsites, 4 w/hookups for water/electricity/sewer, 18 w/hookups for water/electricity, 26 RV sites w/no hookups, plus 15 tent sites, reservation information - (503)381-2275, showers, wheelchair access, laundry, groceries, trout pond, stream, swimming, fishing, playfield, playground, elev. 4300', $$-$$$.
Northwest of Fort Klamath. State 62 northwest 5.0 miles. Park is located 1 mile south of Crater Lake National Park.

FORT CREEK RESORT (Private)
50 campsites, 13 w/hookups for water/electricity/sewer, 8 w/hookups for water/electricity, plus 29 tent units, reservation information - (503)381-2349, showers, laundry, swimming pool, playfield, playground, stream, fishing, elev. 4100', $$$.
South of Fort Klamath. State 62 south 1.5 miles.

FORT KLAMATH LODGE & RV PARK (Private)
16 campsites, 11 w/hookups for water/electricity/sewer, plus 5 tent units, reservation information - (503)381-2234, showers, laundry, groceries, river, fishing, elev. 4100', $$-$$$.
In Fort Klamath. On State 62 near city center.

WILSON'S COTTAGES & CAMP (Private)
15 campsites, reservation information - (503)381-2209, store, creek fishing, cross country skiing, snowmobile trails, ski rental, $$.
Northwest of Ft. Klamath. State 62 northwest 5.0 miles. Park is located less than a mile from Crater Lake National Park.

FOSSIL (D-8)

FOSSIL MOTEL & TRAILER PARK (Private)
12 trailer sites w/hookups for water/electricity/sewer, reservation information - (503)763-4075, stream, fishing, elev. 3000', $$-$$$.
At Fossil. Located on State 19 at Fossil Junction.

SHELTON (Oregon State Park)
36 primitive campsites, trailers to 30', picnic area, hiking, $$.
Southeast of Fossil. State 19 southeast 10.0 miles.

FOX (E-9)

THE HITCHING POST (Private)
17 trailer sites w/hookups for water/electricity/sewer, reservation information - (503)421-3344, showers, laundry, elev. 4000', $$.
Northeast of Fox. US 395 north 8.0 miles to Long Creek.

FRENCHGLEN (E-11)

FISH LAKE (BLM)
22 units, trailers to 24', lake, water, hiking trails, boat ramp, boating, swimming, fishing, elev. 7500', $.

Southeast of Frenchglen. Located 8.0 miles east of State 205 out of Frenchglen on Steens Mountain Loop Road.

JACKMAN PARK (BLM)
5 units, water, hiking, bird watching, elev. 8100', $.
Southeast of Frenchglen. Located 22.0 miles east of State 205 out of Frenchglen on Steens Mountain North Loop Road.

PAGE SPRINGS (BLM)
25 units, trailers to 24', water, hiking, nearby bird watching, fishing, elev. 4339', $.
Southeast of Frenchglen. Located 3.0 miles east of State 205 across the Malheur National Wildlife Refuge.

STEENS MOUNTAIN RESORT CAMP & CAMPER CORRAL (Private)
97 campsites, 55 w/hookups for water/electricity/sewer, plus 42 w/hookups for water/electricity, reservation information - (503)493-2415, showers, laundry, groceries, trailer waste disposal, river, swimming, fishing, hiking, elev. 4100', $$.
Southeast of Frenchglen. Located 3.0 miles southeast on Fishlake Road.

GARDINER (A-10)

LOST LAKE (Siuslaw National Forest)
4 units, trailers to 22', boat launch, fishing, within Oregon Dunes National Recreation Area, elev. 100', $.
Northwest of Gardiner. US 101 northwest 9.0 miles.

GARIBALDI (A-8)

BAR VIEW JETTY COUNTY PARK (Tillamook County)
250 campsites, 40 w/hookups for water/electricity/sewer, 20 w/hookups for electricity, plus 190 tent units, reservation information - (503)322-3477, showers, trailer waste disposal, ocean access, swimming, fishing, playground, hiking, $$.
North of Garibaldi. US 101 north 2.0 miles.

BIAK BY THE SEA MOTOR HOME PARK (Private)
41 campsites, 35 w/hookups for water/electricity/sewer/cable tv, plus 6 tent units, trailers to 35', reservation information - (503)322-3206, laundry, ocean access, swimming, fishing, boat launch, boat rental, $$.
In Garibaldi. West of city center 1 block on 7th Street.

GATES (C-9)

GATES TRAILER RANCH (Private)
14 campsites, information - (503)897-3353, showers, laundry, tv hookup, groceries, playground, fishing, $$.
In Gates. Located right in Gates on State 22.

GLIDE (B-11)

CAVITT CREEK (BLM)
8 units, trailers okay, picnic area, drinking water, swimming, fishing, nature study, elev. 1100', $$.
South of Glide. Campground is located 8.0 miles south of Glide on Cavitt Creek County Road.

LAKE IN THE WOODS (Umpqua National Forest)
11 units, shelter, trailers to 18', picnic area, well, lake - no motors, flush toilets, boating, fishing, hiking trails to Hemlock & Yakso Waterfalls plus Hemlock Lake, elev. 3200', $-$$.
East of Glide. Take Little River Road #17 east 20.0 miles, FSR 27 north 7.0 miles.

WOLF CREEK (Umpqua National Forest)
9 units, trailers to 35', 2 group sites, group reservations - (503)496-3532, piped water, flush toilets, picnic facilities, play areas, swimming, fishing, hiking, elev. 1100', $-$$$.
Southeast of Glide. Take Little River Road #17 southeast 12.4 miles. Campground is located 1 mile east of Job Corp Center on Little River Road.

GOLD BEACH (A-12)

AGNESS RV PARK (Private)
84 campsites, 53 w/hookups for water/electricity/sewer/cable tv, plus 31 w/hookups for electricity only, reservations - (503)247-2813, showers, laundry, groceries, trailer waste disposal, river, swimming, fishing, boat launch, hiking, $$$.
Northeast of Gold Beach. Just before the bridge take Jerry's Flat Road east toward Agness, campground is 28.0 miles.

ANGLERS TRAILER VILLAGE (Private)
49 trailer sites w/hookups for water/electricity/sewer/cable tv, no tents, reservation information - (503)247-7922, showers, laundry, rec room, $$.
East of Gold Beach. Located 3.5 miles east of US 101 on the south bank of Rogue River via Jerry's Flat Road.

ARIZONA BEACH (Private)
127 campsites, 11 w/hookups for water/electricity/sewer, 85 w/hookups for water/electricity, plus 31 tent units, reservations - (503)332-6491, showers, laundry, groceries, trailer waste disposal, ocean access, stream, swimming, fishing, playfield, $$-$$$.
North of Gold Beach. US 101 north 14.0 miles.

FOUR SEASONS RV RESORT (Private)
45 campsites w/hookups for water/electricity/sewer/cable tv, reservation information - (503)247-7959, showers, laundry, groceries, trailer waste disposal, river, swimming, fishing, boat launch, playfield, hiking, $$-$$$.
East of Gold Beach. US 101 to north end of Rogue River Bridge, Rogue River Road east 3.5 miles, North Bank Rogue Road southeast 3.0 miles to campground.

HONEY BEAR CAMPGROUND (Private)
150 campsites, 55 w/hookups for water/electricity/sewer/cable tv, 18 w/hookups for water/electricity, plus 77 tent units, reservation information - (503)247-2765, wheelchair access, showers, laundry, groceries, trailer waste disposal, ocean access, stream, swimming, fishing, playfield, playground, hiking, nearby golf, $$-$$$.
North of Gold Beach. US 101 north 7.0 miles, Ophir Road north 2.0 miles.

HUNTER CREEK RV PARK (Private)
40 campsites w/hookups for water/electricity/sewer, tents okay, reservations - (503)247-2322, showers, laundry, tv hookup, rec room, propane, fishing, $$.
At Gold Beach. Take US 101 south .8 mile, Hunter Creek Loop west .8 mile to campground.

INDIAN CREEK RECREATION PARK (Private)
125 campsites, 100 w/hookups for water/electricity/sewer/cable tv, plus 25 tent units, reservation information - (503)247-7704, showers, laundry, groceries, river, fishing, playfield, playground, wheelchair access, $$-$$$.
East of Gold Beach. Leave US 101 at south end of Rogue River bridge, east .5 mile on Jerry's Flat Road.

KIMBALL CREEK BEND RV RESORT (Private)
79 campsites, 66 w/hookups for water/electricity/sewer/satellite tv, plus 13 tent units, reservation information - (503)247-7580, showers, laundry, groceries, trailer waste disposal, propane, ice, river, swimming, fishing, boat launch, playfield, hiking, $$-$$$.

East of Gold Beach. US 101 to north end of Rogue River Bridge, Rogue River Road east 3.5 miles, North Bank Rogue Road southeast 4.5 miles.

LUCKY LODGE RV PARK (Private)
42 campsites, 32 w/hookups for water/electricity/sewer, 4 w/hookups for water/electricity, plus 6 tent units, trailers to 35', reservation information - (503)247-7618, showers, laundry, trailer waste disposal, river, swimming, fishing, boat launch, $$.
East of Gold Beach. US 101 to north end of Rogue River Bridge, Rogue River Road east 3.5 miles, North Bank Rogue Road southeast 4.5 miles.

NESIKA BEACH RV PARK CAMPGROUND (Private)
37 campsites, 17 w/hookups for water/electricity/sewer/tv, 10 w/hookups for water/electricity, plus 10 tent units, trailers to 35', reservation information - (503)247-6077, showers, laundry, groceries, ocean access, fishing, $$.
North of Gold Beach. US 101 north 7.0 miles, Nesika Road .7 mile southwest to campground.

OCEANSIDE RV CAMP (Private)
95 campsites, 35 w/hookups for water/electricity/sewer/cable tv, plus 60 w/hookups for water/electricity/cable tv, reservation information - (503)247-2301, showers, tackle shop, ocean access, river, fishing, boat launch, $$.
At Gold Beach. Take Port of Gold Beach exit off US 101 and head west .5 mile to the South Jetty.

QUOSATANA (Siskiyou National Forest)
42 units, trailers to 32', piped water, river, flush toilets, wheelchair access, trailer waste disposal, boat launch, boating, swimming, fishing, on recreational section of Wild & Scenic Rogue River, elev. 100', $$.
Northeast of Gold Beach. CR 595 northeast 4.2 miles, FSR 33 northeast 10.0 miles.

GOLD HILL (B-12)

GOLD'N ROGUE KOA (Private)
90 campsites, 20 w/hookups for water/electricity/sewer, 30 w/hookups for water/electricity, 24 w/hookups for water, plus 16 tent units, reservations - (503)855-7710, showers, cable tv, laundry, groceries, propane, trailer waste disposal, swimming pool, stream, playground, $$$.
At Gold Hill. Leave I-5 at Gold Hill exit #40, head north .3 mile to Blackwell Road, travel east .2 mile to campground.

LAZY ACRES MOTEL & RV PARK (Private)
30 campsites w/hookups for water/electricity/sewer, plus tent sites, reservation information - (503)855-7000, river, swimming, fishing, playfield, playground, $$-$$$.
West of Gold Hill. Leave I-5 at Gold Hill exit #40, head north .3 mile, take State 99 west 1.5 miles to campground.

GOVERNMENT CAMP (C-8)

ALPINE (Mt. Hood National Forest)
7 units, trailers to 18', piped water, elev. 5400', $$.
Northeast of Government Camp. US 26 east .8 mile, State 173 northeast 4.6 miles. Located 1 mile below Timberline Lodge National Historic Site.

CLACKAMAS LAKE (Mt. Hood National Forest)
47 units, trailers to 18', well, lake - speed limits, elev. 3400', $$.
Southeast of Government Camp. US 26 southeast 15.0 miles, FSR 42 south 8.0 miles, FSR 4270 east .5 mile.

CLEAR LAKE (Mt. Hood National Forest)
28 units trailers to 22', well, lake, boating, swimming, fishing, water skiing, elev. 3600', $$.
Southeast of Government Camp. US 26 southeast 9.0 miles, FSR 2630 south 1.0 mile, FSR 220 south 1.0 mile.

FROG LAKE (Mt. Hood National Forest)
33 units, trailers to 18', well, lake - no motors, boating, swimming, fishing, elev. 3800', $$.
Southeast of Government Camp. US 26 southeast 7.0 miles, FSR 2610 southeast 1.0 mile, FSR 230 south .5 mile.

GONE CREEK (Mt. Hood National Forest)
50 units, trailers to 32', piped water, lake - speed limits, boating, swimming, fishing, elev. 3200', $$.
South of Government Camp. US 26 southeast 15.0 miles, FSR 42 south 8.0 miles, FSR 57 west 3.5 miles.

JOE GRAHAM HORSE CAMP (Mt. Hood National Forest)
14 units, trailers to 32', reservations advisable - (503)328-6211, elev. 3400', $$.
South of Government Camp. US 26 southeast 15.0 miles, FSR 42 south 8.0 miles.

HOOD VIEW (Mt. Hood National Forest)
43 units, trailers to 32', piped water, lake - speed limits, boating, swimming, fishing, elev. 3200', $$.

South of Government Camp. US 26 southeast 15.0 miles, FSR 42 south 8.0 miles, FSR 57 west 4.0 miles.

LITTLE CRATER (Mt. Hood National Forest)
16 units, trailers to 18', picnic area, well, stream, elev. 3200', $$.
South of Government Camp. US 26 southeast 15.0 miles, FSR 42 south 6.0 miles, FSR 58 west 2.7 miles, FSR 230 west .3 mile.

LOWER TWIN (Mt. Hood National Forest)
5 tent units, fishing, hike-in only, elev. 4200', $$.
Southeast of Government Camp. US 26 east 2.0 miles, State 35 north to Frog Lake Turnoff, take trail to this camp on Lower Twin Lake.

OAK FORK (Mt. Hood National Forest)
47 units, trailers to 22', well, lake - speed limits, boating, swimming, fishing, elev. 3200', $$.
South of Government Camp. US 26 southeast 15.0 miles, FSR 42 south 8.0 miles, FSR 57 west 3.0 miles, FSR 170 north .5 mile.

PINE POINT (Mt. Hood National Forest)
20 units, trailers to 32', piped water, lake - speed limit, boat launch, boating, fishing, swimming, hiking trail, elev. 3200', $$.
South of Government Camp. US 26 southeast 15.0 miles, FSR 42 south 8.0 miles, FSR 57 west 5.0 miles to campground.

STILL CREEK (Mt. Hood National Forest)
27 units, trailers to 18', piped water, fishing, elev. 3700', $$.
Southeast of Government Camp. US 26 southeast 1.2 miles, FSR 2650 south .5 mile.

TRILLIUM LAKE (Mt. Hood National Forest)
39 units, trailers to 32', piped water, lake - no motors, wheelchair access, boat launch, boating, swimming, fishing, bicycling, elev. 3600', $$.
Southeast of Government Camp. US 26 southeast 2.2 miles, FSR 2656 south 1.3 miles.

GRANTS PASS (B-12)

BEND O' THE RIVER CAMPGROUND (Private)
25 campsites, 10 w/hookups for water/electricity/sewer, 10 w/hookups for water/electricity, plus 5 tent units, reservation information - (503)479-2547, showers, laundry, groceries, playground, trailer waste disposal, river, swimming, fishing, nearby boat launch, $$.

West of Grants Pass. Take G Street 7.5 miles west (becomes Upper & Lower River Roads), campground is located just past milepost #7.

BIG PINE (Siskiyou National Forest)
14 units, trailers to 22', picnic area, piped water, fishing, outstanding ponderosa pine stand, barrier-free trail, elev. 2400', $.
West of Grants Pass. I-5 north 3.4 miles, CR 2-6 northwest 12.4 miles, FSR 355 southwest 12.8 miles.

GRANTS PASS OVER-NITERS (Private)
40 trailer sites, 29 w/hookups for water/electricity/sewer, plus 11 w/hookups for water/electricity, reservation information - (503)479-7289, showers, laundry, ice, propane, swimming pool, $$-$$$.
Northwest of Grants Pass. I-5 north 3.0 miles to Merlin exit #61, east to Frontage Road, north .5 mile.

GRIFFIN PARK (Josephine County)
18 campsites, 14 w/hookups for water/electricity/sewer, plus 4 tent units, reservations - (503)474-5285, showers, trailer waste disposal, river, swimming, fishing, boat launch, playfield, playground, hiking, $$.
Southwest of Grants Pass. US 199 approximately 4.0 miles west, Riverbanks Road 2.5 miles to campground.

HAVE-A-NICE DAY CAMPGROUND (Private)
45 campsites, 15 w/hookups for water/electricity/sewer/cable tv, 19 w/hookups for water/electricity, 5 w/hookups for water only, plus 6 tent sites, reservation information - (503)582-1421, showers, laundry, ice, playground, trailer waste disposal, river, swimming, fishing, boat launch, hiking, $$-$$$.
Southeast of Grants Pass. I-5 southeast 8.0 miles to Rogue River exit #48, southwest .1 mile to Rogue River Highway (Old Highway 99), west 1.5 miles to campground.

INDIAN MARY PARK (Josephine County)
91 campsites, 42 w/hookups for water/electricity/sewer, plus 49 tent units, trailers to 35', showers, ice, river, swimming, fishing, boat launch, playfield, playground, hiking, $$.
Northwest of Grants Pass. I-5 north to Merlin exit #61, Merlin-Galice Road west 7.6 miles to campground.

LES CLARE RV PARK & CAMPGROUND (Private)
47 campsites, 29 w/hookups for water/electricity/sewer/cable tv, 8 w/hookups for water/electricity/cable tv, plus 10 tent units, reservations - (503)479-0046, showers, laundry, ice, trailer waste disposal, river, sandy beach, fishing, $$-$$$.

Southeast of Grants Pass. I-5 south to exit #58, State 99 south 3.0 miles, Rogue River Highway (Old Highway 99) east 2.5 miles, located at 2956 Rogue River Highway.

RIVERFRONT RV TRAILER PARK (Private)
27 campsites, 19 w/hookups for water/electricity/sewer/cable tv, 2 w/hookups for water/electricity/cable tv, plus 6 tent units, reservation information - (503)582-0985, showers, laundry, ice, trailer waste disposal, river, swimming, fishing, boat launch, $$-$$$.
Southeast of Grants Pass. I-5 southeast 8.0 miles to Rogue River exit #48, southwest .1 mile to Rogue River Highway (Old Highway 99), west 2.0 miles.

ROGUE VALLEY OVERNIGHTERS (Private)
80 trailer sites w/hookups for water/electricity/sewer, reservation information - (503)479-2208, showers, cable tv, laundry, playground, trailer waste disposal, $$$.
In Grants Pass. I-5 south to exit #58, south 1 block to NW 6th Street, located at 1806 NW 6th Street.

SCHROEDER (Josephine County)
30 trailer sites w/hookups for water/electricity/sewer, trailers to 35', showers, tennis, playfield, playground, river, fishing, boat launch, $$.
West of Grants Pass. Located 4.0 miles west on Schroeder Lane.

SELMAC LAKE (Josephine County)
96 campsites, trailers to 40', information - (503)474-5285, showers, trailer waste disposal lake, swimming, fishing, boat launch, playfield, playground, hiking, $$.
Southwest of Grants Pass. US 199 southwest 23.0 miles from Grants Pass on Lakeshore Drive.

SUNNY VALLEY KOA (Private)
72 campsites, 11 w/hookups for water/electricity/sewer, plus 61 w/hookups for water/electricity, reservation information - (503)479-0209, showers, laundry, game room, groceries, trailer waste disposal, swimming pool, playfield, playground, $$$.
North of Grants Pass. I-5 north 17.0 miles to Sunny Valley exit #71 and campground.

VALLEY OF THE ROGUE (Oregon State Park)
174 campsites, 97 w/hookups for water/electricity/sewer, 55 w/hookups for electricity, plus 21 tent units, group campsites, maximum site 75', group picnic area, wheelchair access, showers, trailer waste disposal, boat launch, fishing, $$-$$$.
East of Grants Pass. I-5 south/east 12.0 miles to campground.

WHITE HORSE (Josephine County)

39 campsites, 8 w/hookups for water/electricity/sewer, 2 w/hookups for electricity, plus 29 tent units, trailers to 35', reservation information - (503)474-5285, showers, river, fishing, boat launch, playground, hiking, $$.

In Grants Pass. At city center take G Street west to Upper River Road, head north 6.0 miles to campground.

GRESHAM (B-8)

BELLACRES MOBILE ESTATE (Private)

12 trailer sites w/hookups for water/electricity/sewer, trailers to 35', no tents, adults only, reservation information - (503)665-4774, showers, laundry, game room, lounge, $$$.

In Gresham. From I-84 take Wood Village exit, follow NE 238th Drive south 2.6 miles (road becomes 242nd then Hogan Drive) to NE Division Street, proceed .6 mile east to mobile park.

OXBOW (Multnomah County)

45 campsites, trailers to 30', no pets, river, fishing, boat launch, playfield, playground, wheelchair access, golden age passports honored, hiking, $$.

East of Gresham. Take Division Street 8.0 miles east of Gresham to campground.

ROLLING HILLS MOBILE TERRACE (Private)

101 trailer sites w/hookups for water/electricity/sewer/cable tv, plus 8 tent units, reservation information - (503)666-7282, showers, laundry, trailer waste disposal, swimming pool, game room, wheelchair access, $$$.

West of Gresham. Leave I-84 westbound at Sandy Blvd. exit #15, campground is west .7 mile at 20145 NE Sandy Blvd.

HAINES (E-9)

ANTHONY LAKE (Wallowa-Whitman National Forest)

37 campsites, trailers to 22', piped water, 20 acre lake - no motors, wheelchair access includes trails & fishing, boat launch, boat rental, ice, cafe/snack bar, boating, swimming, good fishing, hiking, cool in summer, elev. 7100', $$.

Northwest of Haines. CR 1146 northwest 17.0 miles, FSR 73 west 7.0 miles.

GRANDE RONDE LAKE (Wallowa-Whitman National Forest)
8 units, 2 group sites, trailers to 18', picnic area, piped water, 10 acre lake - no motors, boat launch, boating, swimming, fishing, cool in summer, elev. 7200', $.
Northwest of Haines. CR 1146 northwest 17.0 miles, FSR 73 west 8.5 miles, FSR 43 northwest .5 mile.

MUD LAKE (Wallowa-Whitman National Forest)
14 units, trailers to 18', piped water, small lake, boating, swimming, fishing, cool in summer, periodic mosquito problems, elev. 7100', $.
Northwest of Haines. CR 1146 northwest 17.0 miles, FSR 73 west 7.3 miles.

HALFWAY (F-9)

LAKE FORK (Hells Canyon National Recreation Area)
11 units, trailers to 22', well, stream, fishing, hiking, elev. 3200', $.
Northeast of Halfway. State 86 east 9.2 miles, FSR 39 north 8.3 miles.

HAMMOND (A-7)

QUINNAT CHARTER & RV PARK (Private)
20 trailer sites w/hookups for water/electricity/sewer, reservations - (503)861-1292, ice, bait, charter fishing trips, $$$.
In Hammond. Located 300' south of boat launch ramp in Hammond.

HEBO (A-8)

HEBO LAKE (Siuslaw National Forest)
16 units, trailers to 18', picnic area w/shelter, piped water, lake - no motors, boating, swimming, fishing, hiking, elev. 1600', $$.
East of Hebo. US 101 north .1 mile, State 22 southeast .3 mile, FSR 14 east 5.0 miles.

HEPPNER (D-8)

ANSON WRIGHT COUNTY PARK (Morrow County)
24 campsites, 15 w/hookups for water/electricity/sewer, plus 9 tent units, trailers to 30', showers, stream, fishing, playground, hiking, wheelchair access, elev. 2300', $$.
South of Heppner. State 207 south 27.0 miles.

CUTSFORTH COUNTY PARK (Morrow County)
35 campsites, 20 w/hookups for water/electricity/sewer, plus 15 tent units, trailers to 30', showers, lake, fishing, hiking, elev. 3400', $$.
Southeast of Heppner. Willow Creek Highway 20.0 miles southeast.

HERMISTON (E-7)

BUTTERCREEK RECREATIONAL COMPLEX (Private)
24 trailer sites w/hookups for water/electricity/sewer, reservation information - (503)567-5469, showers, laundry, groceries, trailer waste disposal, restaurant/lounge, $$.
Southwest of Hermiston. Leave I-84 at exit #182, located at junction with State 207.

HAT ROCK CAMPGROUND (Private)
60 campsites, 27 w/hookups for water/electricity/sewer, plus 33 w/hookups for water/electricity, reservation information - (503)567-4188, showers, laundry, groceries, swimming pool, playfield, trailer waste disposal, river, swimming, fishing, boat launch, $$-$$$.
Northeast of Hermiston. US 395 north 5.0 miles. US 730 east 8.0 miles, Hat Rock State Park Road 1.0 mile north.

HOOD RIVER (C-8)

KINGSLEY (Mt. Hood National Forest)
11 tent units, piped water, lake, fishing, elev. 2800', $.
South of Hood River. Take FSR N20 for 12 miles to campground.

ROUTSON PARK (Hood River County)
20 campsites, reservations - (503)386-6323, drinking water, flush toilets, stream, fishing, $.
South of Hood River. State 35 south 7.0 miles.

TOLL BRIDGE PARK (Hood River County)
20 trailer sites w/hookups for water/electricity/sewer, reservation information - (503)386-6323, showers, wheelchair access, trailer waste disposal, playfield, playground, hiking, river, fishing, $$.
South of Hood River. State 35 south 18.0 miles.

TUCKER PARK (Hood River County)
44 campsites, 15 w/hookups for water/electricity, plus 28 tent sites, reservations - (503)386-6323, showers, playground, picnic shelter, windsurfing, nearby fishing, $$-$$$.
South of Hood River. Take Tucker Road south 6.0 miles to campground.

VIENTO (Oregon State Park)
75 campsites, 58 w/hookups for electricity, plus 17 tent units, maximum site 30', picnic area, showers, stream, hiking, $$-$$$.
West of Hood River. I-84 west 8.0 miles to campground.

HUNTINGTON (F-9)

FAREWELL BEND (Oregon State Park)
96 campsites, 53 w/hookups for electricity, plus 43 primitive campsites, group sites, maximum site 56', picnic area, showers, trailer waste disposal, boat launch, fishing, swimming, Oregon Trail display, $$-$$$.
Southeast of Huntington. I-84 southeast 5.0 miles to campground.

SPRING (BLM)
14 campsites, trailers to 30', water, boating, swimming, picnic sites, boat launch, elev. 2500', $.
Northeast of Huntington. Take Snake River Road northeast 4.0 miles. Gravel road not advised for trailers.

IDANHA (C-9)

MARION FORKS (Willamette National Forest)
8 units, trailers to 22', piped water, stream, swimming, fishing, hiking, salmon hatchery adjacent to campground, elev. 2500', $$.
Southeast of Idanha. State 22 southeast 12.0 miles, FSR 502 southeast .1 mile.

MOUNTAIN VIEW MOBILE PARK (Private)
28 campsites, 14 w/hookups for water/electricity/sewer/cable tv, plus 14 tent sites, reservation information - (503)854-3774, river, water sports, fishing, hiking, $$.
In Idanha. From city center head east 1 block on State 22, take Church Street 2 blocks south, Willow Street 2 blocks east, and Mountain Avenue 1 block to park.

RIVERSIDE (Willamette National Forest)
37 units, trailers to 22', piped water, on North Santiam River, fishing, hiking, elev. 2400', $$.
Southeast of Idanha. State 22 southeast 9.6 miles.

WHISPERING FALLS (Willamette National Forest)
12 units, trailers to 22', piped water, flush toilets, on North Santiam River, waterfalls across river, fishing, elev. 1900', $$.
East of Idanha. State 22 east 4.1 miles.

IDLEYLD PARK (B-11)

BOGUS CREEK (Umpqua National Forest)
15 units, trailers to 32', picnic facilities, piped water, flush toilets, whitewater boating, flyfishing, hiking, elev. 1100', $$.
East of Idleyld Park. State 138 east 14.0 miles.

CANTON CREEK (Umpqua National Forest)
5 units, some trailers to 24', picnic area w/shelter, piped water, flush toilets, swimming, on Steamboat Creek, nearby flyfishing, hiking, elev. 1200', $.
East of Idleyld Park. State 138 east 18.0 miles, FSR 38 northeast .4 mile.

EAGLE ROCK (Umpqua National Forest)
25 units, trailers to 24', well, access to North Umpqua River, white water boating, hiking, flyfishing, adjacent to Boulder Creek Wilderness, elev. 1676', $-$$.
East of Idleyld Park. State 138 east 30.0 miles.

HORSESHOE BEND (Umpqua National Forest)
27 units, 1 group site - reservation required - (503)496-3532, trailers to 24', picnic facilities, piped water, on North Umpqua River, flush toilets, wheelchair access, boat launch, boating, flyfishing, hiking, elev. 1300', $$-$$$.
East of Idleyld Park. State 138 east 25.6 miles, FSR 4750 south .1 mile, FSR 4750-001 southwest .3 mile.

MILLPOND (BLM)
12 units, trailers okay, group picnic area w/shelters, drinking water, swimming, hiking, fishing, nature study, elev. 1100', $$.
Northeast of Idleyld Park. Take Rock Creek Road 5.0 miles northeast to campground.

POOLE CREEK (Umpqua National Forest)
59 units, trailers to 22', reservations - (800)283-2267, piped water, on west shore of Lemolo Lake, boat launch, boating, swimming, fishing, water skiing, elev. 4200', $$.
East of Idleyld Park. State 138 east 49.4 miles, Lemolo Lake Road north 4.2 miles to campground.

ROCK CREEK (BLM)
17 units, trailers okay, picnic area, drinking water, swimming, fishing, nature study, elev. 1200', $$.
Northeast of Idleyld Park. Take Rock Creek Road 8.0 miles northeast to campground.

SUSAN CREEK (BLM)
33 units, trailers okay, drinking water, swimming, hiking, $$.
East of Idleyld Park. State 138 east 2.0 miles.

IRRIGON (E-7)

COUNTRY GARDEN ESTATES (Private)
4 trailer sites w/hookups for water/electricity/sewer, pull-thrus, reservation information - (503)922-4614, fishing, $$.
West of Irrigon. Old Highway 30 west 1.0 mile to park.

JACKSONVILLE (B-12)

BEAVER SULFER (Rogue River National Forest)
4 units, trailers to 18', picnic area, well, stream, elev. 2100', $.
Southwest of Jacksonville. State 238 southwest 8.0 miles, CR 10 south 9.0 miles, FSR 20 east 3.0 miles. Also accessible via Upper Applegate Road.

CANTRALL-BUCKLEY PARK (Jackson County)
25 campsites, trailers to 25', information - (503)776-7001, showers, stream, swimming, fishing, playground, hiking, $$.
Southwest of Jacksonville. State 238 southwest 13.0 miles.

FLUMET FLAT (Rogue River National Forest)
23 units, trailers to 22', piped water, flush toilets, wheelchair access, river, groceries, gasoline, ice, showers, laundry, interpretive trail, cafe/snack bar, swimming, fishing, hiking, elev. 1700', $$.
Southwest of Jacksonville. State 238 southwest 8.0 miles, CR 859 south 9.9 miles, FSR 1090 1.2 miles to campground.

FRENCH GULCH CAMP & TRAILHEAD (Rogue River National Forest)
9 units, trailers to 18', well, lake, wheelchair access, hiking elev. 2000', $.
Southwest of Jacksonville. State 238 southwest 8.0 miles, CR 10 southwest 14.0 miles, FSR 1075 east 1.5 miles.

SQUAW LAKES (Rogue River National Forest)
16 tent units, picnic area, well, lake - no motors, boating, swimming, fishing, hiking, remote, elev. 3000', $-$$.
Southwest of Jacksonville. State 238 southwest 8.0 miles, CR 10 southwest 14.0 miles, FSR 1075 southeast 8.0 miles to campground.

JOHN DAY (E-10)

CLYDE HOLLIDAY (Oregon State Park)
30 campsites w/hookups for electricity, maximum site 60', picnic area, wheelchair access, showers, trailer waste disposal, fishing, $$$.
West of John Day. US 26 west 7.0 miles.

JOSEPH (F-8)

BLACKHORSE (Hells Canyon National Recreation Area)
17 units, trailers to 32', piped water, river, fishing, elev. 4000', $.
Southeast of Joseph. State 350 east 7.7 miles, FSR 39 southeast 28.7 miles.

COVERDALE (Hells Canyon National Recreation Area)
10 units, trailers to 32', piped water, river, fishing, elev. 4300', $.
Southeast of Joseph. State 350 east 7.7 miles, FSR 39 southeast 28.8 miles, FSR 3960 southwest 4.1 miles.

HIDDEN (Hells Canyon National Recreation Area)
10 units, trailers to 32', piped water, river, fishing, hiking, elev. 4400', $.
Southeast of Joseph. State 350 east 7.7 miles, FSR 39 southeast 28.8 miles, FSR 3960 southwest 7.0 miles.

INDIAN CROSSING (Hells Canyon National Recreation Area)
15 units, trailers to 32', well, river, fishing, trailhead into Eagle Cap Wilderness Area, elev. 4500', $.
Southeast of Joseph. State 350 east 7.7 miles, FSR 39 southeast 28.8 miles, FSR 3960 southwest 8.8 miles.

LICK CREEK (Hells Canyon National Recreation Area)
12 units, trailers to 32', piped water, fishing, hiking, elev. 5400', $.
Southeast of Joseph. State 350 east 7.7 miles, FSR 39 southeast 14.9 miles.

OLLOKOT (Hells Canyon National Recreation Area)
12 units, trailers to 32', well, river, fishing, elev. 4000', $.
Southeast of Joseph. State 350 east 7.7 miles, FSR 39 southeast 28.8 miles.

WALLOWA LAKE (Oregon State Park)
210 campsites, 121 w/hookups for water/electricity/sewer, plus 89 tent units, group sites, maximum site 90', mail reservations available, picnic area, wheelchair access, showers, trailer waste disposal, lake, boating, fishing, swimming, hiking into Eagle Cap Wilderness, $$-$$$.
South of Joseph. Follow road south around Wallowa Lake 6.0 miles to campground.

JUNTURA (E-10)

CHUKAR PARK (BLM)
16 units, water, swimming, hiking trails, elev. 3100', $.
North of Juntura. West on US 20 to Beulah Reservoir Road, 6.0 miles to campground.

OASIS CAFE/MOTEL/RV PARK (Private)
22 trailer sites w/hookups for water/electricity/sewer, reservation information - (503)277-3605, river, fishing, restaurant, elev. 2900', $$.
In Juntura. Located on US 20 in Juntura.

KENO (C-12)

KENO CAMP (Pacific Power)
26 campsites, picnic area, showers, trailer waste disposal, on Klamath River, boat launch, fishing, swimming, $.
Northwest of Keno. State 66 approximately 2.0 miles northwest.

TOPSY (BLM)
15 primitive tent sites, no drinking water, picnic facilities, boat launch, boating, swimming, elev. 3500', $.
West of Keno. State 66 west 6.0 mile, Topsy County Road south 1.0 mile to campground.

KIMBERLY (D-9)

ASHER'S RV PARK (Private)
20 campsites w/hookups for electricity, tents okay, reservations - (503)934-2712, pit toilets, play area, hiking, fishing, nearby store, fossil hunting area, $-$$.
At Kimberly. Located on State 19 near John Day Fossil Beds.

KLAMATH FALLS (C-12)

ASPEN POINT (Winema National Forest)
61 units, trailers to 22', piped water, flush toilets, trailer waste disposal, at Lake of the Woods Recreation Area, boat launch, boating, swimming, fishing, trail to Mountain Lakes Wilderness, elev. 5000', $$.
Northwest of Klamath Falls. State 140 northwest 32.6 miles, FSR 3704 south .6 mile.

FOURMILE LAKE (Winema National Forest)
25 units, trailers to 20', horse facilities, trailhead access to Skylakes Wilderness, well, fishing, boating, swimming, elev. 5800', $.
Northwest of Klamath Falls. State 140 northwest 35.0 miles, FSR 3661 5.5 miles to campground.

HARRIMAN SPRINGS RESORT & MARINA (Private)
23 campsites, 17 w/hookups for water/electricity/sewer, plus 5 tent units, reservation information - (503)356-2323, showers, laundry, trailer waste disposal, lake, swimming, fishing, boat launch, boat rental, lounge, hiking, elev. 4100', $$.
Northwest of Klamath Falls. State 140 northwest 28.0 miles, Rocky Point Road north 1.5 miles.

KLAMATH FALLS KOA (Private)
73 campsites, 36 w/hookups for water/electricity/sewer, 30 w/hookups for water/electricity, plus 7 tent units, reservations - (503)884-4644, showers, laundry, groceries, trailer waste disposal, propane, swimming pool, stream, playground, elev. 4100', $$$.
In Klamath Falls. State 140 to Klamath Falls Lakeview exit, 5th Street to Washburn, left to Shasta Way, located at 3435 Shasta Way.

LAKE OF THE WOODS (Winema National Forest)
Campsites, picnic area, boat launch, hiking, $$.
Northwest of Klamath Falls. State 140 northwest 35.0 miles.

LAKE OF THE WOODS RESORT (Private)
45 campsites, 30 w/hookups for water/electricity/sewer, plus 15 tent units, trailers to 35', reservation information - (503)949-8300, showers, laundry, groceries, trailer waste disposal, lake, restaurant/lounge, swimming, fishing, boat launch, boat rental, hiking, elev. 5000', $$.
Northwest of Klamath Falls. State 140 west 33.0 miles to milepost #36, south 1.0 mile on Lake of the Woods Road, west .5 mile to campground.

MT. VIEW RV PARK (Private)
25 units w/hookups for water/electricity/sewer, reservations - (503)884-5978, showers, laundry, trailer waste disposal, fishing, $$-$$$.
In Klamath Falls. Located at 6660 S. 6th Street in downtown Klamath Falls.

NORTH HILLS MOBILEHOME PARK (Private)
15 spaces w/hookups for water/electricity/sewer, reservation information - (503)884-9068, tv hookup, laundry, trailer waste disposal, swimming, fishing, golf, $$.
In Klamath Falls. Located at 3611 Highway 97 North.

OREGON MOTEL 8 RV PARK (Private)
55 campsites, 29 w/hookups for water/electricity/sewer, 4 w/hookups for water/electricity, plus 22 tent units, reservation information - (503)882-0482, showers, laundry, swimming pool, therapy pool, game room, elev. 4200', $$$.
North of Klamath Falls. US 97 north 3.0 miles, on east side of road.

ROCKY POINT RESORT & MARINA (Private)
35 campsites, 19 w/hookups for water/electricity/sewer, 10 w/hookups for water/electricity, plus 6 tent units, reservation information - (503)356-2287, showers, laundry, trailer waste disposal, river, lake, swimming, fishing, boat launch, tackle shop, paddleboat rental, lounge, hiking, elev. 4200', $$-$$$.
Northwest of Klamath Falls. State 140 northwest 28.0 miles, Rocky Point Road north 3.0 miles to campground.

SUNSET (Winema National Forest)
67 units, trailers to 22', piped water, lake, flush toilets, boat launch, boating, swimming, fishing, water skiing, adjacent to Mountain Lakes Wilderness, at Lake of the Wood Recreation Area, elev. 5000', $$.
Northwest of Klamath Falls. State 140 northwest 32.6 miles, FSR 3704 south 1.0 mile.

TINGLEY LAKE ESTATES (Private)
14 campsites, 4 w/hookups for water/electricity/sewer, 6 w/hookups for water/electricity, plus 4 tent units, reservation information - (503)882-8386, showers, laundry, trailer waste disposal, pond, swimming, fishing, boat rental, playground, elev. 4100', $$.
South of Klamath Falls. US 97 south 7.0 miles to Midland, Old Midland Road 2.0 miles east, Tingley Lane .5 mile south.

WISEMAN'S MOBILE COURT (Private)
20 trailer sites w/hookups for water/electricity/sewer, reservation information - (503)883-8621, showers, laundry, trailer waste disposal, elev. 4200', $$.
In Klamath Falls. US 97 east 5.0 miles to 6th Street, located at 6800 S. 6th Street.

LA GRANDE (E-8)

HILGARD JUNCTION (Oregon State Park)
18 primitive campsites, maximum site 30', picnic area, wheelchair access, trailer waste disposal, fishing, Oregon Trail display, $$.
Northwest of La Grande. I-84 northwest 8.0 miles to campground.

HOT LAKE RV RESORT (Private)
100 units w/hookups for water/electricity/sewer, reservation information - (503)963-5253, showers, laundry, pool, spa, mineral baths, massage therapy, mini mart, $$$.
Southeast of La Grande. I-84 to exit #265, State 203 southeast 5.0 miles.

STONEWOOD RV PARK (Private)
102 sites, reservation information - (503)963-8121, showers, playground, rec room, trailer waste disposal, swimming, fishing, golf, $$-$$$.
In La Grande. Located at 1809 26th Street.

SUNDOWNER MOBILE HOME PARK (Private)
24 trailer sites w/hookups for water/electricity/sewer, no tents, reservation information - (503)963-2648, showers, laundry, trailer waste disposal, elev. 2800', $$$.
In La Grande. State 82 east .3 mile, Holmes Street south .2 mile.

LAKESIDE (A-11)

NORTH LAKE RESORT & MARINA (Private)
100 campsites, 5 w/hookups for water/electricity/sewer, 31 w/hookups for water/electricity, plus 64 tent units, reservation information - (503)759-3515, showers, groceries, lake, swimming, fishing, boat launch, boat rental, playground, $$.
In Lakeside. US 101 to Lakeside exit, .5 mile east to N. Lake Avenue, .5 mile east to 2090 North Lake Avenue.

SEADRIFT MOTEL & CAMPGROUND (Private)
42 trailers sites, 39 w/hookups for water/electricity/sewer/cable tv, plus 3 w/hookups for water/electricity, no tents, reservation information - (503)759-3102, showers, laundry, trailer waste disposal, playground, $$.
Northwest of Lakeside. US 101 north .3 mile past Lakeside exit.

LAKEVIEW (D-12)

GOOSE LAKE (Oregon State Park)
48 campsites w/hookups for electricity, trailers to 50', boat launch, fishing, $$$.
South of Lakeview. US 395 south 15.0 miles to campground.

HUNTER'S RV (Private)
23 sites, 10 w/hookups for water/electricity/sewer, plus 13 w/hookups for water/electricity, reservation information - (503)947-4968, showers, groceries, trailer waste disposal, therapy pool, ponds, lounge, playground, elev. 5000', $$-$$$.
North of Lakeview. US 395 north 2.0 miles.

JUNIPERS RESERVOIR RV RESORT (Private)
40 campsites, 25 w/hookups for water/electricity/sewer, plus 15 w/hookups for water/electricity, reservation information - (503)947-2050, showers, laundry, trailer waste disposal, reservoir, stream, fishing, hiking, wheelchair access, wildlife viewing, $$$.
West of Lakeview. State 140 west 10.0 miles, located in the middle of an 8,000 acre cattle ranch in a wildlife viewing area.

PARKWAY MOTEL & RV PARK (Private)
19 campsites, 13 w/hookups for water/electricity/sewer, 1 w/hookups for electricity only, plus 5 tent units, reservation information - (503)947-2707, showers, elev. 4800', $$-$$$.
In Lakeview. West of US 395/State 140 junction, on State 140, 2 blocks from junction.

VALLEY FALLS STORE & CAMPGROUND (Private)
16 campsites, 6 w/hookups for water/electricity/sewer, 1 w/hookups for water/electricity, 1 w/hookups for water only, plus 8 tent units, reservation information - (503)947-2052, groceries, playground, hiking, elev. 4200', $$.
North of Lakeview. US 395 north 23.0 miles, located at junction with State 31.

LANGLOIS (A-11)

LANGLOIS TRAVEL PARK (Private)
20 campsites, 10 w/hookups for water/electricity/sewer, plus 10 tent units, reservation information - (503)348-2256, showers, laundry, nearby wind surfing, $$.
In Langlois. Located at south end of town on US 101.

PINE SPRINGS KOA (Private)
72 campsites, 11 w/hookups for water/electricity/sewer, 17 w/hookups for water/electricity, plus 48 tent units, reservations - (503)348-2358, showers, laundry, groceries, propane, trailer waste disposal, pond, playground, hiking, $$-$$$.
South of Langlois. US 101 south 3.0 miles.

LaPINE (D-10)

ALLEN'S RIVERVIEW TRAILER PARK (Private)
25 campsites, 18 w/hookups for water/electricity/sewer/cable tv, plus 7 tent units, reservation information - (503)536-2382, showers, laundry, river, swimming, fishing, elev. 4300', $$.
North of La Pine. US 97 north 2.6 miles to Wickiup Junction, Burgess Road west 1.0 mile, Huntington Road north 1.0 mile.

CHIEF PAULINA HORSE CAMP (Deschutes National Forest)
14 units, trailers to 32', reservations required - (503)388-5674, in Newberry Crater, elev. 6300', $$.
Northeast of LaPine. US 97 north 5.0 miles, CR 21 east 15.0 miles.

CINDER HILL (Deschutes National Forest)
109 units, trailers to 32', piped water, flush toilets, boat launch, boating, fishing, in Newberry Crater, elev. 6300', $$.
East of LaPine. US 97 north 5.0 miles, CR 21 east 18.0 miles to campground. At east end of East Lake.

CULTUS LAKE (Deschutes National Forest)
54 units, trailers to 22', picnic area, well, lake, boating, swimming, fishing, water skiing, elev. 4700', $$.

Northwest of LaPine. US 97 northeast 2.4 miles, CR 43 west 9.0 miles, FSR 42 west 8.0 miles, CR 46 north 6.4 miles, FSR 463 west 1.0 mile.

DESCHUTES BRIDGE (Deschutes National Forest)
15 units, trailers to 22', picnic area, on Deschutes River, fishing, elev. 4600', $.
Northeast of LaPine. US 97 northeast 2.4 miles, CR 43 east 9.0 miles, FSR 42 west 8.0 miles, CR 46 north 10.0 miles.

EAST LAKE (Deschutes National Forest)
31 units, trailers to 32', piped water, on East Lake - speed limits, flush toilets, boat launch, boating, fishing, in Newberry Crater, elev. 6300', $$.
Northeast of LaPine. US 97 north 5.0 miles, CR 21 east 17.0 miles. Located on southwest side of East Lake.

EAST LAKE RESORT & RV PARK (Private)
38 trailer sites w/hookups for water/electricity/sewer, trailers to 35', tents okay, reservation information - (503)536-2230, showers, laundry, groceries, trailer waste disposal, playground, lake, swimming, fishing, boat launch, boat rental, hiking, elev. 6300', $$$.
Northeast of LaPine. US 97 north 6.0 miles, Paulina/East Lake Road 18.0 miles east.

FAR-E-NUF TRAILER PARK (Private)
18 trailer sites w/hookups for water/electricity/sewer/cable tv, reservations - (503)536-2265, showers, laundry, ice, trailer waste disposal, elev. 4200', $$.
North of LaPine. US 97 north 2.6 miles to Wickiup Junction, Burgess Road 2.5 miles west, Pine Forest Road .7 mile south, Wright Road 1 block to campground.

GULL POINT (Deschutes National Forest)
5 units, 15 group sites, trailers to 32', picnic area, piped water, on Wickiup Reservoir, flush toilets, boating, swimming, fishing, water skiing, elev. 4300', $$.
West of LaPine. US 97 northeast 2.4 miles, CR 43 west 9.0 miles, FSR 42 west 5.4 miles, FSR 4260 south 3.5 miles. Located on north side of Wickiup Reservoir.

HOT SPRINGS (Deschutes National Forest)
43 units, trailers to 32', piped water, on East Lake - speed limits, fishing, in Newberry Crater, elev. 6300', $$.
East of LaPine. US 97 north 5.0 miles, CR 21 east 17.6 miles. Campground is located on south side of East Lake.

LAPINE (Oregon State Park)
145 campsites, 95 w/hookups for water/electricity/sewer, plus 50 w/hookups for electricity only, maximum site 85', picnic area, wheelchair access, showers, trailer waste disposal, boating, fishing, $$-$$$.
North of LaPine. US 97 northeast 6.0 miles, LaPine Recreation Area Road 3.2 miles west.

LAVA LAKE (Deschutes National Forest)
45 units, trailers to 22', picnic area, well, lake - speed limits, trailer waste disposal, boat launch, boat rental, boating, fishing, hiking, elev. 4800', $$.
Northwest of LaPine. US 97 northeast 2.4 miles, CR 43 west 9.0 miles, CR 42 west 8.0 miles, CR 46 north 13.5 miles, FSR 500 northeast 1.0 mile.

LAVA LAKE RV CAMPGROUND (Private)
24 campsites w/hookups for water/electricity/sewer, tents okay, reservation information - (503)382-9443, showers, laundry, propane & gas, groceries, trailer waste disposal, lake, swimming, fishing, boat launch, boat rental, hiking, elev. 4700', $$.
Northwest of LaPine. US 97 north 3.0 miles, Pringle Falls Highway northwest 9.0 miles, Cascade Lakes Highway west/north 26.0 miles.

LITTLE CRATER (Deschutes National Forest)
51 units, trailers to 32', well, on Paulina Lake - speed limits, boat launch, boating, fishing, in Newberry Crater, elev. 6300', $$.
East of LaPine. US 97 north 5.0 miles, CR 21 east 15.0 miles. Campground is located on east shore of Paulina Lake.

NORTH DAVIS CREEK (Deschutes National Forest)
17 units, trailers to 22', picnic area, well, on Wickiup Reservoir, boat launch, boating, fishing, water skiing, elev. 4400', $$.
West of LaPine. US 97 northeast 2.4 miles, CR 43 west 9.0 miles, CR 42 west 8.0 miles, CR 46 south 4.0 miles. Located between two springs at west end of Wickiup Reservoir.

PAULINA LAKE (Deschutes National Forest)
71 units, trailers to 32', piped water, on Paulina Lake - speed limits, flush toilets, boat launch, boating, fishing, in Newberry Crater, elev. 6300', $$.
East of LaPine. US 97 north 5.0 miles, CR 21 east 13.1 miles. Campground is located on south shore of Paulina Lake.

PRAIRIE (Deschutes National Forest)
14 units, trailers to 32', well, stream, fishing, elev. 4400', $.
Northeast of LaPine. US 97 north 5.0 miles, CR 21 southeast 3.0 miles.

PRAIRIE GROUP AREA (Deschutes National Forest)
Group campsites, reservations required - (503)388-5674, stream, fishing, elev. 4300', $$.
Northeast of LaPine. US 97 north 5.0 miles, CR 21 southeast 2.5 miles.

QUINN RIVER (Deschutes National Forest)
41 units, trailers to 32', picnic area, well, river, boating, fishing, on Crane Prairie Reservoir - speed limits, historic site, elev. 4400', $$.
Northwest of LaPine. US 97 northeast 2.4 miles, CR 43 west 9.0 miles, FSR 42 west 8.0 miles, CR 46 north 4.0 miles. Located at mouth of Quinn River, on Crane Prairie Reservoir, near Billy Quinn Historical Grave Site.

ROCK CREEK (Deschutes National Forest)
32 units, trailers to 22', well, on Crane Prairie Reservoir - speed limits, boating, fishing, elev. 4400', $$.
Northwest of LaPine. US 97 northeast 2.4 miles, CR 43 west 9.0 miles, FSR 42 west 8.0 miles, CR 46 north 2.4 miles.

ROSLAND (Deschutes National Forest)
11 units, trailers to 22', no drinking water, on Little Deschutes River, swimming, fishing, elev. 4200', $.
North of LaPine. US 97 northeast 2.4 miles, CR 43 west 1.5 miles.

ROUNDUP TRAVEL TRAILER PARK (Private)
27 campsites, 23 w/hookups for water/electricity/sewer, plus 4 w/hookups for water/electricity, reservation information - (503)536-2378, showers, laundry, trailer waste disposal, elev. 4300', $$$.
In LaPine. From city center take Huntington Road south 1 block, then Finley Butte Road east 1 block to campground..

SOUTH TWIN LAKE (Deschutes National Forest)
21 units, trailers to 22', piped water, lake - no motors, flush toilets, boating, swimming, fishing, elev. 4300', $$.
Southwest of LaPine. US 97 northeast 2.4 miles, CR 43 west 9.0 miles, FSR 42 west 5.4 miles, FSR 4260 south 1.6 miles.

WEST SOUTH TWIN (Deschutes National Forest)
22 units, 2 group sites, trailers to 22', piped water, on Deschutes River channel - speed limits, flush toilets, boat launch, boat rental, cafe/snack bar, boating, swimming, fishing, elev. 4300', $$.
West of LaPine. US 97 northeast 2.4 miles, CR 43 west 9.0 miles, CR 42 west 5.4 miles, FSR 4260 south 1.7 miles.

LINCOLN CITY (A-9)

COYOTE ROCK RV PARK (Private)
58 campsites, 38 w/hookups for water/electricity/sewer/cable tv, plus 20 w/hookups for water/electricity/cable tv, reservation information - (503)996-6824, showers, ice, river, fishing, boat launch, boat rental, $$-$$$.
Southeast of Lincoln City. US 101 south 1.5 miles, State 229 east 1.0 mile.

DEVIL'S LAKE (Oregon State Park)
100 campsites, 32 w/hookups for water/electricity/sewer, plus 68 tent units, group campsites, mail reservations available, maximum site 62', wheelchair access, showers, boat launch, on East Devil's Lake, boating, fishing, swimming, $$-$$$.
At Lincoln City. Campground is at Lincoln City off US 101, follow signs.

LINCOLN CITY KOA (Private)
85 campsites, 23 w/hookups for water/electricity/sewer/cable tv, 29 w/hookups for water/electricity, plus 32 tent units, reservations - (503)994-2961, showers, laundry, groceries, game room, rec room w/kitchen, propane, trailer waste disposal, playground, $$$.
Northeast of Lincoln City. US 101 north 4.0 miles, East Devils Lake Road southeast 1.0 miles.

SALMON RIVER EVERGREEN PARK (Private)
32 campsites, 25 w/hookups for water/electricity/sewer, plus 7 tent units, reservation information - (503)994-3116, showers, laundry, groceries, trailer waste disposal, river, fishing,, hiking, $$-$$$.
Northeast of Lincoln City. US 101 north 5.0 miles, State 18 east 6.0 miles.

SPORTSMAN'S LANDING (Private)
30 trailer sites w/hookups for water/electricity/sewer/cable tv, reservation information - (503)996-4225, laundry, river, fishing, boat launch & rental, $$.
South of Lincoln City. US 101 south 5.0 miles, State 229 east 3.9 miles.

LOWELL (B-10)

BEDROCK (Willamette National Forest)
20 units, trailers to 22', picnic area, well, stream, swimming, fishing, hiking, elev. 1100', $-$$.

Northeast of Lowell. CR 6220 north 1.8 miles, CR 6240 east 9.9 miles, FSR 181 east 4.8 miles.

BIG POOL (Willamette National Forest)
5 tent units, piped water, stream, swimming, fishing, elev. 1000', $.
Northeast of Lowell. CR 6220 north 1.8 miles, CR 6240 east 9.9 miles, FSR 181 east 1.7 miles.

CLARK CREEK (Willamette National Forest)
5 group sites w/shelters, reservations required - (503)937-2129, no trailers, well, wheelchair access, interpretive services, hiking, $$$.
West of Lowell. CR 6220 north 1.8 miles, CR 6240 east 8.0 miles, FSR 18 east 3.0 miles.

PUMA (Willamette National Forest)
11 units, trailers to 18', well, stream, swimming, fishing, hiking, elev. 1100', $.
Northeast of Lowell. CR 6220 north 1.8 miles, CR 6240 east 9.9 miles, FSR 181 east 6.5 miles.

WINBERRY CREEK (Willamette National Forest)
6 units, 2 group sites, trailers to 18', well, fishing, swimming, hiking, elev. 1100', $-$$$.
East of Lowell. CR 6220 north 1.8 miles, CR 6240 east .4 mile, CR 62450 southeast 5.8 miles, FSR 191 southeast 3.5 miles.

MADRAS (D-9)

CANYON COURT & RV PARK (Private)
35 campsites, reservation information - (503)553-1011, pull thrus, tents okay, showers, laundry, tv, trailer waste disposal, nearby fishing, $-$$.
In Madras. Located at 7228 NW US Highway 26, in Madras.

HAYSTACK RESERVOIR (Ochoco National Forest)
24 units, trailers to 22', piped water, flush toilets, lake, boat launch, boating, swimming, fishing, water skiing, elev. 2900', $$-$$$.
South of Madras. US 97 south 9.3 miles, CR 6 southeast 3.3 miles, FSR 58 north .6 mile.

MADRAS/CULVER KOA (Private)
81 campsites, 16 w/hookups for water/electricity/sewer, 46 w/hookups for water/electricity, plus 19 tent units, reservations - (503)546-3073, showers, laundry, groceries, trailer waste disposal, swimming pool, playground, elev. 2800', $$-$$$.

Southwest of Madras. US 97 south 9.0 miles, Jericho Lane east .5 mile.

THE COVE PALISADES (Oregon State Park)
272 campsites, 87 w/hookups for water/electricity/sewer, 91 w/hookups for electricity only, plus 94 tent units, group campsites, maximum site 60', mail reservations available, picnic area, wheelchair access, showers, trailer waste disposal, boat launch, fishing, swimming, hiking trails, at confluence of Crooked/ Deschutes/Metolius Rivers, $$-$$$.
Southwest of Madras. Just south of Madras leave US 97 and head east 5.0 miles, road will veer south, campground is 10.0 miles past this point. Route is marked by signs.

MAPLETON (A-10)

ARCHIE KNOWLES (Siuslaw National Forest)
9 units, trailers to 18', picnic area, piped water, stream, flush toilets, elev. 100', $$.
East of Mapleton. State 126 east 3.0 miles.

CLAY CREEK (BLM)
20 units, trailers okay, group picnic area w/shelters, drinking water, boating, swimming, fishing, nature study, elev. 500', $$.
Southeast of Mapleton. State 126 east 12.5 miles, Siuslaw River Road south 16.0 miles.

MAPLE-LANE TRAILER PARK & MARINA (Private)
46 campsites w/hookups for water/electricity/sewer, reservation information - (503)268-4822, showers, river, fishing, boat launch, $$.
In Mapleton. Located on State 126 at milepost #14.

WHITTAKER CREEK (BLM)
31 units, trailers okay, picnic area, drinking water, boat launch, non-motorized boating only, swimming, fishing, nature study, elev. 300', $$.
East of Mapleton. State 126 southeast 14.0 miles, Whittaker Creek Road to campground.

MAUPIN (D-8)

BEAR SPRINGS (Mt. Hood National Forest)
21 units, trailers to 18', piped water, elev. 3200', $$.
Northwest of Maupin. State 216 northwest 25.0 miles.

MAUPIN CITY PARK (City)
27 trailer sites w/hookups for water/electricity/sewer, trailers to 24', trailer waste disposal, river, fishing, $-$$.
In Maupin. Located in downtown Maupin.

McKENZIE BRIDGE (C-10)

BELKNAP WOODS RESORT (Private)
31 campsites, 23 w/hookups for water/electricity/sewer, plus 8 w/hookups for water/electricity, reservations required - (503)822-3512, showers, laundry, trailer waste disposal, swimming pool, therapy pool, river, fishing, hiking, $$.
East of McKenzie Bridge. State 126 east 5.0 miles, Belknap Springs Road north .3 mile.

COLDWATER COVE (Willamette National Forest)
35 units, 2 group sites, trailers to 22', well, lake - no motors, groceries, boat launch, boat rental, cafe/snack bar, boating, fishing, hiking, wheelchair access - includes trails, elev. 3100', $.
Northeast of McKenzie Bridge. State 126 northeast 14.2 miles, FSR 1372 southeast .1 mile.

ICE CAP CREEK (Willamette National Forest)
22 units, trailers to 18', piped water, flush toilets, near Carmen Reservoir - no motors, Koosah & Sahalie Falls nearby, fishing, hiking, elev. 3000', $$.
Northeast of McKenzie Bridge. State 126 northeast 19.2 miles, FSR 14071 northeast .1 mile.

McKENZIE BRIDGE (Willamette National Forest)
20 units, trailers to 22', well, on McKenzie River, boating, fishing, elev. 1400', $.
West of McKenzie Bridge. State 126 west 1.0 mile.

OLALLIE (Willamette National Forest)
17 units, trailers to 22', at confluence of McKenzie River & Olallie Creek, boating, fishing, elev. 2000', $.
Northeast of McKenzie Bridge. State 126 northeast 11.1 miles.

PARADISE (Willamette National Forest)
64 units, trailers to 22', piped water, group picnic area, flush toilets, on McKenzie River, fishing, hiking, elev. 1600', $$.
East of McKenzie Bridge. State 126 east 3.5 miles.

TRAIL BRIDGE (Willamette National Forest)
24 units, trailers to 32', picnic area, piped water, flush toilets, lake - speed limits, boating, fishing, elev. 2000', $.

Northeast of McKenzie Bridge. State 126 northeast 13.2 miles, FSR 1477 southwest .2 mile.

McMINNVILLE (B-8)

MULKEY RV PARK (Private)
50 campsites, 12 w/hookups for water/electricity/sewer, 12 w/hookups for water/electricity, plus 26 tent sites, reservation information - (503)472-2475, showers, river, fishing, $$.
Southwest of McMinnville. State 18 southwest 4.0 miles.

MEHAMA (C-9)

FISHERMEN'S BEND (BLM)
38 units, 22 w/hookups for water, plus 16 tent sites, group campsites & picnic area by reservation only - (503)399-5646, drinking water, flush toilets, showers, boat launch, on North Santiam River, fishing, nature study, basketball & volleyball courts, ball diamonds, horseshoe pits, trailer waste disposal, elev. 750', $$.
Southeast of Mehama. State 22 east 8.5 miles, campground is 1.5 miles west of Mill City.

JOHN NEAL MEMORIAL PARK (Linn County)
40 campsites, trailers to 22', playground, playfield, river, boat launch, fishing, hiking, $$.
Southeast of Mehama. South 1.0 mile to Lyons, east 1.5 miles to Memorial Park Road, north to park.

MOSIER (C-8)

AMERICAN ADVENTURE (Private)
350 campsites, 250 w/hookups for water/electricity, plus 100 tent sites, information - (503)478-3750, showers, picnic area, laundry, play area, wheelchair access, trailer waste disposal, pond fishing, swimming, hiking, spa, mini mart, golf course, $$-$$$.
In Mosier. Located at 2350 Carroll Road, in Mosier.

MYRTLE CREEK (B-11)

MILLSITE PARK & RV PARK (Private)
11 campsites w/hookups for water/electricity, tents okay, reservation information - (503)863-3171, showers, wheelchair access, playground, trailer waste disposal, river, fishing, trails, $$$.

In Myrtle Creek. Leave I-5 at exit #108, in Myrtle Creek take 4th Street to park. Located at 441 4th Street.

NEWBERG (B-8)

CHAMPOEG (Oregon State Park)
48 campsites w/hookups for electricity, maximum site 50', group campsites, group picnic area, wheelchair access, showers, trailer waste disposal, boating, fishing, bicycle paths, hiking trails, historic area - site of Oregon's first government, interpretive center, $$$.
Southeast of Newberg. Campground is located off US 99W, approximately 7.0 miles southeast of Newberg and is also accessible via I-5.

NEWPORT (A-9)

AGATE BEACH TRAILER & RV PARK (Private)
30 campsites, 21 w/hookups for water/electricity/sewer/cable tv, 9 w/hookups for water/electricity/cable tv, no tents, reservation information - (503)265-7670, showers, laundry, trailer waste disposal, lounge, near ocean beaches, $$-$$$.
North of Newport. US 101 north 3.0 miles.

BEVERLY BEACH (Oregon State Park)
279 campsites, 52 w/hookups for water/electricity/sewer, 75 w/hookups for electricity, plus 152 tent units, group campsites, mail reservations available, maximum site 65', picnic area, wheelchair access, showers, trailer waste disposal, fishing, ocean access, beachcombing, hiking, $$-$$$.
North of Newport. US 101 north 7.0 miles.

HARBOR VILLAGE TRAILER PARK (Private)
140 trailer sites w/hookups for water/electricity/sewer/cable tv, no tents, reservation information - (503)265-5088, showers, laundry, groceries, ocean access, fishing, boat rental, lounge, $$-$$$.
East of Newport. US 20 east .5 mile, SW Moore Drive south .5 mile, SE Bay Blvd. east 1 block.

SOUTH BEACH (Oregon State Park)
254 campsites w/hookups for electricity, group sites, mail reservations available, maximum site 60', wheelchair access, showers, trailer waste disposal, ocean access, beachcombing, fishing, hiking, $$$.
South of Newport. US 101 south 2.0 miles to campground.

SOUTH BEACH MARINA RV PARK (Port of Newport)
60 trailer sites w/hookups for water/electricity/sewer/cable tv, tents okay, reservation information - (503)867-3321, showers, laundry, playground, wheelchair access, groceries, trailer waste disposal, river, fishing, boat launch, lounge, $$-$$$.
In Newport. Leave US 101 at south end of Yaquina Bay Bridge on Marine Science Center exit, park is .5 mile east.

SPORTSMAN'S TRAILER PARK (Private)
36 trailer sites, 33 w/hookups for water/electricity/sewer, plus 3 w/hookups for water/electricity, no tents, reservation information - (503)867-3330, ocean access, river, fishing, boat launch, boat rental, $$.
In Newport. Leave US 101 at south end of Yaquina Bay Bridge on Marine Science Center exit, park is north 1 block.

NORTH BEND (A-11)

BLUEBILL LAKE (Siuslaw National Forest)
18 units, 1 group site, trailers to 22', piped water, flush toilets, lake, fishing, hiking, ocean beach & dunes access, elev. 100', $$.
Northwest of North Bend. US 101 north 2.5 miles, CR 609 west .8 mile, FSR 1099 northwest 2.3 miles.

HORSEFALL BEACH (Siuslaw National Forest)
34 campsites, trailers okay, water, ocean beach access, ORV access to sand dunes, elev. 100', $$.
North of North Bend. US 101 north 4.0 miles, Horsefall Dunes Road to campground.

HORSEFALL STAGING (Siuslaw National Forest)
90 campsites, trailers okay, showers, ORV access to sand dunes, elev. 100', $$.
North of North Bend. US 101 north 4.0 miles, Horsefall Dunes Road to campground.

SPINREEL (Siuslaw National Forest)
37 campsites, trailers okay, drinking water, ORV access to sand dunes, trail, elev. 100', $$.
North of North Bend. US 101 north 8.0 miles to campground.

THE FIRS TRAILER PARK (Private)
25 trailer sites w/hookups for water/electricity/sewer/cable tv, reservation information - (503)756-6274, showers, laundry, $-$$.
North of North Bend. US 101 north 7.0 miles, Wildwood Drive east 1.1 mile.

WILD MARE HORSE CAMP (Siuslaw National Forest)
15 campsites, trailers okay, horse corrals, drinking water, no ORV, elev. 100', $$.
North of North Bend. US 101 north 4.0 miles, Horsefall Dune Road to campground.

OAKRIDGE (C-10)

BLACK CANYON (Willamette National Forest)
71 units, trailers to 22', picnic area, piped water, wheelchair access - includes trails & fishing, river - speed limit, boat launch, boating, fishing, swimming, hiking, at head of Lookout Point Reservoir, elev. 1000', $$-$$$.
Northwest of Oakridge. State 58 northwest 8.5 miles.

BLUE POOL (Willamette National Forest)
22 units, trailers to 18', picnic area, piped water, flush toilets, river, fishing, swimming, near McCredie Hot Springs, elev. 1900', $$.
Southeast of Oakridge. State 58 southeast 8.8 miles.

GOLD LAKE (Willamette National Forest)
25 units, trailers to 18', picnic area, well, lake - no motors, boat launch, boating, swimming, hiking, flyfishing only, elev. 4800', $$.
Southeast of Oakridge. State 58 southeast 25.6 miles, FSR 500 northeast 2.2 miles.

HAMPTON (Willamette National Forest)
5 units, trailers to 32', well, river, boat launch, boating, swimming, fishing, water skiing, elev. 1100', $.
Northwest of Oakridge. State 58 northwest 10.0 miles.

ISLET (Willamette National Forest)
55 units, 3 group sites, trailers to 22', piped water, flush toilets, trailer waste disposal, lake - speed limits, boat launch, boating, swimming, fishing, hiking, elev. 5400', $$.
East of Oakridge. State 58 southeast 23.1 miles, FSR 5897 northeast 10.5 miles, FSR 5898 northwest 1.7 miles, FSR 5898 southwest 1.7 miles.

NORTH WALDO (Willamette National Forest)
58 units, trailers to 22', piped water, flush toilets, trailer waste disposal, lake - speed limits, boat launch, boating, swimming, fishing, hiking, elev. 5400', $$.
East of Oakridge. State 58 southeast 23.1 miles, FSR 5897 northeast 10.5 miles, FSR 5898 northwest 1.5 miles, FSR 515 northwest .6 mile.

PACKARD CREEK (Willamette National Forest)
33 units, trailers to 32', picnic area, piped water, lake, wheelchair access includes trails, boat launch, boating, swimming, water skiing, fishing, hiking, elev. 1600', $$-$$$.
Southeast of Oakridge. State 58 southeast 2.2 miles, CR 360 southeast .5 mile, FSR 21 south 5.2 miles.

SALMON CREEK FALLS (Willamette National Forest)
15 units, trailers to 18', picnic area, well, fishing, swimming, elev. 1500', $$.
East of Oakridge. CR 149 east 3.0 miles, FSR 24 northeast 3.7 miles.

SAND PRAIRIE (Willamette National Forest)
20 units, trailers to 32', piped water, flush toilets, wheelchair access includes trails, river, near head of Hills Creek Reservoir, nearby boat launch, swimming, fishing, elev. 1600', $$-$$$.
South of Oakridge. State 58 southeast 2.2 miles, CR 360 southeast .5 mile, FSR 21 south 11.6 miles.

SHADOW BAY (Willamette National Forest)
92 units, 11 large group sites, trailers to 40', reservations advised - (503)782-2291, piped water, flush toilets, trailer waste disposal, lake - speed limits, boat launch, boating, swimming, fishing, elev. 5400', $$-$$$.
East of Oakridge. State 58 southeast 23.1 miles, FSR 5897 northeast 6.5 miles, FSR 5896 northwest 2.0 miles.

SHADY DELL (Willamette National Forest)
9 units, trailers to 18', well, stream, fishing, elev. 1000', $.
Northwest of Oakridge. State 58 northwest 7.0 miles.

ONTARIO (F-10)

COUNTRY CAMPGROUNDS (Private)
15 campsites w/hookups for water/electricity/sewer, tent sites available, reservations - (503)889-6042, showers, laundry, trailer waste disposal, picnic area, hiking, fishing, $-$$.
At Ontario. Located 2.0 miles west of Ontario Airport at 660 Sugar Avenue.

IDLE WHEELS (Private)
6 campsites w/hookups for water/electricity/sewer, reservations - (503)889-8433, showers, laundry, trailer waste disposal, $$.
In Ontario. Located at 198 SE 5th Street, in Ontario.

PACIFIC CITY (A-8)

CAPE KIWANDA RV PARK (Private)
135 campsites, 95 w/hookups for water/electricity/sewer, plus 40 w/hookups for water/electricity, reservation information - (503)965-6230, showers, laundry, cable tv, groceries, playground, trailer waste disposal, ocean access, swimming, fishing, boat launch, $$-$$$.
North of Pacific City. At city center take Brooten Road west .2 mile, then proceed north 1.0 mile to campground.

ISLAND PARK (Tillamook County)
40 campsites, trailer waste disposal, ocean access, pond, swimming, fishing, boat launch, $$.
North of Pacific City. US 101 north 5.0 miles, at Sandlake.

PACIFIC CITY TRAILER PARK (Private)
15 trailer sites w/hookups for water/electricity/sewer, adults only, reservation information - (503)965-6820, cable tv, showers, laundry, trailer waste disposal, river, fishing, $$.
In Pacific City. At city center take Pacific Avenue east 1 block.

RAINES RESORT (Private)
14 campsites, 12 w/hookups for water/electricity/sewer, plus 2 tent units, reservation information - (503)965-6371, laundry, river, fishing, boat launch, boat rental, $$.
In Pacific City. At city center take Brooten Road west .2 mile, then proceed north .8 mile, just past the bridge take Ferry Street west .1 mile.

RIVERVIEW LODGE CAMPGROUND (Private)
12 campsites w/hookups for water/electricity, reservation information - (503)965-6000, showers, river, swimming, fishing, boat rental, $-$$.
In Pacific City. Leave US 101 at northern Pacific City exit, campground is west 1.0 mile.

SAND BEACH (Siuslaw National Forest)
101 units, trailers to 32', piped water, flush toilets, trailer waste disposal, boating, fishing, Pacific Ocean & sand dunes access, ORV area, elev. 100', $.
North of Pacific City. CR 536 west .2 mile, CR 535 north 8.4 miles, CR 503 west 1.0 mile, FSR S3001 southwest .5 mile.

SAND BEACH PARKING (Siuslaw National Forest)
100 units, trailers to 32', piped water, flush toilets, no tables, boating, fishing, Pacific Ocean & sand dunes access, ORV area, elev. 100', $-$$.

North of Pacific City. CR 536 west .2 mile, CR 535 north 8.4 miles, CR 503 southwest 1.8 miles.

WEBB PARK (Tillamook County)
30 campsites, trailer waste disposal, ocean access, fishing, boat launch, $$.
North of Pacific City. At city center take Brooten Road west .2 mile then north 2.0 miles to park.

WOOD PARK (Tillamook County)
10 campsites, 5 w/hookups for water/electricity/sewer, plus 5 tent sites, river, fishing, $$.
103North of Pacific City. Take Brooten Road west .2 mile then north 1.0 miles.

PARKDALE (C-8)

LOST LAKE (Mt. Hood National Forest)
76 units, trailers to 22', piped water, lake - no motors, wheelchair access, groceries, ice, showers, boat launch, interpretive services, boat rental, cafe/snack bar, boating, swimming, fishing, hiking, bicycling, elev. 3200', $$.
Southwest of Parkdale. State 281 north 6.0 miles, CR N22 southwest 10.0 miles, FSR 13 southwest 4.0 miles.

LOST LAKE GROUP CAMP (Mt. Hood National Forest)
12 group sites, trailers to 22', reservations required - (503)666-0701, piped water, showers, groceries, ice, lake - no motors, boat launch, interpretive services, boat rental, swimming, fishing, hiking, bicycling, elev. 3200', $$$.
Southwest of Parkdale. State 281 north 6.0 miles, CR N22 southwest 10.0 miles, FSR 13 southwest 4.0 miles.

POLALLIE (Mt. Hood National Forest)
10 units, trailers to 18', well, river, swimming, fishing, elev. 3000', $$.
South of Parkdale. State 35 southeast 14.0 miles.

ROBINHOOD (Mt. Hood National Forest)
24 units, trailers to 18', picnic area, wheelchair access, well, river, swimming, fishing, hiking, elev. 3600', $$.
Southeast of Parkdale. State 35 south 12.0 miles.

SHERWOOD (Mt. Hood National Forest)
18 units, trailers to 18', picnic area, well, river, wheelchair access, fishing, hiking, elev. 3000', $$.
South of Parkdale. State 35 south 8.0 miles.

WAHTUM LAKE (Mt. Hood National Forest)
8 tent units, fishing, lake, hike-in only, elev. 3700', $$.
Northwest of Parkdale. State 281 north 6.0 miles, CR 501 south-
west 5.0 miles, FSR N13/1300 west 5.0 miles, FSR N18/1820
northwest 8.0 miles, FSR N20/2820620 to Wahtum Lake, trail .3
mile to lakeside tent units.

PAULINA (D-10)

SUGAR CREEK (Ochoco National Forest)
10 units, trailers to 22', picnic area, swimming, bicycling, elev.
4000', $.
Northeast of Paulina. CR 380 east 3.5 miles, CR 113 north 6.5
miles, FSR 158 east 1.8 miles.

WOLF CREEK (Ochoco National Forest)
17 units, trailers to 22', piped water, bicycling, elev. 4100', $.
Northeast of Paulina. CR 380 east 3.5 miles, CR 113 north 6.6
miles, FSR 142 north 1.6 miles, campground road north .2 mile.

PENDLETON (E-7)

ARROWHEAD RV PARK (Private)
100 trailer sites w/hookups for water/electricity/sewer, reserva-
tions - (503)276-8080, wheelchair access, groceries, ice, propane,
gas & diesel, cafe, elev. 2600', $$.
East of Pendleton. I-84 east 4.0 miles to exit #216, Market Road
.1 mile northeast.

BROOKE TRAILER COURT (Private)
18 campsites, 16 w/hookups for water/electricity/sewer, plus 2
w/hookups for water/electricity, reservation information -
(503)276-5353, showers, laundry, ice, on river, fishing, $$-$$$.
In Pendleton. I-84 to exit #210, State 11 northeast .8 mile, SE
Court Avenue 2.5 miles west, SE 8th Street north 2 blocks.

EMIGRANT SPRINGS (Oregon State Park)
51 campsites, 18 w/hookups for water/electricity/sewer, plus 33
tent units, group campsites, maximum site 60', group picnic
area, showers, Oregon Trail display, located in ponderosa pine
forest, $$-$$$.
Southeast of Pendleton. I-84 southeast 26.0 miles to campground.

RV PARK (Private)
61 campsites, 31 w/hookups for water/electricity/sewer/cable tv, plus 30 w/hookups for water/electricity, trailers to 35', no dogs, information - (503)276-5408, showers, laundry, playground, trailer waste disposal, $$$.
In Pendleton. I-84 to exit #210, State 11 to Byers Avenue, located at 1500 SE Byers Avenue.

PHILOMATH (A-9)

ALSEA FALLS (BLM)
16 units, trailers okay, picnic area, drinking water, swimming, hiking, geology, fishing, nature study, elev. 800', $$.
Southwest of Philomath. State 34 southwest 19.0 miles to Alsea, follow South Fork Alsea Road southeast to campground which is about 8.0 miles west of Glenbrook.

MARYS PEAK (Siuslaw National Forest)
3 tent units, picnic area, hiking, elev. 3500', $.
Southwest of Philomath. US 20 west 1.0 miles, State 34 southwest 9.1 miles, FSR 3010 northwest 9.2 miles.

PORT ORFORD (A-11)

AGATE BEACH TRAILER PARK (Private)
14 campsites, 12 w/hookups for water/electricity/sewer, plus 2 w/hookups for water/electricity, reservation information - (503)332-3031, ocean access, lake, agate hunting, beachcombing, surf fishing, $$.
In Port Orford. US 101 to 12th Street, west .7 mile to park.

CAPE BLANCO (Oregon State Park)
58 campsites w/hookups for electricity, maximum site 70', picnic area, wheelchair access, showers, trailer waste disposal, fishing, ocean access, black sand beach, beachcombing, hiking, access to the Oregon Coast Trail, historic Hughes House. $$$.
Northwest of Port Orford. US 101 north 4.0 miles, follow signs west 5.0 miles to campground.

ELK RIVER RV CAMPGROUND (Private)
50 campsites w/hookups for water/electricity/sewer, tents okay, pull thrus, information - (503)332-2255, showers, laundry, trailer waste disposal, on Elk River, fishing, boat access, $$-$$$.
North of Port Orford. US 101 north 3.0 miles, Elk River Road 1.7 miles to campground.

EVERGREEN PARK (Private)
15 trailer sites w/hookups for water/electricity/sewer, reservation information - (503)332-5942, showers, laundry, trailer waste disposal, $$.
In Port Orford. US 101 to 9th Street, west 2 blocks.

HUMBUG MOUNTAIN (Oregon State Park)
108 campsites, 30 w/hookups for water/electricity/sewer, plus 78 tent units, maximum site 55', picnic area, wheelchair access, showers, trailer waste disposal, fishing, ocean access, beachcombing, hiking, access to the Oregon Coast Trail, $$-$$$.
South of Port Orford. US 101 south 6.0 miles.

PORT ORFORD RV TRAILER VILLAGE (Private)
49 campsites, 40 w/hookups for water/electricity/sewer, plus 9 w/hookups for water/electricity, reservation information - (503)332-1041, showers, cable tv, laundry, ice, public kitchen, rec room, trailer waste disposal, $$-$$$.
In Port Orford. US 101 to north end of town, Madrona Avenue east 1 block, Port Orford Loop .5 mile north.

PORTLAND (B-8)

AINSWORTH (Oregon State Park)
45 campsites w/hookups for water/electricity/sewer, maximum site 60', picnic area, showers, trailer waste disposal, hiking, access to Columbia Gorge Trail, $$$.
East of Portland. Take US 30's scenic route east 37.0 miles to campground which is located just west of US 30's remerging with I-84.

JANTZEN BEACH RV PARK (Private)
165 trailer sites w/hookups for water/electricity/sewer, no tents, reservation information - (503)289-7626 or (800)443-7248, showers, laundry, ice, swimming pool, tennis, playground, rec room, nearby shops, $$$.
In Portland. I-5 north to Jantzen Beach exit #308, North Hayden Island Drive west .5 mile.

PORTLAND - FAIRVIEW RV PARK (Private)
220 campsites w/hookups for water/electricity/sewer, reservations - (503)661-1047, showers, laundry, trailer waste disposal, pool, rec room, satellite tv, pets okay, lake fishing, horseshoes, $$$.
East of Portland. I-84 to Parkrose exit, Sandy Blvd. 2.0 miles. Located at 21401 NE Sandy Blvd.

SOUTHGATE MOBILE HOME & RV PARK (Private)
25 trailer sites w/hookups for water/electricity/sewer, reservation information - (503)771-5262, showers, laundry, $$$.
In Portland. I-205 to Foster Avenue exit, west to 82nd Avenue, turn left on 82nd Avenue, located at 7911 SE 82nd Avenue.

TALL FIRS MOBILE HOME & RV PARK (Private)
7 trailer sites w/hookups for water/electricity/sewer, no tents, reservation information - (503)761-8210, laundry, $$$.
In Portland. I-205 to Division exit, located at 15656 SE Division.

TOWN & COUNTRY MOBILE ESTATES (Private)
21 campsites w/hookups for water/electricity/sewer, reservation information - (503)771-1040, showers, laundry, tv, rec room, groceries, trailer waste disposal, $$-$$$.
In Portland. I-205 to Foster Avenue exit, west to 82nd Avenue, turn left on 82nd Avenue, located at 9911 SE 82nd Avenue.

TRAILER PARK OF PORTLAND (Private)
120 trailer sites, 100 w/hookups for water/electricity/sewer/cable tv, plus 20 w/hookups for water/electricity, no tents, reservations - (503)692-0225, showers, laundry, groceries, trailer waste disposal, river, fishing, playground, $$-$$$.
Southeast of Portland. I-5 to exit #289, Nyberg Road (State 212) east .2 mile to campground.

POWERS (A-11)

DAPHNE GROVE (Siskiyou National Forest)
17 units, trailers to 18', drinking water, river, swimming, fishing, hiking, elev. 800', $.
South of Powers. CR 90 southeast 4.2 miles, FSR 333 south 10.4 miles.

POWERS COUNTY PARK (Coos County)
60 campsites, 40 w/hookups for water/electricity, plus 20 tent sites, showers, playground, tennis, trailer waste disposal, lake - no motors, fishing, swimming, horseshoes, hiking, $$.
In Powers. Located 1.0 miles north of city center.

PRAIRIE CITY (E-9)

DEPOT PARK (Prairie City)
21 campsites, 16 w/hookups for water/electricity/sewer, plus 9 tent sites, showers, trailer waste disposal, hiking, $$.
In Prairie City. Leave US 26 on Main Street, park is .5 mile.

PRINEVILLE (E-10)

ANTELOPE RESERVOIR (Ochoco National Forest)
24 units, trailers to 32', picnic area, well, lake, boat launch, boating, swimming, fishing, elev. 4600', $.
Southeast of Prineville. CR 380 southeast 29.0 miles, FSR 17 south 11.0 miles, FSR 17 east .3 mile.

CHIMNEY ROCK RECREATION SITE (BLM)
33 units, trailers to 30', water, picnic facilities, fishing in Crooked River, elev. 1500', $.
South of Prineville. State 27 south 12.0 miles.

CRYSTAL CORRAL PARK (Private)
42 campsites, 16 w/hookups for water/electricity/sewer, 7 w/hookups for water/electricity, plus 20 tent units, reservation information - (503)447-5932, showers, laundry, groceries, lake, swimming, fishing, boat launch, elev. 3200', $-$$.
East of Prineville. US 26 east 6.5 miles.

LAKESHORE MOTOR PARK (Private)
64 campsites, 43 w/hookups for water/electricity/sewer, 4 w/hookups for electricity, plus 17 tent units, reservation information - (503)447-6059, showers, laundry, groceries, trailer waste disposal, lake, swimming, fishing, boat launch, boat rental, lounge, playground, elev. 3100', $$-$$$.
East of Prineville. US 26 east 7.0 miles.

OCHOCO DIVIDE (Ochoco National Forest)
28 units, trailers to 22', piped water, elev. 4700', $.
Northeast of Prineville. US 26 northeast 30.8 miles, FSR 550 southeast .1 mile. Campground is at summit of Ochoco Pass.

OCHOCO LAKE (Oregon State Park)
22 primitive campsites, maximum site 30', drinking water, picnic area, boat launch, fishing, hiking trails, $$-$$$.
East of Prineville. State 26 east 7.0 miles to campground.

PRINEVILLE RESERVOIR (Oregon State Park)
70 campsites, 22 w/hookups for water/electricity/sewer, plus 48 tent units, mail reservations available, maximum site 40', picnic area, showers, boat launch, fishing, swimming, $$-$$$.
Southeast of Prineville. US 26 east 1.0 mile, Prineville Reservoir Road 16.0 miles southeast to campground.

PRINEVILLE RESERVOIR RESORT (Private)
73 campsites w/hookups for water/electricity, reservations - (503)447-7468, showers, groceries, trailer waste disposal, lake, swimming, fishing, boat launch, boat rental, elev. 3100', $$$.
Southeast of Prineville. US 26 east 1.0 mile, Prineville Reservoir Road 18.0 miles southeast.

WALTON LAKE (Ochoco National Forest)
23 units, trailers to 22', picnic area, piped water, lake - no motors, boating, fishing, swimming, hiking trails, elev. 5000', $$.
Northeast of Prineville. US 26 east 16.7 miles, CR 123 northeast 8.5 miles, FSR 22 6.2 miles, FSR 2220 .3 mile to campground.

WILDCAT (Ochoco National Forest)
17 units, trailers to 32', picnic area, well, stream, hiking, adjacent to Mill Creek Wilderness, elev. 3700', $.
Northeast of Prineville. US 26 east 9.2 miles, CR 122 northeast 8.9 miles, FSR 33 2.0 miles, FSR 300 east .2 mile.

PROSPECT (C-11)

ABBOTT CREEK (Rogue River National Forest)
21 units, trailers to 22', picnic area, well, fishing, elev. 3100', $.
North of Prospect. State 62 north 6.8 miles, FSR 68 northwest 3.4 miles.

FAREWELL BEND (Rogue River National Forest)
61 units, trailers to 22', piped water, river, flush toilets, fishing, elev. 3400', $$.
North of Prospect. State 62 north 11.6 miles.

HAMAKER (Rogue River National Forest)
10 tent units, well, river, fishing, hiking, elev. 4000', $.
North of Prospect. State 62 north 12.0 miles, State 230 north 11.0 miles, FSR 6530 southeast .6 mile, FSR 900 south .6 mile.

MT. HOME MOBILE VILLAGE (Private)
7 campsites, tents okay, reservation information - (503)560-3504, showers, laundry, fishing, $$-$$.
In Prospect. Take 1st Street to Mill Creek Drive, campground is located at 51 Mill Creek Drive.

UNION CREEK (Rogue River National Forest)
72 units, trailers to 18', picnic area, piped water, fishing, hiking, elev. 3200', $.
North of Prospect. State 62 north 10.8 miles, FSR 3136 west .2 mile.

RAINIER (B-7)

HUDSON/PARCHER PARK (Columbia County)
18 campsites w/hookups for water/electricity, plus tent area, playfield, playground, trailer waste disposal, $$.
North of Rainier. Located 1 mile off State 30.

REDMOND (D-10)

CROOKED RIVER RANCH (Private)
96 campsites, 37 w/hookups for water/electricity/sewer, 45 w/hookups for water/electricity, plus 14 tent units, reservation information - (503)923-1441, restaurant/lounge, showers, laundry, groceries, swimming pool, playground, golf course, trailer waste disposal, river, fishing, hiking, elev. 2600', $$-$$$.
Northwest of Redmond. US 97 north 6.0 miles, Lower Bridge Road northwest 7.0 miles to Crooked River Ranch.

DESERT TERRACE (Private)
20 trailer sites w/hookups for water/electricity/sewer, reservation information - (503)548-2546, showers, laundry, elev. 3000', $$$.
South of Redmond. US 97 south 3.0 miles.

GRANDMA & GRANDPA'S RV PARK (Private)
33 campsites, 31 w/hookups for water/electricity/sewer, 1 w/hookups for water/electricity, plus 1 w/hookups for electricity only, reservation information - (503)923-0868, wheelchair access, showers, laundry, trailer waste disposal, propane, fishing, nearby golf & skiing, $$.
South of Redmond. Located just south of Redmond along US 97.

REEDSPORT (A-11)

COHO MARINA & RV PARK (Private)
49 trailer sites w/hookups for water/electricity/sewers, no tents, trailers to 35', reservations - (503)271-5411, showers, trailer waste disposal, river, fishing, boat launch, $$$.
In Reedsport. Located at center of town on US 101, at 16th Street.

EAST SHORE RECREATION SITE (BLM)
8 tent units, picnic facilities, boating, fishing, swimming, elev. 500', $$.
South of Reedsport. US 101 south, located near Siskiyou National Forest.

LOON LAKE (BLM)
59 units, trailers okay, picnic area, drinking water, boat launch, boating, swimming, hiking, berry picking, geology, fishing, nature study, elev. 700', $$-$$$.
Southeast of Reedsport. State 38 about 12.0 miles to Mill Road, campground is 7.0 miles along this road.

LOON LAKE LODGE RESORT (Private)
100 campsites, 37 w/hookups for water/electricity, reservations - (503)599-2244, groceries, restaurant/lounge, lake, swimming, fishing, boat launch, boat rental, hiking, $$.
Southeast of Reedsport. State 38 east 13.0 miles, CR 3 south 8.2 miles.

NORTH EEL CREEK (Siuslaw National Forest)
52 units, trailers to 22', piped water, stream, flush toilets, hiking, elev. 100', $$.
Southwest of Reedsport. US 101 southwest 12.1 miles.

SALBASGEON MOTEL & RV PARK (Private)
6 trailer sites w/hookups for water/electricity/sewer, no tents, reservation information - (503)271-2025, river, swimming, fishing, boat launch, $$.
East of Reedsport. State 38 east 7.5 miles.

SURFWOOD CAMPGROUND (Private)
163 campsites, 101 w/hookups for water/electricity/sewer, 40 w/hookups for water/electricity, plus 22 tent units, reservation information - (503)271-4020, showers, laundry, groceries, swimming pool, playground, tennis, trailer waste disposal, stream, $$.
Southwest of Reedsport. US 101 south 2.0 miles.

TAHKENITCH LAKE (Siuslaw National Forest)
35 units, trailers to 22', piped water, flush toilets, hiking, elev. 100', $$.
North of Reedsport. US 101 north 7.0 miles, FSR 1090 west .1 mile.

TAHKENITCH LANDING (Siuslaw National Forest)
26 campsites, trailers okay, boat launch, fishing, elev. 100', $$.
North of Reedsport. US 101 north 8.0 miles to campground.

UMPQUA BEACH RESORT (Private)
75 campsites w/hookups for water/electricity/sewer, reservation information - (503)271-3443, showers, laundry, groceries, ocean access, stream, swimming, fishing, boat launch, playground, $$-$$$.
Southwest of Reedsport. US 101 southwest 4.0 miles to Winchester Bay, Salmon Harbor Drive southwest 1.0 mile.

UMPQUA LIGHTHOUSE (Oregon State Park)
64 campsites, 22 w/hookups for water/electricity/sewer, plus 42 tent units, maximum site 45', picnic area, showers, boat launch, fishing, sand dunes, hiking trails, $$-$$$.
South of Reedsport. US 101 south 6.0 miles.

WILLIAM M. TUGMAN (Oregon State Park)
115 campsites w/hookups for electricity, maximum site to 50', picnic area, wheelchair access, showers, trailer waste disposal, boat launch, fishing, swimming, $$$.
South of Reedsport. US 101 south 8.0 miles to campground.

WINDY COVE COUNTY PARK (Douglas County)
2 camp areas offer 68 sites w/hookups for water/electricity /sewer/cable tv, plus 33 tent units, showers, ocean access, lake, swimming, fishing, playground, wheelchair access, $$.
Southwest of Reedsport. US 101 southwest 4.0 miles to Winchester Bay, Salmon Harbor Drive .3 mile west.

REMOTE (A-11)

REMOTE CAMPGROUND & CABINS (Private)
17 campsites w/hookups for water/electricity/sewer, trailers to 35', reservation information - (503)572-5105, showers, laundry, groceries, river, swimming, fishing, $$.
East of Remote. State 42 east 1.0 mile.

SLEEPY HOLLOW RV PARK (Private)
12 trailer sites, 9 w/hookups for water/electricity/sewer, plus 3 w/hookups for water/electricity, reservation information - (503)572-2141, showers, laundry, ice, river, swimming, fishing, $$-$$$.
West of Remote. State 42 west 8.5 miles, located east of bridge.

RHODODENDRON (C-8)

CAMP CREEK (Mt. Hood National Forest)
30 units, trailers to 22', flush toilets, fishing, hiking, elev. 2200', $$.
Southeast of Rhododendron. US 26 southeast 2.9 miles, Camp Creek FSR south .1 mile to campground.

TOLLGATE (Mt. Hood National Forest)
23 units, trailers to 22', stream, wheelchair access, fishing, hiking, borders Tollgate Observation Site, elev. 1700', $$.
Southeast of Rhododendron. US 26 southeast .5 mile.

RICHLAND (F-9)

EAGLE VALLEY RV & MOBILE HOME PARK (Private)
60 campsites, 25 w/hookups for water/electricity/sewer, plus 35 tent sites, reservation information - (503)893-6161, showers, laundry, ice, trailer waste disposal, RV parts & sales, playground, playfield, wheelchair access, $$-$$$.
At Richland. State 86 east .2 mile, located near milepost #42.

RICKREALL (B-9)

POLK COUNTY FAIRGROUNDS (Polk County)
242 campsites, 218 w/hookups for electricity only, plus 24 pull-thrus w/hookups for water/electricity, tents okay, reservation information - (503)623-3048, showers, $$.
At Rickreall. State 99 west to fairgrounds.

ROGUE RIVER (B-12)

CIRCLE W CAMPGROUND (Private)
25 campsites, 15 w/hookups for water/electricity/sewer/cable tv, plus 10 w/hookups for water/electricity/cable tv, reservation information - (503)582-1686, showers, laundry, ice, trailer waste disposal, mini store, propane, river, swimming, fishing, playground, $$-$$$.
At Rogue River. I-5 to exit #48 to State 99, west 1.0 mile to campground.

ROSEBURG (B-11)

JOHN P. AMACHER PARK (Douglas County)
30 campsites, 20 w/hookups for water/electricity/sewer, plus 10 tent units, showers, river, fishing, boat launch, playground, wheelchair access, $$.
North of Roseburg. I-5 north to exit #129, park is .3 mile south.

NEBO TRAILER PARK (Private)
25 trailer sites w/hookups for water/electricity/sewer, no tents, reservation information - (503)673-4108, showers, laundry, ice, trailer waste disposal, $$$.
In Roseburg. I-5 to exit #125, Garden Valley Blvd. east .8 mile, NE Stephens Street (State 99) north .7 mile to campground.

SHER RON ESTATES MOBILE PARK (Private)
10 sites, reservation information - (503)678-7571, showers, tv hookup, laundry, rec room, fishing, nearby golf, $$-$$$.
In Roseburg. Located at 25 SW Manor Loop, in Roseburg.

TWIN RIVERS VACATION PARK (Private)
85 campsites, 72 w/hookups for water/electricity/sewer, 8 w/hookups for water/electricity, plus 5 w/hookups for water only, reservation information - (503)673-3811, showers, laundry, groceries, river, swimming, fishing, boat ramp, playground, $$-$$$.
In Roseburg. I-5 to exit #125, Garden Valley Road west 5.0 miles, Old Garden Valley Road west 1.5 miles.

WHISTLER'S BEND (Douglas County)
23 rustic campsites, showers, river, fishing, boat launch, playground, $$.
Northeast of Roseburg. State 138 northeast 15.0 miles, Whistler's Bend Road to campground.

SALEM (B-9)

ELKHORN VALLEY (BLM)
23 units, trailers okay, water, swimming, elev. 1000', $.
East of Salem. State 22 east 24.0 miles, Elkhorn Road north 10.0 miles.

FOREST GLEN (Private)
100 campsites w/hookups for water/electricity/sewer, reservation information - (503)363-7616, showers, laundry, ice, therapy pool, game room, trailer waste disposal, miniature golf, hiking, $$$.
South of Salem. I-5 south 5.0 miles to Turner/Sunnyside exit #248, east over freeway, Enchanted Way south .5 mile.

KOA SALEM, INC. (Private)
204 campsites, 118 w/hookups for water/electricity/sewer, 47 w/hookups for water/electricity, 7 w/hookups for water, plus 32 tent units, reservations - (503)581-6736, showers, laundry, groceries, trailer waste disposal, lake, swimming, fishing, game room, playground, $$-$$$.
In Salem. I-5 to exit #253, State 22 southeast .2 mile, Lancaster Drive SE .05 mile south.

SILVER FALLS (Oregon State Park)
105 campsites, 53 w/hookups for electricity, plus 51 tent units, maximum site 60', group sites, picnic area, wheelchair access, showers, trailer waste disposal, waterfalls, swimming, fishing, horse camp, hiking, $$-$$$.
East of Salem. State 214 east approximately 26.0 miles; campground can also be reached from Silverton.

TRAILER PARK VILLAGE (Private)
22 trailer sites w/hookups for water/electricity/sewer, adults only, no pets, no tents, information - (503)393-7424, showers, laundry, ice, $$$.
In Salem. I-5 to exit #258, State 99E north .5 mile to campground.

SAUVIE ISLAND (B-8)

REEDER BEACH RV PARK (Private)
30 campsites, 21 w/hookups for water/electricity/sewer, plus 9 w/hookups for water/electricity, reservations recommended - (503)621-3970, tents okay, showers, laundry, wheelchair access, trailer waste disposal, river, fishing, picnic supplies, ice, $$-$$$.
On Sauvie Island. Located on Columbia River side of island at 26048 NW Reeder Beach Road.

SCAPPOOSE (B-7)

AIRPORT PARK (Columbia County)
6 campsites w/hookups for water/electricity, plus tent area, playground, $$.
North of Scappoose. Located .8 mile off State 30, north of Scappoose.

SEASIDE (A-7)

CIRCLE CREEK CAMPGROUND (Private)
24 campsites w/hookups for water/electricity/sewer, reservations - (503)738-6070, tents okay, showers, $$-$$$.
South of Seaside. US 101 south 1.0 mile.

VENICE RV PARK (Private)
26 trailer sites w/hookups for water/electricity/sewer/cable tv, no tents, reservation information - (503)738-8851, showers, laundry, trailer waste disposal, picnic area, river, fishing, $$$.
In Seaside. Located at south end of Newana River Bridge in Seaside at 1032 24th Avenue.

SELMA (A-12)

GRANTS PASS/REDWOOD HIGHWAY KOA (Private)
41 campsites, 26 w/hookups for water/electricity, plus 15 w/hookups for water only, reservations - (503)476-6508, showers, laundry, groceries, trailer waste disposal, propane, stream, playfield, playground, $$$.
Northeast of Selma. US 199 northeast 7.0 miles, located between mileposts #14 and #15.

THE LAST RESORT (Private)
40 campsites, 5 w/hookups for water/electricity/sewer, 18 w/hookups for water/electricity, plus 16 tent units, reservations - (503)597-4989, showers, laundry, groceries, rec room, snack bar, year-round fishing, boat rental, horse rental, $$.
East of Selma. US 199 to Lake Selmac Junction, Lake Shore Drive 2.5 miles east.

SISTERS (D-10)

BIG LAKE (Willamette National Forest)
21 units, trailers to 18', piped water, flush toilets, lake, boat launch, boating, swimming, fishing, water skiing, nearby trailheads to Mt. Washington Wilderness & Patjens Lake, elev. 4600', $$.
West of Sisters. US 20 west 21.7 miles, FSR 2690 south 3.4 miles.

BLUE BAY (Deschutes National Forest)
19 units, 6 group sites, trailers to 22', piped water, on Suttle Lake - speed limits, boat launch, boating, swimming, fishing, water skiing, hiking, elev. 3400', $$-$$$.
Northwest of Sisters. US 20 northwest 13.0 miles, FSR 2070 southwest 1.0 mile.

BLUE LAKE RESORT (Private)
38 campsites, 9 w/hookups for water/electricity/sewer, 16 w/hookups for water/electricity, plus 12 w/hookups for water only, reservation information - (503)595-6671, showers, ice, trailer waste disposal, Suttle Lake - speed limits, swimming, fishing, boat launch, boat rental, playground, hiking, elev. 3500', $$-$$$.
Northwest of Sisters. US 20 northwest 13.0 miles to Blue Lake Junction, Suttle Lake Forest Road west 2.5 miles.

CIRCLE 5 TRAILER PARK (Private)

24 trailer sites, 20 w/hookups for water/electricity/sewer, plus 3 w/hookups for water/electricity, reservation information - (503)549-3861, showers, laundry, trailer waste disposal, elev. 3200', $$$.
Southeast of Sisters. US 20 southeast .7 mile.

COLD SPRING (Deschutes National Forest)

23 units, trailers to 22', well, stream, elev. 3400', $$-$$$.
West of Sisters. State 242 west 5.0 miles.

INDIAN FORD (Deschutes National Forest)

15 units, 10 group sites, trailers to 22', well, stream, fishing, elev. 3200', $$.
Northwest of Sisters. US 20 northwest 5.0 miles, turn on FSR 11 to campground.

LINK CREEK (Deschutes National Forest)

25 units, 8 group sites, trailers to 22', piped water, on Suttle Lake - speed limits, boating, swimming, fishing, water skiing, hiking, elev. 3400', $$.
Northwest of Sisters. US 20 northwest 13.0 miles, FSR 2070 northwest 2.0 miles.

SCOUT LAKE (Deschutes National Forest)

6 units, 7 group sites, trailers to 22', reservations required - (503)549-2111, piped water, lake - no motors, boating, swimming, fishing, hiking, elev. 4000', $$-$$$.
West of Sisters. US 20 northwest 13.0 miles, FSR 2070 southwest 1.0 mile, FSR 2066 south .5 mile.

SISTERS KOA (Private)

57 campsites, 18 w/hookups for water/electricity/sewer, 24 w/hookups for water/electricity, plus 15 tent units, reservations - (503)549-3021, showers, cable tv, laundry, groceries, propane & gas, trailer waste disposal, spa, restaurant, video rental, pond, swimming, fishing, mini golf, playfield, playground, elev. 3200', $$$.
Southeast of Sisters. US 20 southeast 4.0 miles.

SOUTH SHORE (Deschutes National Forest)

31 units, 8 group sites, trailers to 22', piped water, on Suttle Lake - speed limits, boat launch, boating, swimming, fishing, water skiing, hiking trails, elev. 3400', $$.
Northwest of Sisters. US 20 northwest 13.0 miles, FSR 2070 northwest 1.5 miles.

SUTTLE LAKE (Deschutes National Forest)
7 tent units, picnic area, community kitchen, flush toilets, boat launch, boating, fishing, swimming, water skiing, hiking, elev. 3400', $$.
Northwest of Sisters. US 20 northwest 13.0 miles, FSR 2070 to east end of lake and campground.

SPRAY (D-9)

BULL PRAIRIE (Umatilla National Forest)
28 units, trailers to 32', piped water, Bull Prairie Lake, fishing, trail, picnic area, elev. 4000', $.
Northeast of Spray. State 19 east 2.5 miles, State 207 north 12.0 miles, FSR 2039 northeast 3.0 miles, FSR 30 southeast .5 mile.

SPRINGFIELD (B-10)

CHALET VILLAGE ANNEX (Private)
24 trailer sites w/hookups for water/electricity/sewer, no tents, reservation information - (503)747-8311, showers, $$$.
East of Springfield. I-5 to exit #194, State 126 east 7.0 miles, Main Street west 1 block to 54th Street.

SUNRIVER (D-10)

TWIN LAKES RESORT (Private)
23 trailer sites w/hookups for water/electricity/sewer, reservation information (503)385-2188, no tents, showers, toilets, groceries, tackle shop, restaurant, row boat rental, paddle boat rental,, picnic tables, on South Twin Lake - no gas motors allowed, lake fishing, hiking, $$$.
Southwest of Sunriver. Located across highway from Wickiup Reservoir, on South Twin Lake, along Cascade Loop Highway.

SUTHERLIN (B-11)

HI-WAY HAVEN RV PARK (Private)
84 campsites, 34 w/hookups for water/electricity/sewer, plus 50 w/hookups for water/electricity, reservation information - (503)459-4557, tents okay, showers, tv cable, laundry, wheelchair access, rec room, groceries, trailer waste disposal, fishing, golf, $$-$$$.
Located in Sutherlin. Located at 609 Fort McKay Road, in Sutherlin.

TYEE (BLM)
9 units, water, swimming, elev. 200', $$.
Northwest of Sutherlin. State 138 northwest 12.0 miles to
Bullock Bridge, CR 57 north .5 mile to campground.

SWEET HOME

CASCADIA (Oregon State Park)
26 primitive sites, maximum site 35', group picnic area,
wheelchair access, fishing, hiking trails, $$.
East of Sweet Home. US 20 east 14.0 miles.

DIAMOND HILL RV PARK & CAMPGROUND (Private)
93 campsites, 24 w/hookups for water/electricity/sewer, 24
w/hookups for water/electricity, plus 45 w/hookups for water
only, reservations - (503)995-8050, showers, laundry, groceries,
swimming pool, playground, trailer waste disposal, $$-$$$.
Southwest of Sweet Home. State 228 east 19.0 miles to I-5, south
8.0 miles to exit #209, campground is west 1 block. (Also accessible from Harrisburg; located 5.0 miles east.)

FERNVIEW (Willamette National Forest)
11 units, trailers to 18', well, river, wheelchair access, swimming,
fishing, trailers, elev. 1400', $.
East of Sweet Home. US 20 east 23.5 miles.

HOUSE ROCK (Willamette National Forest)
17 tent units, picnic area, well, wheelchair access, river, swimming, fishing, hiking, located in virgin old growth douglas fir,
elev. 1600', $$.
East of Sweet Home. US 20 east 26.5 miles, FSR 2044 southeast
.1 mile.

LOST PRAIRIE (Willamette National Forest)
10 units, trailers to 22', well, stream, wheelchair access, historic
site, hiking, elev. 3300', $$.
East of Sweet Home. US 20 east 39.2 miles.

SUNNYSIDE PARK/FOSTER RESERVOIR (Linn County)
137 campsites, 63 w/hookups for water/electricity, plus 74 tent
units, picnic area, showers, trailer waste disposal, lake, beach,
fishing, boat launch, wheelchair access, playfield, moorage
w/handicap accessible dock, $$.
East of Sweet Home. US 20 east 3.0 miles to Green Peter Dam
exit, proceed north to park.

TROUT CREEK (Willamette National Forest)
24 units, trailers to 22', well, wheelchair access, swimming, fishing, nearby trailhead to wilderness, elev. 1300', $$.
East of Sweet Home. US 20 east 18.7 miles.

WHITCOMB CREEK (Linn County)
39 campsites, drinking water, lake, swimming, fishing, boat launch, hiking, $-$$.
East of Sweet Home. US 20 east 3.0 miles to Green Peter Dam exit, north 9.0 miles to park.

YELLOWBOTTOM (BLM)
23 units, trailers okay, picnic area, drinking water, swimming, fishing, nature study, elev. 1500', $.
Northeast of Sweet Home. State 20 east 3.0 miles to Foster; campground is 26.0 miles northeast of Foster, go past the reservoir and follow the Quartzville Road to camp.

YUKWAH (Willamette National Forest)
20 units, trailers to 32', well, river, wheelchair access, swimming, fishing, nature trail, elev. 1300', $$.
East of Sweet Home. US 20 east 19.3 miles.

TALENT (B-12)

HOLIDAY RV PARK (Private)
110 trailer sites w/hookups for water/electricity/sewer, no tents, reservation information - (503)535-2183, showers, laundry, groceries, swimming pool, stream, wheelchair access, $$$.
Northwest of Talent. Located on west side of I-5 at exit #24.

PEAR TREE CENTER (Private)
31 units w/hookups for water/electricity/sewer/cable tv, no tents, reservation information - (503)535-4445, showers, laundry, wheelchair access, mini mart, restaurant, pool, spa, playground, gas & propane, $$$.
Northeast of Talent. Located on east side of I-5 at exit #24.

THE DALLES (C-8)

BOB'S BUDGET RV & TRAILER PARK (Private)
20 trailer sites w/hookups for water/electricity/sewer, reservations - (503)739-2829, showers, laundry, teepee rentals, $$.
East of The Dalles. I-84 east 24.0 miles to Rufus exit #109, Old Highway 30 west .5 mile, Wallace Street .2 mile south.

DESCHUTES RIVER (Oregon State Park)
34 primitive campsites, maximum site 30', fishing, hiking trails, Oregon Trail display, $$.
East of The Dalles. I-84 east 17.0 miles to campground.

LEPAGE PARK (Corps)
10 campsites, reservation information - (503)296-1181, showers, trailer waste disposal, on John Day River, swimming, fishing, boat launch, $$.
East of The Dalles. I-84 east 28.0 miles to exit #104, follow signs .2 mile to park; located 4.0 miles east of Rufus.

LONE PINE RV PARK (Private)
22 trailer sites w/hookups for water/electricity/sewer, reservation information - (503)296-9133, showers, laundry, river, fishing, playground, $$$.
In The Dalles. I-84 to exit #87, located near north end of overpass.

MEMALOOSE (Oregon State Park)
110 campsites, 43 w/hookups for water/electricity/sewer, plus 67 tent units, maximum site 60', wheelchair access, showers, trailer waste disposal, $$-$$$.
West of The Dalles. I-84 west 11.0 miles; this campground is only accessible from I-84 westbound.

PHILIPPI PARK (Corps)
10 campsites, on John Day River, boat-in access only, fishing, swimming, $.
East of The Dalles. I-84 east 28.0 miles to exit #104, follow signs .2 mile to LePage Park. Philippi's boat- in campground is located 4.0 miles upstream on the John Day River.

TIDEWATER (A-10)

BLACKBERRY (Siuslaw National Forest)
31 sites, trailers to 32', picnic area, piped water, along Alsea River, flush toilets, boat launch, boating, swimming, fishing, elev. 100', $$.
Southeast of Tidewater. State 34 southeast 6.0 miles.

SLIDE (Siuslaw National Forest)
6 tent units, well, stream, fishing, elev. 100', $.
Southeast of Tidewater. State 34 southeast 5.0 miles.

RIVEREDGE (Siuslaw National Forest)
1 group shelter, reservations required - (503)487-5811, piped water, stream, wheelchair access includes trail, boat launch, boating, swimming, fishing, hiking, elev. 200', $$.
Southeast of Tidewater. State 34 southeast 11.0 miles.

TILLAMOOK (A-8)

BAY SHORE TRAILER PARK (Private)
58 campsites, 53 w/hookups for water/electricity/sewer, plus 3 w/hookups for water/electricity, no tent sites, trailers to 40', reservation information - (503)842-7774, showers, laundry, ice, ocean access, stream, fishing, boat launch, boat rental, $$-$$$.
West of Tillamook. Netarts Highway west 6.0 miles, Bilyeu Ave. .3 mile to park.

BIG SPRUCE TRAILER PARK (Private)
23 trailer sites w/hookups for water/electricity/sewer, plus 3 tent sites, trailers to 40', reservation information - (503)842-7443, showers, laundry, ocean access, stream, swimming, fishing, boat launch, $$.
West of Tillamook. Netarts Highway west 6.5 miles.

CAPE LOOKOUT (Oregon State Park)
250 campsites, 53 w/hookups for water/electricity/sewer, plus 197 tent units, maximum site 60', group campsites, mail reservations available, picnic area, wheelchair access, showers, trailer waste disposal, hiking trail, ocean beach, beachcombing, fishing, $$-$$$.
Southwest of Tillamook. Leave US 101 at Tillamook and head southwest 12.0 miles to campground.

HAPPY CAMP (Private)
34 trailer sites w/hookups for water/electricity, no tents, reservations - (503)842-4012, playfield, trailer waste disposal, ocean access, swimming, fishing, boat launch, boat rental, $$.
West of Tillamook. Netarts Highway west 7.0 miles.

IDAVILLE TRAILER COURT (Private)
4 trailer sites w/hookups for water/electricity/sewer, reservation information - (503)842-4910, showers, laundry, groceries, trailer waste disposal, fishing, nearby golf, $$.
In Tillamook. Located in Tillamook at 7475 Alderbrook Road.

JETTY FISHERY (Private)
30 campsites, 15 w/hookups for water/electricity, plus 15 tent units, reservation information - (503)368-5746, groceries, ocean access, river, swimming, fishing, boat launch, boat rental, $$.
North of Tillamook. US 101 north 18.0 miles.

KILCHIS RIVER PARK (Tillamook County)
40 campsites, trailer waste disposal, river, swimming, fishing, boat launch, playfield, playground, hiking. $$.
Northeast of Tillamook. US 101 north .5 mile of Tillamook Cheese Factory, Kilchis River Road 7.0 miles northeast.

PACIFIC CAMPGROUND (Private)
67 campsites, 28 w/hookups for water/electricity/sewer/cable tv, 4 w/hookups for water/electricity, 5 w/hookups for electricity only, plus 30 tent units, reservations - (503)842-5201, showers, ice, $-$$.
North of Tillamook. US 101 north 2.0 miles.

SHOREWOOD TRAVEL TRAILER VILLAGE (Private)
21 trailer sites, 6 w/hookups for water/electricity/sewer, plus 15 w/hookups for water/electricity, no tents, reservation information - (503)355-2278, showers, laundry, ice, trailer waste disposal, ocean access, swimming, fishing, playground, some ocean front sites, $$-$$$.
North of Tillamook. US 101 north 12.7 miles, southwest 3 blocks at Shorewood sign.

TILLAMOOK KOA (Private)
85 campsites, 13 w/hookups for water/electricity/sewer, 65 w/hookups for water/electricity, 5 w/hookups for water, plus 2 tent units, reservations - (503)842-4779, showers, laundry, groceries, playground, cable tv, trailer waste disposal, river, fishing, hiking, propane, $$$.
South of Tillamook. US 101 south 6.0 miles.

TRASK RIVER MOTOR HOME PARK (Private)
14 campsites, 9 w/hookups for water/electricity/sewer, plus 5 w/hookups for water/electricity, reservations - (503)842-6142, showers, laundry, river, fishing, $$-$$$.
In Tillamook. Located at 3370 Geinger Road, in Tillamook.

TILLER (B-11)

TILLER RV PARK (Private)
16 campsites w/hookups for water/electricity/sewer, information - (503)825-3789, river, fishing, $$.
In Tiller. Located at 300 Terry Lane, in Tiller.

TOLLGATE (E-7)

JUBILEE LAKE (Umatilla National Forest)
51 units, trailers to 22', picnic area, piped water, flush toilets, lake - no motors, hiking, elev. 4700', $$.
Northeast of Tollgate. FSR 64 northeast 12.0 miles to campground.

TARGET MEADOWS (Umatilla National Forest)
20 units, trailers to 22', picnic area, piped water, hiking, elev. 4800', $.
North of Tollgate. FSR 6401 north 2.2 miles.

TYGH VALLEY (D-8)

BEAVERTAIL (BLM)
21 units, trailers okay, drinking water, boating, hiking, geology, fishing, swimming, nature study, elev. 500', $.
Northeast of Tygh Valley. State 216 east 5.0 miles to Sherar's Bridge, take Deschutes River Road north of Sherar's Bridge 12.0 miles to campground.

HUNT PARK/WASCO COUNTY FAIRGROUNDS (Wasco County)
150 trailer sites w/hookups for water/electricity, reservation information - (503)483-2288, showers, wheelchair access, playground, playfield, trailer waste disposal, stream, fishing, $-$$.
In Tygh Valley. Located on Fairground Road, 2.0 miles west of US 197.

MACKS CANYON (BLM)
16 units, trailers okay, picnic area, drinking water, boat launch, boating, hiking, geology, fishing, nature study, elev. 500', $.
Northeast of Tygh Valley. State 216 east 5.0 miles to Sherar's Bridge, take Deschutes River Road north of Sherar's Bridge, campground is 20.0 miles north.

UKIAH (E-8)

UKIAH-DALE FOREST (Oregon State Park)
25 primitive campsites, trailers to 25', fishing, on North Fork John Day River, $.
Southwest of Ukiah. US 395 southwest 3.0 miles to campground.

UMATILLA (E-7)

SHADY REST RV PARK (Private)
24 trailer sites, 18 w/hookups for water/electricity/sewer, plus 6 w/hookups for water/electricity, reservation information - (503)922-5041, showers, laundry, swimming pool, $$.
West of Umatilla. US 730 west .4 mile to park.

UNION (F-8)

CATHERINE CREEK (Oregon State Park)
18 primitive campsites, maximum site 30', picnic area, wheelchair access, fishing, $$.
Southeast of Union. State 203 southeast 8.0 miles to campground.

UNITY (E-9)

UNITY LAKE (Oregon State Park)
21 campsites, 10 w/hookups for electricity, plus 11 tent units, maximum site 60', picnic area, wheelchair access, showers, trailer waste disposal, boat launch, swimming, fishing, $$-$$$.
Northwest of Unity. Campground is located approximately 2.5 miles northwest of Unity, off US 26.

UNITY MOTEL & TRAILER PARK (Private)
10 trailer sites w/hookups for water/electricity/sewer, reservation information - (503)446-3431, showers, laundry, trailer waste disposal, elev. 4000', $$.
In Unity. US 26 to east end of town.

VALE (F-10)

BULLY CREEK RESERVOIR (Malheur County)
66 campsites, 64 w/hookups for electricity, reservation information - (503)473-2969, showers, trailer waste disposal, lake, swimming, fishing, boat launch, $-$$.
West of Vale. Graham Road west 9.0 miles.

LAKE OWYHEE (Oregon State Park)
40 campsites, 10 w/hookups for electricity, plus 30 tent units, maximum site 55', picnic area, showers, trailer waste disposal, boat launch, fishing, $$-$$$.
South of Vale. Head south out of Vale on the road to Lake Owyhee State Park, it's approximately 41.0 miles. This campground is also accessible from Ontario.

LAKE OWYHEE RESORT (Private)

100 seasonal campsites, 5 w/hookups for water/electricity/sewer, 35 w/hookups for water/electricity, plus 60 tent units, trailers to 35', reservations - (503)372-2444, groceries, lounge, lake, swimming, fishing, boat launch, boat rental, $$.
South of Vale. Head south out of Vale on the road to Lake Owyhee State Park, it's approximately 38.0 miles. Also accessible from Ontario.

PROSPECTOR TRAVEL TRAILER PARK (Private)

34 campsites, 24 w/hookups for water/electricity/sewer, 4 w/hookups for water/electricity, plus 6 w/hookups for electricity only, reservation information - (503)473-3879, showers, laundry, ice, trailer waste disposal, $$.
In Vale. At US 20/26 junction take US 26 north .1 mile to Hope Street, park is 1 block east.

SUCCOR CREEK (Oregon State Park)

19 primitive campsites, picnic area, hiking trails, colorful rock formations, $$.
Southeast of Vale. Head south out of Vale on the road to Lake Owyhee State Park, after about 15.0 miles head east 2.0 miles to State 201, follow this 13.0 miles south to Succor Creek State Recreation Area Road. Follow this southwest; you will reach the campground after 16.5 miles.

WESTERNER MOTOR HOME PARK (Private)

15 campsites, 10 w/hookups for water/electricity/sewer, plus 5 w/out hookups, reservation information - (503)473-3947, showers, laundry, trailer waste disposal, river, swimming, fishing, $$.
In Vale. Located at junction of US 20 and US 26.

VERNONIA (B-7)

ANDERSON PARK (Columbia County)

24 campsites, 16 w/hookups for water/electricity/sewer, plus 8 w/hookups for water only, trailer waste disposal, river, fishing, playfield, playground, $-$$.
In Vernonia. Located 2 blocks east of State 47 on Jefferson.

BIG EDDY (Columbia County)

40 campsites, 10 w/hookups for water/electricity, 10 w/hookups for electricity only, plus 20 tent units, trailer waste disposal, river, fishing, boat launch, playground, $$.
North of Vernonia. State 47 north 8.0 miles.

WALDPORT (A-10)

ALSEA BAY TRAILER PARK (Private)
15 trailer sites w/hookups for water/electricity/sewer, reservation information - (503)563-2250, showers, river, swimming, fishing, hiking, $$$.
In Waldport. US 101 north .5 mile, located at northern end of bridge.

BEACHSIDE (Oregon State Park)
80 campsites, 26 w/hookups for electricity, plus 55 tent units, mail reservations available, maximum site 30', picnic area, showers, ocean access, beachcombing, fishing, $$-$$$.
South of Waldport. US 101 south 4.0 miles to campground.

CHINOOK TRAILER PARK (Private)
20 trailer sites w/hookups for water/electricity/sewer, plus 5 tent units, adults only, reservation information - (503)563-3485, showers, laundry, river, fishing, $$$.
East of Waldport. State 34 east 3.3 miles.

DRIFT CREEK LANDING (Private)
60 trailer sites, 52 w/hookups for water/electricity/sewer, plus 8 w/hookups for water/electricity, no tents, reservation information - (503)563-3610, showers, laundry, river, fishing, boat launch, boat rental, $$-$$$.
East of Waldport. State 34 east 3.7 miles.

FISHIN' HOLE PARK & MARINA (Private)
23 campsites, 11 w/hookups for water/electricity, reservation information - (503)563-3401, showers, cable tv, spring water, laundry, river, fishing, crabbing, boat launch, boat rental, $$-$$$.
East of Waldport. State 34 east 3.8 miles.

HANDY HAVEN RV PARK (Private)
11 trailer sites w/hookups for water/electricity/sewer/cable tv, no tents, reservation information - (503)563-4286, showers, laundry, groceries, trailer waste disposal, $$$.
In Waldport. Near city center, just east of US 101.

HAPPY LANDING RV PARK & MARINA (Private)
29 campsites, 17 w/hookups for water/electricity/sewer, plus 12 w/hookups for water/electricity, reservation information - (503)528-3300, showers, laundry, river, fishing, boat launch, boat rental, $$$.
East of Waldport. State 34 east 7.0 miles.

KING SILVER TRAILER PARK (Private)
33 campsites, 19 w/hookups for water/electricity/sewer, 9 w/hookups for water/electricity, plus 5 tent units, trailers to 35', reservation information - (503)563-3502, ice, tackle shop, RV/marine supplies, covered moorage, river, fishing, boat launch, boat rental, $$-$$$.
East of Waldport. State 34 east 3.6 miles.

KOZY KOVE MARINA & RV PARK (Private)
34 campsites, 27 w/hookups for water/electricity/sewer/cable tv, plus 7 tent sites, reservation information - (503)528-3251, showers, laundry, groceries, trailer waste disposal, restaurant/lounge, river, fishing, boat launch, boat rental, $$-$$$.
East of Waldport. State 34 east 9.5 miles.

OAKLAND'S FISH CAMP (Private)
17 trailer sites w/hookups for water/electricity/sewer, trailers to 35', adults only, no tents, reservation information - (503)563-5865, laundry, river, fishing, boat launch, boat rental, restaurant, $$.
East of Waldport. State 34 east 4.1 miles.

SEAL ROCKS TRAILER COVE (Private)
44 campsites, 30 w/hookups for water/electricity/sewer, plus 14 w/hookups for electricity, trailers to 35', reservations - (503)563-3955, showers, trailer waste disposal, ocean access, swimming, fishing, clamming, $$-$$$.
North of Waldport. US 101 north 4.8 miles, near Seal Rock.

TAYLORS LANDING (Private)
27 campsites, 21 w/hookups for water/electricity/sewer, plus 6 w/hookups for water/electricity, reservation information - (503)528-3388, showers, laundry, river, fishing, boat rental, hiking, $$-$$$.
East of Waldport. State 34 east 7.2 miles.

TILLICUM BEACH (Siuslaw National Forest)
57 units, trailers to 32', piped water, flush toilets, ocean view campsites, fishing, elev. 100', $$.
South of Waldport. US 101 south 4.7 miles.

WAMIC (C-8)

PINE HOLLOW LAKESIDE RESORT (Private)
120 campsites, 38 w/hookups for water/electricity/sewer, 62 w/hookups for water/electricity, plus 20 tent units, reservations - (503)544-2271, showers, laundry, groceries, trailer waste disposal, lake, swimming, fishing, boat launch, boat rental, restaurant/lounge, $$-$$$
Northwest of Wamic. Pine Hollow Reservoir Road 3.5 miles northwest.

ROCK CREEK RESERVOIR (Mt. Hood National Forest)
33 units, trailers to 32', piped water, lake - no motors, wheelchair access, boating, fishing, elev. 2200', $$.
West of Wamic. CR 226 west 6.0 miles, FSR 48 southwest 1.2 miles, FSR 4820 west .2 mile, FSR 120 north .2 mile.

WARM SPRINGS (C-9)

KAH-NEE-TA (Private)
69 trailer sites, 29 w/hookups for water/electricity/sewer/cable tv, 10 w/out hookups, plus 28 tent sites, group area, reservation information - (800)831-0100, showers, laundry, ice, trailer waste disposal, swimming pool, therapy pool, river, fishing, boat rental, horse rental, lounge, tennis, golf, mini golf, playground, hiking, $$-$$$.
North of Warm Springs. Take Kah-Nee-Ta Road north off US 97 for 11.0 miles.

WELCHES (C-8)

GREEN CANYON (Mt. Hood National Forest)
15 units, trailers to 32', piped water, on Salmon River, wheelchair access, fishing, hiking, elev. 1600', $$.
South of Welches. US 26 east 1.0 mile, FSR 2168 south 4.6 miles. Located near Zigzag.

McNEIL (Mt. Hood National Forest)
34 units, trailers to 32', piped water, near Sandy River, fishing, bicycling, elev. 2000', $$.
Northeast of Welches. US 26 east 1.0 mile, CR 18 northeast 4.8 miles, FSR 17 east .8 mile, FSR 1825 east .2 mile.

MT. HOOD RV VILLAGE (Private)

420 campsites w/hookups for water/electricity/sewer, reservation information - (503)622-4011, wheelchair access, showers, indoor pool, cable tv, weight room, sauna, hot tub, laundry, groceries, propane, fishing for steelhead & salmon, nearby golf & skiing, $$$.
West of Welches. US 26 west 2.0 miles to campground.

RILEY (Mt. Hood National Forest)

14 units, trailers to 22', piped water, stream, horse unloading & hitchracks, nearby horse trails, fishing, hiking, elev. 2100', $$.
Northeast of Welches. US 26 east 1.0 mile, CR 18 northeast 4.8 miles, FSR 1825 east 1.2 miles, FSR 382 southeast .1 mile.

WESTFIR (C-10)

KIAHANIE (Willamette National Forest)

20 units, trailers to 18', river, fly fishing only, elev. 2200', $$.
Northeast of Westfir. FSR 19 northeast 19.3 miles.

WESTON (E-7)

VILLADOM MOBILE HOME PARK (Private)

11 trailer sites w/hookups for water/electricity/sewer, no tents, reservation information - (503)938-7247, showers, laundry, groceries, swimming pool, $$.
North of Weston. State 11 north 10.0 miles, located at junction with Crockett Road.

WOODWARD (Umatilla National Forest)

18 units, trailers to 22', picnic area, piped water, hiking, elev. 4950', $.
East of Weston. State 204 east 17.5 miles.

WHITE CITY (C-12)

BOB'S RV PARK (Private)

37 campsites, 30 w/hookups for water/electricity/sewer, plus 7 w/hookups for water/electricity, reservation information - (503)878-2400, showers, laundry, river, fishing, boat launch, playfield, playground, hiking, $$.
Northeast of White City. State 62 northeast 19.0 miles.

DOE POINT (Rogue River National Forest)
25 units, trailers to 22', piped water, lake - speed limits, flush toilets, boating, swimming, fishing, hiking, bicycling, elev. 4600', $$.
East of White City. State 140 east 28.2 miles, on Fish Lake.

FISH LAKE (Rogue River National Forest)
17 units, trailers to 22', piped water, lake - speed limits, flush toilets, boat launch, boating, swimming, fishing, hiking, elev. 4600', $$.
East of White City. State 140 east 29.7 miles, on Fish Lake.

FISH LAKE RESORT (Private)
60 trailer sites, 45 w/hookups for water/electricity/sewer, plus 15 w/out hookups, reservations - (503)949-8500, showers, laundry, groceries, fishing supplies, cafe, complete game room, trailer waste disposal, on Fish Lake, swimming, fishing, boat launch, boat rental, hiking, elev. 4600', $$.
East of White City. State 140 east 30.0 miles.

JOSEPH P. STEWART (Oregon State Park)
201 campsites, 151 w/hookups for electricity, plus 50 tent units, group campsites, maximum site 80', picnic area, wheelchair access, trailer waste disposal, boat launch, marina, fishing, swimming, 8 miles of hiking/bike trails, access to Upper Rogue River Trail & Pacific Crest Trail, bicycle path, $$-$$$.
Northeast of White City. State 62 northeast 25.0 miles to campground.

LILO'S HACIENDA RV PARK (Private)
30 trailer sites w/hookups for water/electricity/sewer, reservations - (503)878-2749, showers, laundry, Mexican restaurant/lounge, river, swimming, fishing, nearby boat launch, $$.
Northeast of White City. State 62 northeast 13.0 miles, located near Rogue River bridge at milepost #20.

MEDFORD OAKS CAMPARK (Private)
80 campsites, 20 w/hookups for water/electricity/sewer, 37 w/hookups for water/electricity, plus 23 tent units, reservations - (503)826-5103, showers, picnic pavilion, dance floor, laundry, groceries, trailer waste disposal, swimming pool, pond, fishing, playfield, playground, $$-$$$.
East of White City. State 140 east 6.8 miles.

ROGUE ELK CAMPGROUND (Jackson County)
31 campsites, trailers okay, reservation information - (503)776-7001, showers, trailer waste disposal, river, swimming, fishing, boat launch, playground, hiking, $$.
Northeast of White City. State 62 northeast 18.0 miles.

SHADY TRAILS (Private)

50 campsites, 20 w/hookups for water/electricity/sewer/cable tv, plus 30 w/hookups for water/electricity, reservations - (503)878-2206, showers, groceries, trailer waste disposal, river, fishing, boat launch, playground, $$-$$$.
Northeast of White City. State 62 northeast 16.0 miles.

WOODBURN (B-8)

WOODBURN I-5 RV PARK (Private)

150 campsites w/hookups for water/electricity/sewer/cable tv, reservation information - (503)981-0002, wheelchair access, showers, laundry, swimming, playground, rec room, groceries, nearby golf, $$$.
At Woodburn. Take exit #271 off I-5 at Woodburn. Located on west side of freeway.

YACHATS (A-10)

CAPE PERPETUA (Siuslaw National Forest)

37 units, 1 group site, reservations required - (503)563-3211, trailers to 22', piped water, stream, flush toilets, trailer waste disposal, interpretive services, fishing, hiking, Pacific Ocean access, elev. 100', $$-$$$.
South of Yachats. US 101 south 2.7 miles.

ROCK CREEK (Siuslaw National Forest)

16 units, trailers to 22', piped water, flush toilets, fishing, Pacific Ocean access, elev. 100', $$.
South of Yachats. US 101 south 10.0 miles.

SEA PERCH RV PARK & CAMPGROUND (Private)

48 campsites, 21 w/hookups for water/electricity/sewer/cable tv, plus 27 w/hookups for water/electricity/cable tv, tents okay, reservations - (503)547-3505, showers, laundry, groceries, ocean access, swimming, fishing, $$-$$$.
South of Yachats. US 101 south 6.5 miles.

YAMHILL (B-8)

FLYING "M" RANCH (Private)

100 campsites, reservation information - (503)662-3222, restaurant, lounge - live music, horse back riding, pond, fishing, river, $$-$$$.
In Yamhill. Located in Yamhill at 23029 Flying "M" Road.

WHERE TO FIND WASHINGTON'S IMPROVED CAMPGROUNDS

WASHINGTON MAP

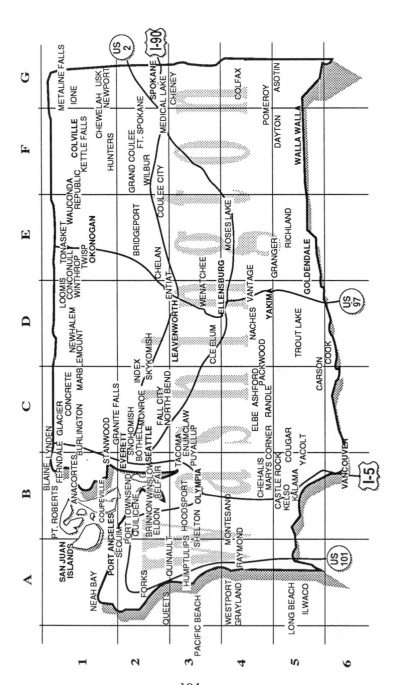

ANACORTES (B-1)

FERN HILL CAMPGROUND & RV PARK (Private)
102 campsites, 25 w/hookups for water/electricity/sewer, 35 w/hookups for water/electricity, plus 45 tent sites, reservations - (206)384-2622, showers, laundry, ice, playfield, playground, trailer waste disposal, mini mart, propane, $$-$$$.
South of Anacortes. State 20 south to junction with Oak Harbor, State 20 west .8 mile, Miller Road west 1 block to campground.

WASHINGTON PARK (City of Anacortes)
75 campsites, 46 w/hookups for water/electricity, plus 29 tent units, showers, laundry, playfield, playground, trailer waste disposal, ocean access, swimming, fishing, boat launch, hiking, $$.
In Anacortes. State 20 to 12th Street, west 2.0 miles to Y, veer left .3 mile to park.

ASHFORD (C-4)

BIG CREEK (Gifford Pinchot National Forest)
30 units, trailers to 22', piped water, stream, fishing, hiking, elev. 1800', $$.
Southeast of Ashford. State 706 east 2.3 miles, County Road south 1.4 miles, FSR 52 east .5 mile. Located near Nisqually entrance to Mt. Rainier National Park.

ASOTIN (G-5)

FIELDS SPRING STATE PARK (Washington State Parks)
20 units, some trailers - no hookups, community kitchen/shelter, wheelchair access, trailer waste disposal, short hike up Puffer Butte for view of three states, birdwatching, wildflowers, winter sports, $$.
Southwest of Asotin. State 129 southwest 23.5 miles to campground road.

BELFAIR (B-2)

BELFAIR STATE PARK (Washington State Parks)
133 units, 47 w/hookups for water/electricity/sewer, picnic shelter, trailer waste disposal, open play area, fishing, clamming, $$.
Southwest of Belfair. State 300 southwest 3.0 miles to campground.

ILLAHEE STATE PARK (Washington State Parks)
33 units, some trailers - no hookups, group sites - reservations advised - (206)478-4661, community kitchen/shelter, boat launch, pier fishing, $$-$$$.
Northeast of Belfair. State 3 northeast 12.0 miles, State 304 east 3.0 miles, State 303 north 2.0 miles, State 306 east 2.0 miles.

JARRELL COVE STATE PARK (Washington State Parks)
20 units, some trailers - no hookups, picnic shelter, wheelchair access, groceries nearby, fishing, $$.
Southwest of Belfair. State 3 southwest 17.0 miles, park road 7.0 miles east.

MANCHESTER STATE PARK (Washington State Parks)
53 units, some trailers - no hookups, picnic shelter, wheelchair access, trailer waste disposal, historic buildings, scuba diving area, fishing, $$.
Northeast of Belfair. State 3 northeast 8.0 miles, State 160 for 4.0 miles to Port Orchard, take the road around the point about 6.0 miles to park.

NORSELAND MOBILE ESTATES & RV PARK (Private)
21 trailer sites w/hookups for water/electricity/sewer, no tents, reservation information - (206)674-2874, showers, laundry, rec room, $$.
Northeast of Belfair. State 3 northeast 4.0 miles.

PENROSE POINT STATE PARK (Washington State Park)
85 units, some trailers - no hookups, group sites - reservations advised - (206)884-2514, community kitchen, trailer waste disposal, on Carr Inlet in Puget Sound, fishing, clamming, nearby boat launch, $$-$$$.
South of Belfair. State 3 south 4.0 miles, State 302 southeast 12.0 miles, Longbranch road south 7.0 miles.

ROBIN HOOD VILLAGE (Private)
14 trailer sites w/hookups for water/electricity, reservation information - (206)898-2163, showers, laundry, ocean access, fishing, $$.
Southwest of Belfair. State 3 south 1.0 mile, State 106 southwest 13.5 miles.

SHERWOOD HILLS ADULT RV PARK (Private)
33 trailer sites w/hookups for water/electricity/sewer, adults only, reservation information - (206)275-3155, groceries, trailer waste disposal, lake, fishing, $$$.
South of Belfair. State 3 south 2.2 miles, located in Allyn near city center.

TWANOH STATE PARK (Washington State Parks)

47 units, 9 trailer sites w/hookups for water/electricity/sewer, group sites - reservations advised - (206)275-2222, community kitchen/shelter, wheelchair access, on Hood Canal, boat launch, fishing, swimming, water skiing, tennis court, horseshoe pits, groceries, $$-$$$.
West of Belfair. State 106 west 8.0 miles.

BLAINE (B-1)

BAYWOOD PARK (Private)

100 campsites w/hookups for water/electricity/sewer, reservation information - (206)371-7211, showers, laundry, lounge, playfield, playground, trailer waste disposal, $$$.
West of Blaine. I-5 north to exit #270, Birch Bay-Lynden Road west 3.2 miles.

BIRCH BAY STATE PARK (Washington State Parks)

170 units, 20 trailer sites w/hookups for water/electricity, group sites - reservations advised (206)366-5944, wheelchair access, picnic shelter, trailer waste disposal, scuba diving area, fishing, birdwatching, hiking, $$-$$$.
South of Blaine. Campground is located 8.0 miles south of Blaine along water.

BIRCH BAY TRAILER PARK (Private)

290 trailer sites, 200 w/hookups for water/electricity/sewer, plus 50 w/hookups for water/electricity, 40 w/out hookups, reservation information - (206)371-7922, showers, laundry, rec room, groceries, satellite tv, propane, trailer waste disposal, ocean access, swimming, fishing, $$$.
Southwest of Blaine. Leave I-5 at exit #270, Birch Bay-Lynden Road 4.0 miles west, south to 8080 Harborview Road.

EVERGREEN MANOR & RV PARK (Private)

16 trailer sites w/hookups for water/electricity/sewer, no tents, reservation information - (206)384-1241, laundry, $$$.
Southeast of Blaine. I-5 south to exit #266, Grandview Road east .5 mile, Enterprise Road .01 mile to park.

PLAZA RV & MOBILE HOME PARK (Private)

20 campsite, 10 w/hookups for water/electricity/sewer, 10 w/hookups for water/electricity, plus tenting area, reservations - (206)371-7822, showers, laundry, playfield, trailer waste disposal, $$-$$$.
Southwest of Blaine. Leave I-5 at exit #270, Birch Bay-Lynden Road 2.0 miles east.

BOTHELL (B-2)

LAKE PLEASANT RV PARK (Private)
196 units, 56 w/hookups for water/electricity/sewer, 120 w/hookups for water/electricity, plus 20 tent sites, reservations - (206)487-1785, pull-thrus, tv, showers, laundry, spa, nearby golf, $$-$$$.
At Bothell. I-5 to I-405 to exit #26, Bothell Highway 1.0 mile south to park.

BRIDGEPORT (E-2)

BRIDGEPORT STATE PARK (Washington State Parks)
30 units, 20 w/hookups for water/electricity, group sites - reservations advised - (509)686-7231, community kitchen, trailer waste disposal, on Lake Rufus Woods, boat launch, fishing, golf nearby, $$-$$$.
North of Bridgeport. State 173 to State 17, north 1.5 miles to park.

ROCK GARDEN RV PARK (Private)
20 campsites, 12 w/hookups for water/electricity/sewer, plus 8 w/hookups for water/electricity, reservation information - (509)686-5343, showers, laundry, trailer waste disposal, river, fishing, playfield, playground, $$.
Northeast of Bridgeport. State 173 northwest 2.5 miles.

WATERFRONT MARINA (City of Bridgeport)
14 trailer sites w/hookups for water/electricity/sewer, showers, covered picnic area, playground, trailer waste disposal, river, fishing, boat launch, $$.
In Bridgeport. Located in town at Columbia Avenue & 7th Street.

BRINNON (B-2)

COLLINS (Olympic National Forest)
16 units, trailers to 21', well, river, swimming, fishing, Duckabush Trailhead nearby, elev. 200', $.
West of Brinnon. US 101 south 2.0 miles, FSR 2510 west 4.8 miles.

COVE TRAILER PARK (Private)
35 trailer sites w/hookups for water/electricity/sewer, no tents, reservations - (206)796-4723, showers, laundry, groceries, trailer waste disposal, ocean access, fishing. $$.
North of Brinnon. US 101 north 3.0 miles.

DOSEWALLIPS STATE PARK (Washington State Parks)
129 units, 40 w/hookups for water/electricity/sewer, group sites - reservations advised (206)796-4415, wheelchair access, trailer waste disposal, access to Dosewallips River & Hood Canal, fishing, clamming, oyster gathering, $$-$$$.
South of Brinnon. Take US 101 south 1.0 mile past Brinnon to campground.

ELKHORN (Olympic National Forest)
20 units, trailers to 22', well, river, swimming, fishing, hiking, elev. 600', $.
Northwest of Brinnon. US 101 north 1.0 mile, FSR 261 west 10.0 miles.

SEAL ROCK (Olympic National Forest)
41 units, trailers to 32', piped water, on Hood Canal, flush toilets, wheelchair access, boating, swimming, fishing, elev. 100', $$.
North of Brinnon. US 101 north 2.0 miles.

BURLINGTON (C-1)

BAYVIEW STATE PARK (Washington State Parks)
99 units, 9 w/hookups for water/electricity/sewer, community kitchen, on Padilla Bay, play area, $$.
West of Burlington. State 20 west approximately 6.0 miles; campground is 1.3 miles north of highway.

BURLINGTON/CASCADE KOA (Private)
87 campsites, 30 w/hookups for water/electricity/sewer, 25 w/hookups for water/electricity, 8 w/hookups for electricity, plus 24 tent units, reservations - (206)724-5511, wheelchair access, showers, laundry, cable tv, propane, groceries, indoor heated swimming pool, sauna, hot tubs, rec room, playfield, playground, trailer waste disposal, steam, fishing, $$$.
In Burlington. I-5 north to exit #232, Cook Road east .2 mile, Old Highway 99 north 3.5 miles.

CEDAR GROVE SHORES RV PARK (Private)
26 campsites w/hookups for water/electricity/sewer, reservation information - (206)652-7083, showers, rec room, laundry, cable tv, playfield, lake, 2 docks on lake, swimming, fishing, boat launch, $$$.
South of Burlington. I-5 south to exit #206, Lakewood Road 5.0 miles west, 52nd Avenue NW .5 mile south.

JIM MARION'S LAKE MARTHA RV PARK (Private)
23 campsites w/hookups for water/electricity/sewer, information - (206)652-8412, showers, laundry, trailer waste disposal, swimming, fishing, boat launch, golf, $$$.
South of Burlington. I-5 south to exit #206, Lakewood Road west 6.5 miles, stay left at Y and follow 1.0 mile to park.

KAYAK POINT COUNTY PARK (Snohomish County)
32 sites w/hookups for electricity/gray water, 2 sites have handicap access, reservations for handicap sites - (206)652-7992, flush toilets, picnic area, boat launch, fishing, $$.
South of Burlington. I-5 to exit #199, west on Marine Drive 12.0 miles to park.

LAKE GOODWIN RESORT (Private)
85 campsites, 68 w/hookups for water/electricity/sewer, plus 17 w/hookups for water/electricity, reservation information - (206)652-8169, no pets, groceries, gas, propane, ice, playfield, playground, trailer waste disposal, lake, swimming, fishing, boat launch, boat rental, $$$.
South of Burlington. I-5 south to exit #206, Lakewood Road 5.0 miles west, located at 176th NW.

LAKE McMURRAY RESORT (Private)
32 units w/hookups for water/electricity, reservation information - (206)445-4555, some pull-thrus, tenting area, showers, trailer waste disposal, lake fishing & swimming, boat rental, $$-$$$.
Southeast of Burlington. I-5 south 11.5 miles, State 534 east 5.0 miles, State 9 southeast 1.3 miles, Lakeview Road north .5 mile.

LARRABEE STATE PARK (Washington State Parks)
90 units, 26 w/hookups for water/electricity/sewer, group sites - reservations advised (206)676-2093, community kitchen/shelter, trailer waste disposal, on Samish Bay in Puget Sound, boat launch, fishing, tidal pools, hiking trails access two mountain lakes, $$-$$$.
Northwest of Burlington. State 11 northwest 14.0 miles.

MOUNTAIN VIEW TRAILER PARK (Private)
14 trailer sites w/hookups for water/electricity/sewer, adults only, no tents, reservation information - (206)424-3775, showers, laundry, $$.
South of Burlington. I-5 south to exit #225, west to State 99S, north .01 mile.

RIVERBEND PARK (Private)
105 campsites, 75 w/hookups for water/electricity/sewer, plus 30 tent units, reservation information - (206)428-4044, wheelchair access, showers, laundry, rec room, trailer waste disposal, river, fishing, $$-$$$.
South of Burlington. I-5 south to exit #227, College Way west .01 mile, Freeway Drive .5 mile north to campground.

WILDWOOD RESORT (Private)
155 sites, 78 w/hookups for water/electricity/sewer, plus 77 w/out hookups, some pull-thrus, reservation information - (206)595-2311, no pets, flush toilets, groceries, rec hall, lake fishing & swimming, play area, boat launch, moorage, water skiing, boat rentals, $$-$$$.
Northeast of Burlington. I-5 north approximately 13.0 miles to exit #240, Cain Lake Road east .5 mile, north at the Y for .2 mile to resort.

CARSON (C-5)

ALEGRIA RV PARK (Private)
59 units, 19 RV sites, plus 40 tent sites, reservation information - (509)427-8982, showers, laundry, play area, picnic area, store, fishing, $$-$$$.
North of Carson. Wind River Highway north 1.5 miles, follow blue signs.

BEAVER (Gifford Pinchot National Forest)
27 units, trailers to 25', group sites - reservation information (509)427-5645, piped water, flush toilets, wheelchair access, swimming, hiking, berry picking, fishing, mushroom area, near Trapper Creek Wilderness & Government Mineral Springs, elev. 1100', $-$$$.
Northwest of Carson. CR 30 northwest 12.2 miles to campground.

CARSON HOT SPRINGS (Private)
14 RV sites, tenting area, reservations - (509)427-8292, showers hot springs, therapy baths, picnic area, handicap access, trailer waste disposal, fishing, hiking, $$.
In Carson. At flashing yellow light go up hill to 4 way stop, go past golf course, take an immediate left and go down hill to resort.

LEWIS & CLARK CAMPGROUND/RV PARK (Private)

60 campsites, 20 w/hookups for water/electricity/sewer, plus 40 w/hookups for water/electricity, reservation information - (509)427-5559, showers, laundry, rec room, trailer waste disposal, river, fishing, hiking, 9 hole golf course next door to park, $$$.

Southwest of Carson. State 14 west to milepost #37, park is located about 1.0 mile west of North Bonneville on Evergreen Drive.

PANTHER CREEK (Gifford Pinchot National Forest)

33 units, trailers to 25', well, stream, fishing, hiking, berry & mushroom picking, Pacific Crest Trail nearby, horse trails & loading ramp, elev. 1000', $$.

North of Carson. CR 92135 northwest 9.0 miles, FSR 6517 east 1.5 miles, FSR 65 south .1 mile.

PARADISE CREEK (Gifford Pinchot National Forest)

42 units, trailers to 25', well, river, wheelchair access, fishing, hiking, berry & mushroom picking, Lava Butte Trailhead, elev. 1500', $$.

North of Carson. CR 92135 northwest 13.8 miles, FSR 30 north 6.3 miles.

CASTLE ROCK (B-5)

COWLITZ RESORT & RV PARK (Private)

25 campsites w/hookups for water/electricity/sewer, reservation information - (206)864-6611, showers, trailer waste disposal, on Cowlitz River, boat launch, fishing, $$.

Northeast of Castle Rock. I-5 north to exit #59, located at 162 Cowlitz Loop in Toledo.

FROST ROAD TRAILER PARK (Private)

19 trailer sites w/hookups for water/electricity/sewer, reservation information - (206)785-3616, showers, rec room, playfield, trailer waste disposal, $$.

Northeast of Castle Rock. I-5 north to exit #63, east .8 mile, north 1.5 mile, west .5 mile to park.

MERMAC RV PARK & STORE (Private)

10 trailer sites w/hookups for water/electricity/sewer, reservations - (206)274-6785, showers, groceries, $$.

North of Castle Rock. Leave I-5 just north of Castle Rock on exit #52, park is .6 mile.

RIVER OAKS RV PARK (Private)

53 campsites, 12 w/hookups for water/electricity/sewer, 12 w/hookups for water/electricity, plus 29 w/out hookups, tents okay, reservation information - (206)864-2895, showers, laundry, playfield, trailer waste disposal, on Cowlitz River, fishing, boat launch, $$.
Northwest of Castle Rock. I-5 north to exit #59, State 506 west .3 mile.

SCOTTS FRUIT STAND & RV PARK (Private)

50 campsites, 30 w/hookups for water/electricity/sewer, plus 20 w/out hookups, reservation information - (206)262-9220, wheelchair access, showers, hot tub & sauna, laundry, groceries, gas, propane, stream, fishing, $$$.
Northeast of Castle Rock. I-5 to exit #68, US 12 for .8 mile to park.

SEAQUEST STATE PARK (Washington State Parks)

72 units, 16 w/hookups for water/electricity/sewer, group sites - reservations advised (206)274-8633, community kitchen/shelter, trailer waste disposal, across from Silver Lake, fishing, $$-$$$.
East of Castle Rock. Leave I-5 on exit #49, State 504 east 5.0 miles.

SILVER LAKE MOTEL & RESORT (Private)

35 campsites, 7 w/hookups for water/electricity/sewer, 14 w/hookups for water/electricity, plus 14 tent units, reservation information - (206)274-6141, showers, groceries, rec room, on Silver Lake, swimming, fishing, boat launch, boat rental, $$$.
East of Castle Rock. Leave I-5 on exit #49, State 504 east 6.0 miles.

TOUTLE VILLAGE RESTAURANT & RV PARK (Private)

10 trailer sites w/hookups for water/electricity/sewer, reservation information - (206)274-7343, showers, laundry, ice, restaurant, rec room, trailer waste disposal, $$-$$$.
East of Castle Rock. I-5 to exit #49, State 504 east 10.0 miles.

CHEHALIS (B-4)

OFFUT LAKE RESORT & RV PARK (Private)

54 campsites, 35 w/hookups for water/electricity/sewer, 10 w/hookups for electricity, plus 9 tent sites, reservation information - (206)264-2438, showers, laundry, groceries, rec room, playground, trailer waste disposal, lake, swimming, fishing, boat rental, $$-$$$.

Northeast of Chehalis. I-5 north to exit #99, 93rd Avenue east 3.0 miles, Old Highway 99 south 4.0 miles, Offut Lake Road east 1.0 mile, park is just north of here, in Tenino.

RAINBOW FALLS STATE PARK (Washington State Parks)
50 units, group sites - reservations advised (206)291-3767, community kitchen, trailer waste disposal, swinging bridge over Chehalis River, nature trails through old-growth timber, play area, $$-$$$.
West of Chehalis. Take State 6 west from Chehalis approximately 18.0 miles, campground is near Doty.

STAN HEDWALL PARK (City of Chehalis)
29 campsites w/hookups for water/electricity, reservations - (206)748-0271, showers, playfield, playground, trailer waste disposal, river, swimming, fishing, hiking, $$.
In Chehalis. I-5 to exit #76, Rice Road .5 mile west.

TRAILER VILLAGE RV PARK (Private)
16 trailer sites w/hookups for water/electricity/sewer, no tents, pets okay, reservation information - (206)736-9260, showers, $$$.
North of Chehalis. I-5 north to Centralia exit #82, Harrison Street west .5 mile.

CHELAN (E-2)

ALTA LAKE STATE PARK (Washington State Parks)
191 units, 16 w/hookups for water/electricity, group sites - reservations advised (509)923-2473, community kitchen, wheelchair access, trailer waste disposal, fishing, swimming, trail, winter sports, $$-$$$.
North of Chelan. US 97 northeast 17.0 miles, State 153 west 2.0 miles, campground road south 2.0 miles to park.

CITY OF CHELAN LAKESHORE RV PARK (City of Chelan)
160 trailer sites, 151 w/hookups for water/electricity/sewer, plus 9 w/hookups for water/electricity, no tents, no dogs, information - (509)682-5031, reservations by mail only, showers, playground, trailer waste disposal, on Lake Chelan, swimming, fishing, bumper boats, go carts, paddleboat rentals, tennis, mini golf, $$$.
In Chelan. State 150 northwest .1 mile.

LAKE CHELAN STATE PARK (Washington State Parks)

146 units, 17 w/hookups for water/electricity/sewer, wheelchair access, picnic shelter, on 55 mile long Lake Chelan, snack bar, trailer waste disposal, boat launch, scuba diving area, fishing, swimming, water skiing, $$.
West of Chelan. Take road leading around southern side of Lake Chelan, campground is 9.0 miles west of city.

TWENTYFIVE MILE CREEK RESORT (Private)

95 campsites, 13 w/hookups for water/electricity/sewer, 15 w/hookups for water/electricity, plus 67 tent units, reservation information - (509)687-3610, wheelchair access, showers, groceries, swimming pool, trailer waste disposal, lake, swimming, fishing, boat launch, $$-$$$.
Southwest of Chelan. US 97 south to South Shore Road, resort is 19.0 miles west along south shore of Lake Chelan.

TWENTYFIVE MILE CREEK PARK (Washington State Parks)

85 units, 33 w/hookups for water/electricity/sewer, lake, boat launch & dock, swimming, $$.
Northwest of Chelan. Take road leading around southern side of Lake Chelan, campground is 18.0 miles west.

CHENEY (G-3)

BADGER LAKE RESORT (Private)

25 campsites, 20 w/hookups for water/electricity/sewer, plus 5 w/hookups for water/electricity, reservation information - (509)235-2341, tents okay, showers, laundry, groceries, playground, trailer waste disposal, lake, fishing, swimming, boat launch, boat rental, $$.
South of Cheney. Badger Lake Road south 9.5 miles.

BUNKERS RESORT (Private)

30 sites, 15 w/hookups for water/electricity/sewer, plus 15 w/hookups for water/electricity, reservation information - (509)235-5212, showers, groceries, trailer waste disposal, restaurant, on Williams Lake, boat rental, launch & dock, bait & tackle, fishing, swimming, picnic area, hiking, $$-$$$.
Southwest of Cheney. Cheney Plaza Road south 11.5 miles, Williams Lake Road west approximately .5 mile.

PEACEFUL PINES RV PARK (Private)

30 campsites, 10 w/hookups for water/electricity/sewer, 6 w/hookups for water/electricity, plus 14 w/out hookups, tents okay, reservation information - (509)235-4966, showers, trailer waste disposal, $$.
West of Cheney. State 904 west 1.0 mile.

WILLIAMS LAKE RESORT (Private)

150 campsites, 90 w/hookups for water/electricity/sewer, 40 w/hookups for water/electricity, 10 w/hookups for electricity, plus 10 tent sites, reservation information - (509)235-2391, groceries, gas, propane, playground, trailer waste disposal, lake, swimming, fishing, restaurant, boat launch, boat rental, $$-$$$. Southwest of Cheney. Cheney Plaza Road south 11.5 miles, Williams Lake Road west 3.5 miles.

CHEWELAH (F-1)

FORTYNINER CAMPGROUND & MOTEL (Private)

24 campsites w/hookups for water/electricity/sewer, reservation information - (509)935-8613, showers, ice, indoor heated swimming pool, sauna, jacuzzi, rec room, trailer waste disposal, $$. In Chewelah. Located on US 395 at south edge of town.

GRANITE POINT PARK (Private)

59 trailer sites, 53 w/hookups for water/electricity/sewer, 4 w/hookups for water/electricity/ plus 2 w/out hookups, trailers to 35', no pets, no tents, reservation information - (509)233-2100, showers, laundry, groceries, rec room, playfield, playground, lake, swimming, fishing, boat launch, boat rental, $$$. Southeast of Chewelah. US 395 southeast 17.5 miles, located about 1.5 miles south of Loon Lake.

SHORE ACRES RESORT (Private)

35 campsites, 17 w/hookups for water/electricity/sewer, 5 w/hookups for water/electricity, plus 13 tent units, trailers to 30', reservation information - (509)233-2474, showers, groceries, boat gas, playground, trailer waste disposal, lake, swimming, fishing, boat launch, boat rental, $$. South of Chewelah. US 395 southeast 16.0 miles, State 292 west 1.8 miles, Shore Acres Road south 1.8 miles.

SILVER BEACH RESORT (Private)

53 trailer sites, 33 w/hookups for water/electricity/sewer, 14 w/hookups for waste/electricity, plus 6 w/hookups for electricity, trailers to 35', no tents, reservation information - (509)937-2811, showers, laundry, restaurant, groceries, propane, gas, playground, trailer waste disposal, lake, swimming, fishing, boat launch, boat rental, $$$. South of Chewelah. US 395 south 4.0 miles, State 231 south 2.0 miles, Waitts Lake Road west 3.0 miles.

CLE ELUM (D-3)

CLE ELUM RIVER (Wenatchee National Forest)
35 units, group sites, trailers to 22', well, picnic facilities, fishing, hiking, elev. 2200', $.
Northwest of Cle Elum. State 903 northwest 11.2 miles, CR 903 northwest 7.0 miles.

CRYSTAL SPRINGS (Wenatchee National Forest)
20 units, trailers to 22', picnic area w/open-sided group picnic shelter, piped water, fishing, berry & mushroom picking, elev. 2400', $.
Northwest of Cle Elum. I-90 northwest 20.7 miles, FSR 212 northwest .4 mile.

KACHESS (Wenatchee National Forest)
180 units, trailers to 32', reservations - (800)283-CAMP, picnic area, piped water, flush toilets, interpretive trail, on Lake Kachess, berry picking, boat launch, boating, swimming, fishing, water skiing, hiking, elev. 2300', $$.
Northwest of Cle Elum. I-90 northwest 20.7 miles, FSR 49 northeast 5.4 miles. Sometimes closed late in season due to low water.

LAKE EASTON STATE PARK (Washington State Parks)
137 units, 45 w/hookups for water/electricity/sewer, group sites - reservations advised (509)656-2230, wheelchair access, trailer waste disposal, boat launch, fishing, swimming, winter sports, $$-$$$.
Northwest of Cle Elum. I-90 northwest 12.0 miles, campground is located 1.0 mile west of Easton.

MINERAL SPRINGS (Wenatchee National Forest)
12 units, piped water, nearby restaurant/lounge, fishing, elev. 2700', $.
Northeast of Cle Elum. US 97 east 12.0 miles, US 97 north 9.0 miles.

MINERAL SPRINGS RESORT & RV (Private)
15 sites, 8 w/hookups for water/electricity/sewer, plus 7 w/hookups for electricity only, reservation information - (509)857-2361, showers, laundry, restaurant & lounge, hiking, gold panning, agate beds, $$$.
Northeast of Cle Elum. US 97 east 12.0 miles, US 97 north approximately 9.0 miles to resort.

147

RV TOWN INC. (Private)
72 trailer sites, 20 w/hookups for water/electricity/sewers, plus 52 w/hookups for water/electricity, reservation information - (509)656-2360, showers, laundry, groceries, gas, propane, rec room, playground, restaurant, swimming pool, trailer waste disposal, stream, fishing, $$-$$$.
Northwest of Cle Elum. I-90 northwest to exit #70, in Easton.

SALMON LA SAC (Wenatchee National Forest)
127 units, trailers to 22', includes Cayuse Horse Camp's 15 units w/ramp & corrals, reservation information - (800)283-CAMP, picnic area w/open-sided group picnic shelter, piped water, flush toilets, fishing, hiking, trailhead to Cascade Crest Trail & Alpine Lakes Wilderness, elev. 2400', $-$$.
Northwest of Cle Elum. State 903 northwest 11.2 miles, CR 903 northwest 10.7 miles.

SWAUK (Wenatchee National Forest)
23 units, trailers to 22', picnic area, piped water, horseshoe pits, play area & fields, fishing, hiking, elev. 3200', $$.
Northeast of Cle Elum. US 97 east 12.0 miles, US 97 north 10.0 miles.

TANEUM (Wenatchee National Forest)
13 units, picnic area, piped water, hiking, horse & motorcycle trails, stream, fishing, elev. 2400', $.
Southeast of Cle Elum. I-90 southeast 12.0 miles, CR 9123 south 3.0 miles, CR 51 west 2.0 miles, FSR 33 northwest 4.2 miles.

THE LAST RESORT (Private)
8 sites w/hookups for water/electricity, tents okay, reservations - (509)649-2222, picnic area, mini mart, storage, propane, restaurant, lounge, boating on Lake Cle Elum, fishing, hiking, $$-$$$.
Southwest of Cle Elum. I-90 to exit #90, State 903 northwest 4.0 miles, resort road 1.0 mile to lake and resort.

TRAILER CORRAL RV PARK (Private)
30 campsites, 18 w/hookups for water/electricity/sewer, 6 w/hookups for water/electricity, plus 6 w/out hookups, reservations - (509)674-2433, showers, laundry, trailer waste disposal, $$.
East of Cle Elum. I-90 east to exit #85, State 970 east 1.0 mile.

WISH POOSH (Wenatchee National Forest)
39 units, trailers to 22', picnic area, piped water, lake, flush toilets, boat launch, boating, swimming, fishing, water skiing, elev. 2400', $$.
Northwest of Cle Elum. State 903 northwest 10.2 miles, FSR 112 west .1 mile. Sometimes closed late in season due to low water.

COLFAX (G-4)

BOYER PARK & MARINA (Private)
28 campsites, 14 w/hookups for water/electricity/sewer, plus 14 w/hookups for waste/electricity, reservations - (509)397-3208, showers, laundry, ice, restaurant, groceries, trailer waste disposal, on Snake River, swimming fishing, boat launch, $$.
Southwest of Colfax. State 26 west to CR 8000, follow this to CR 8250, park is located 23.0 miles south of Colfax; on Little Goose Pool 2.0 miles downstream from Lower Granite Dam. (Follow any signs directing you to Marina, Almota, Snake River or Lower Granite Dam.)

CITY OF PULLMAN RV PARK (City of Pullman)
24 trailer sites w/hookups for water/electricity/sewer, reservation information - (509)334-4555, swimming pool, playfield, playground, $$.
Southeast of Colfax. US 195 southeast 13.0 miles to Pullman, Grand 2 blocks northeast to Paradise Street, east to Spring Street where you will find signs directing you to City Playfield, park is at south end of Playfield.

COLVILLE (F-1)

BEAVER LODGE RV PARK (Private)
40 campsites, 8 w/hookups for water/electricity/sewer, 4 w/hookups for water/electricity, plus 28 w/out hookups, tents okay, reservation information - (509)684-5657, showers, laundry, deli-snack bar, groceries, gas, propane, on Little Pend Oreille Lake, swimming, fishing, boat launch, canoe & paddle boat rental, tackle store, cross country ski rental, elev. 3300', $$.
East of Colville. State 20 east 25.0 miles.

COLVILLE FAIRGROUNDS RV PARK (Stevens County)
40 trailer sites w/hookups for water/electricity/sewer, wheelchair access, showers, playfield, trailer waste disposal, $$.
In Colville. US 395 to Fairgrounds exit, follow signs.

GILLETTE (Colville National Forest)
30 units, trailers to 32', piped water, flush toilets, wheelchair access, trailer waste disposal, hiking trails, nearby motorcycle trails, bicycling, elev. 3200', $$-$$$.
East of Colville. State 20 east 25.0 miles.

LAKE LEO (Colville National Forest)
8 units, trailers to 18', well, boat launch, boating, swimming, fishing, elev. 3200', $$.
East of Colville. State 20 east 25.0 miles.

LAKE THOMAS (Colville National Forest)
15 tent units, piped water, boating, swimming, fishing, water skiing, nearby motorcycle trails, bicycling, elev. 3200', $$.
East of Colville. State 20 east 25.0 miles.

WILDERNESS WEST RESORT (Private)
65 campsites, 25 w/hookups for water/electricity/sewer, plus 40 tent units, reservation information - (509)732-4263, showers, laundry, groceries, gas, rec room, playfield, trailer waste disposal, on Deep Lake, swimming, fishing, boat launch, boat rental, hiking, elev. 3200', $$.
Northeast of Colville. State 20 east 1.0 mile, Aladdin Road north 30.0 miles to Deep Lake, located on northeast shore.

CONCONULLY (D-1)

ANDY'S RV PARK (Private)
35 trailer sites w/hookups for water/electricity/sewer, companion tents okay, reservations - (509)826-0326, showers, laundry, swimming pool, on Upper & Lower Conconnully Reservoir, fishing, $$.
In Conconully. Located 1 block east of Main Street in Conconully.

COTTONWOOD (Okanogan National Forest)
4 units, trailers to 22', artesian well, stream, fishing, elev. 2700', $.
North of Conconully. CR 2361 north 1.8 miles, FSR 38 north .3 mile.

FLEMING'S HAVEN RESORT (Private)
11 trailer sites w/hookups for water/electricity/sewer, no tents, reservations - (509)826-0813, showers, ice, on Conconully Lake, swimming, fishing, boat launch, boat rental, $$$.
East of Conconully. Upper Conconully Lake Road east 1.0 mile.

JACK'S RV PARK (Private)
66 trailer sites w/hookups for water/electricity/sewer, reservations - (509)826-0132, showers, laundry, swimming pool, trailer waste disposal, on Upper & Lower Conconully Reservoir, stream, fishing, boat rental, $$.
In Conconully. Located 1 block east of Main Street in Conconully.

KOZY CABINS & RV PARK (Private)
12 campsites w/hookups for water/electricity/sewer, tents okay, reservations - (509)826-6780, cable tv, showers, stream, fishing, $$.
In Conconully. Turn right, located at 111 Broadway.

LIARS COVE RESORT (Private)
30 trailer sites w/hookups for water/electricity/sewer, no tents, reservations - (509)826-1288, showers, ice, lake, swimming, fishing, boat launch, boat rental, $$$.
In Conconully. Located at east end of town.

ORIOLE (Okanogan National Forest)
8 units, well, stream, fishing, elev. 2900', $-$$.
Northwest of Conconully. CR 2361 northwest 1.8 miles, FSR 38 northwest .7 mile, FSR 25 northwest .4 mile. Located 3 miles northwest of Conconully State Park.

SALMON MEADOWS (Okanogan National Forest)
7 tent/trailer sites, picnic area, well, stream, hiking trails, elev. 4500', $-$$.
Northwest of Conconully. CR 2361 northwest 1.5 miles, FSR 38 northwest 6.9 miles.

SHADY PINES RESORT (Private)
24 campsites, 20 w/hookups for water/electricity/sewer, plus 4 w/hookups for water/electricity, reservations - (509)826-2287, showers, ice, tackle shop, on Conconully Reservoir, stream, swimming, fishing, boat rental, $$$.
West of Conconully. Located on west shore of Conconully Reservoir about 1.0 mile west of town.

'THE OTHER PLACE' RV PARK (Private)
25 trailer sites w/hookups for water/electricity/sewer, no tents, reservations - (509)826-4231, wheelchair access, showers, nearby lake & fishing, $$.
In Conconully. Located in Conconully east of Main, on A Street.

CONCRETE (C-1)

CLARK'S SKAGIT RIVER RV PARK (Private)
50 trailer sites w/hookups for water/electricity/sewer, reservation information - (206)873-2250, showers, laundry, restaurant, museum, chapel, river, fishing, on Cascade Loop, hiking, wildlife, $$.
East of Concrete. State 20 east 14.5 miles; located 6 miles east of Rockport.

CREEKSIDE CAMPING (Private)
27 campsites, 11 w/hookups for water/electricity/sewer, 13 w/hookups for water/electricity, plus 3 w/out hookups , pets okay, reservations - (206)826-3566, showers, laundry, groceries, playground, trailer waste disposal, stream, fishing, on Cascade Loop, $$.
West of Concrete. State 20 west 7.0 miles, Baker Lake Road north .2 mile. Also accessible off I-5, take exit #232 and follow State 20 east 17.0 miles to Baker Lake Road.

HORSESHOE COVE (Mt. Baker-Snoqualmie National Forest)
34 units, trailers to 22', picnic area, piped water, on Baker Lake, flush toilets, boat launch, boating, swimming, fishing, water skiing, elev. 700', $-$$.
North of Concrete. CR 25 north 9.6 miles, FSR 11 north 2.4 miles, FSR 1118 east 2.0 miles.

HOWARD MILLER STEELHEAD PARK (Skagit County)
60 campsites, 40 w/hookups for water/electricity, plus 20 w/hookups for electricity only, reservation information - (206)853-8808, wheelchair access, picnic shelter, showers, groceries, playground, trailer waste disposal, river, swimming, fishing, boat launch, hiking, on Cascade Loop, $$.
East of Concrete. State 20 east 10.0 miles, past Rockport to Alfred Street and park.

PANORAMA POINT (Mt. Baker-Snoqualmie National Forest)
13 units, trailers to 22', well, on Baker Lake, boat launch, swimming, fishing, water skiing, elev. 700', $-$$.
North of Concrete. CR 25 north 9.6 miles, FSR 11 north 6.4 miles. Campground is located 5 miles east of Mt. Baker.

ROCKPORT STATE PARK (Washington State Parks)
61 units, 50 w/hookups for water/electricity/sewer, group sites - reservations advised (206)853-4705, picnic shelter, wheelchair access includes trail, old growth forest, trailer waste disposal, fishing, hiking, $$-$$$.
East of Concrete. State 20 east 8.0 miles.

TIMBERLINE RV PARK (Private)

35 trailer sites w/hookups for waste/electricity/sewer, reservation information - (206)826-3131, wheelchair access, showers, cable tv, laundry, groceries, propane, rec room, playfield, playground, on Cascade Loop, $$.
West of Concrete. State 20 west 5.0 miles, Russell Road north to Challenger Road, east .3 mile to park at 736 Wilde Road.

WILDERNESS VILLAGE (Private)

38 trailer sites w/hookups for water/electricity/sewer, reservation information - (206)873-2571, showers, laundry, ice, rec room, river, fishing, on Cascade Loop, $$.
East of Concrete. State 20 east 14.0 miles.

COOK (D-6)

HOME VALLEY PARK (Snoqualmie Parks Dept.)

25 units, 20 RV sites, plus 5 tent sites, reservations - (509)427-5141, showers, picnic area, play area, wheelchair access, swimming, fishing, wind surfing, nearby groceries, $-$$.
West of Cook. State 14 west to milepost #50; take a right and follow signs to park.

OKLAHOMA (Gifford Pinchot National Forest)

23 units, trailers to 22', well, on Little White Salmon River, wheelchair access, fishing, elev. 1700', $.
North of Cook. CR 18 north 14.4 miles.

MOSS CREEK (Gifford Pinchot National Forest)

18 units, trailers to 32', piped water, on Little White Salmon River, wheelchair access, fishing, elev. 1400', $.
North of Cook. CR 18 north 8.0 miles to campground.

COUGAR (B-5)

BEAVER BAY CAMP (Pacific Power)

63 campsites, group sites - reservations required (503)243-4778, showers, trailer waste disposal, on Lewis River, boat launch, fishing, swimming, water skiing, $-$$.
East of Cougar. State 503 east 2.0 miles.

COUGAR CAMP (Pacific Power)

45 tent sites, group sites - reservations required (503)243-4778, also has tenting area - reservations advised, showers, on Lewis River, boat launch, fishing, swimming, water skiing, $-$$.
East of Cougar. State 503 east 2.0 miles.

LONE FIR RESORT (Private)
32 campsites w/hookups for water/electricity/sewer, reservations - (206)238-5210, showers, laundry, ice, swimming pool, $$-$$$.
In Cougar. Located on Lewis River Road in Cougar.

SWIFT CAMP (Pacific Power)
93 campsites, picnic area, drinking water, trailer waste disposal, on Lewis River, boat launch, fishing swimming, water skiing, $.
West of Cougar. State 503 west 2.0 miles.

COULEE CITY (E-2)

BLUE LAKE RESORT (Private)
75 campsites, 23 w/hookups for water/electricity/sewer, 33 w/hookups for water/electricity, plus 19 tent units, reservation information - (509)632-5364, showers, groceries, tackle store, playfield, playground, lake, swimming, fishing, boat launch, boat rental, $$.
Southwest of Coulee City. US 2 west 2.0 miles, State 17 south 10.0 miles.

COULEE CITY PARK (Coulee City)
140 campsites, 34 w/hookups for water/electricity/sewer, plus 106 tent units, trailers to 24', reservation information - (509)632-5331, showers, playground, trailer waste disposal, lake, swimming, fishing, boat launch, $-$$.
In Coulee City. Located in Coulee City at northern edge of town.

COULEE LODGE RESORT (Private)
45 campsites, 22 w/hookups for water/electricity/sewer, 11 w/hookups for water/electricity, plus 12 tent units, reservation information - (509)632-5565, wheelchair access, showers, laundry, groceries, trailer waste disposal, lake, swimming, fishing, boat launch, boat rental, $$.
Southwest of Coulee City. US 2 southwest 2.0 miles, State 17 south 8.0 miles.

LAURENTS SUN VILLAGE RESORT (Private)
106 units, 56 w/hookups for water/electricity/sewer, 40 w/hookups for water/electricity, plus 10 tent sites, reservation information - (509)632-5664, pull-thrus, showers, laundry, store, gas, propane, rec room, arcade, lake swimming, boat rentals, water skiing, boat dock, boat launch, playground, fishing, hiking, picnic area, $$-$$$.
South of Coulee City. US 2 west 2.0 miles, State 17 south 8.0 miles, State Park Road east 1.0 mile to resort.

SUN LAKES PARK RESORT (Private)

110 trailer sites w/hookups for water/electricity/sewer, tents okay, reservation information - (509)632-5291, showers, laundry, groceries, tackle store, propane, gas, trailer waste disposal, swimming pool, playfield, lake, swimming, fishing, boat launch, boat rental, mini golf, golf, hiking, $$$.
Southwest of Coulee City. US 2 west 2.0 miles. State 17 south 7.0 miles.

SUN LAKES STATE PARK (Washington State Parks)

193 units, 18 w/hookups for water/electricity/sewer, group sites - reservations advised (509)632-5583, wheelchair access, snackbar, groceries, trailer waste disposal, boat & horse rental, boat launch, fishing, swimming, horse trails, $$-$$$.
Southwest of Coulee City. US 2 west 2.0 miles, State 17 south 5.0 miles.

SUN VILLAGE RESORT (Private)

115 campsites, 95 w/hookups for water/electricity/sewer, plus 20 w/hookups for water/electricity, reservation information - (509)632-5664, showers, laundry, groceries, deli, playfield, playground, trailer waste disposal, lake, swimming, fishing, boat launch, boat rental, $$$.
Southwest of Coulee City. US 2 west 2.0 miles, State 17 south 8.0 miles.

COUPEVILLE (B-1)

DECEPTION PASS STATE PARK (Washington State Parks)

246 tent units, some trailers - no hookups, community kitchen/ shelter, wheelchair access, trailer waste disposal, boat launch/ buoys/floats, fishing, scuba diving area, swimming, $$.
North of Coupeville. Deception State Park is located at the northern end of Whidbey Island, approximately 16.0 miles north of Coupeville.

FORT CASEY STATE PARK (Washington State Parks)

38 units, some trailers - no hookups, wheelchair access, located in historic US Defense Post, boat launch, fishing, scuba diving area, beach access, $$.
South of Coupeville. Located about 3.5 miles south of Coupeville along County Road; or follow State 20 south out of Coupeville and then west to water's edge and campground, approximately 8.0 miles.

FORT EBEY STATE PARK (Washington State Parks)
53 units, some trailers - no hookups, historic WWII defense bunker, beach access, fishing, $$.
Northwest of Coupeville. Located on west side of Whidbey Island, approximately 6.0 miles northwest of Coupeville.

MUTINY BAY RESORT (Private)
25 trailer sites w/hookups for water/electricity/sewer, trailers to 30', no tents, reservation information - (206)321-4500, showers, ice, playfield, tackle store, trailer waste disposal, ocean access, swimming, fishing, $$$.
South of Coupeville. Located in Freeland, 10.0 miles from Clinton Ferry Landing via State 525, Fish Road south 1.0 mile, Mutiny Bay Road to resort.

OAK HARBOR CITY BEACH (Oak Harbor)
55 campsites w/hookups for water/electricity, tents okay, showers, tennis, playground, trailer waste disposal, ocean access, swimming, fishing, boat launch, $$.
North of Coupeville. State 20 north toward Oak Harbor, campground is located just south of Oak Harbor at Pioneer Road.

SOUTH WHIDBEY STATE PARK (Washington State Parks)
60 sites, some trailers - no hookups, group sites - reservations advised (206)321-4559, wheelchair access, trailer waste disposal, scuba diving area, fishing, beachcombing, clamming, $$-$$$.
South of Coupeville. Leave Coupeville on State 20 to State 525, follow this about 6.0 miles where you will find a road leading southwest toward the water and campground.

DAYTON (F-5)

LEWIS & CLARK TRAIL STATE PARK (Washington State Parks)
34 units, some trailers - no hookups, community kitchen/shelter, trailer waste disposal, on historic Lewis & Clark Trail, campfire programs in summer, fishing, winter sports, $$.
Southwest of Dayton. US 12 southwest 5.0 miles.

ELBE (C-4)

COUGAR ROCK CAMPGROUND (Mt. Rainier National Park)
200 campsites, trailers to 30', information - (206)569-2211, trailer waste disposal, hiking, $$.
East of Elbe. State 706 east 22.2 miles, located .8 mile east of Nisqually Entrance.

SUNSHINE POINT (Mt. Rainier National Park)
18 campsites, trailers to 25', on Nisqually River, fishing, $.
East of Elbe. State 706 east 22.6 miles, located .5 mile east of
Nisqually Entrance.

ELDON (B-2)

HAMMA HAMMA (Olympic National Forest)
15 units, trailers to 22', well, river, swimming, fishing, hiking,
bicycling, elev. 600', $.
Northwest of Eldon. US 101 north 1.7 miles, FSR 25 west 6.5
miles. Lena Lakes Trailhead is 2.5 miles west of campground.

ELLENSBURG (D-4)

ELLENSBURG KOA (Private)
140 campsites, 12 w/hookups for water/electricity/sewer, 88
w/hookups for water/electricity, plus 40 tent units, reservations
- (509)925-9319, showers, laundry, groceries, rec room, playfield,
playground, swimming pool, trailer waste disposal, rafting,
horseshoe pits, volleyball court, on river, fishing, $$$.
At Ellensburg. I-90 to exit #106 and campground.

ENTIAT (D-3)

COTTONWOOD (Wenatchee National Forest)
25 units, 1 group site, trailers to 22', well, river, fishing, hiking,
elev. 3100', $.
Northwest of Entiat. US 97 southwest 1.4 miles, Entiat Valley
Road #5100 northwest 39.0 miles.

ENTIAT CITY PARK (City of Entiat)
31 campsites w/hookups for electricity, plus tent area, showers,
playground, trailer waste disposal, lake, swimming, fishing, boat
launch, $$-$$$.
In Entiat. Leave US 97 at Entiat on Lakeshore Drive and follow to
park.

FOX CREEK (Wenatchee National Forest)
9 units, trailers not recommended, well, fishing, elev. 2300', $.
Northwest of Entiat. US 97 southwest 1.4 miles, Entiat Valley
Road #5100 northwest 27.0 miles.

LAKE CREEK (Wenatchee National Forest)
12 units, trailers to 18', well, fishing, hiking, elev. 2400', $.
Northwest of Entiat. US 97 southwest 1.4 miles, Entiat Valley
Road #5100 northwest 28.2 miles.

NORTH FORK (Wenatchee National Forest)
9 units, 1 trailer to 22', river, fishing, trail, elev. 2700', $.
Northwest of Entiat. US 97 southwest 1.4 miles, Entiat Valley
Road #5100 northwest 33.5 miles.

SILVER FALLS (Wenatchee National Forest)
35 units, group camp - reservations required (800)283-CAMP,
trailers to 22', picnic area, well, stream, waterfall, fishing, hiking,
elev. 2400', $$-$$$.
Northwest of Entiat. US 97 southwest 1.4 miles, Entiat Valley
Road #5100 northwest 30.4 miles.

ENUMCLAW (B-3)

IPSUT CREEK (Mt. Rainier National Park)
29 campsites, trailers to 20', hiking, elev. 4400', $.
South of Enumclaw. State 165 south approximately 12.0 miles to
Carbonado, located 5.0 miles east of Mt. Rainier National Park's
Carbon River Entrance on park access road.

KANASKAT/PALMER STATE PARK (Washington State Parks)
54 units, 19 trailer sites w/hookups for electricity, group sites -
reservations advised (206)886-0148, community kitchen/shelter,
wheelchair access, on Green River, boating, fishing, $$-$$$.
Northeast of Enumclaw. State 410 east 1.0 mile, Palmer Road
northeast 9.0 miles.

SILVER SPRINGS (Mt. Baker-Snoqualmie National Forest)
56 units, 4 group sites, trailers to 22', picnic area, water,
wheelchair access, fishing, elev. 2600', $-$$.
Southeast of Enumclaw. State 410 southeast 31.3 miles.
Campground is located 1 mile northwest of Mt. Rainier National
Park boundary.

THE DALLES (Mt. Baker-Snoqualmie National Forest)
45 units, trailers to 22', picnic area, water, stream, fishing, hik-
ing, elev. 2200', $-$$.
Southeast of Enumclaw. State 410 southeast 25.4 miles.
Campground is located 7 miles northwest of Mt. Rainier National
Park boundary.

WHITE RIVER CAMPGROUND (Mt. Rainier National Park)
117 campsites, trailers to 20', on White River, hiking, $$.
West of Enumclaw. State 410 east, located 5.0 miles west of
White River Entrance for Mt. Rainier National Park.

EVERETT (B-2)

SILVER SHORES RV PARK (Private)
83 trailer sites, 57 w/hookups for water/electricity/sewer, 11
w/hookups for water/electricity, plus 15 w/out hookups, reser-
vations - (206)337-8741, showers, laundry, ice, tennis, trailer
waste disposal, on Silver Lake, swimming, fishing, $$$.
In Everett. I-5 to exit #186 to 128th Street, west to 4th Avenue,
north to 112th Street, take this east across freeway, 14th
Avenue/Silver Lake Road south to 11621 West Silver Lake Road
and park.

SMOKEY POINT RV PARK (Private)
109 units, 96 w/hookups for water/electricity/sewer, 6
w/hookups for water/electricity, plus 6 tent units, reservation
information - (206)652-7300, showers, laundry, RV supplies, rec
room, trailer waste disposal, nearby mini mart & restaurant, stay
includes free pass to nearby full service health club, $$-$$$.
Northeast of Everett. I-5 north 14.0 miles to exit #206, located in
Arlington at 17019 28th Drive NE.

FALL CITY (C-2)

SNOQUALMIE RIVER CAMPGROUND (Private)
300 units, 100 w/hookups for water/electricity, plus 200 w/out
hookups, reservation information - (206)222-5545, 25 pull-thrus,
tenting area, group sites, showers, laundry, pavilion, river, fishing, swimming, boating, playground, $$-$$$.
At Fall City. Located on Snoqualmie River at SE 44th Street.

FERNDALE (B-1)

FERNDALE CAMPGROUND (Private)
111 sites, 23 w/hookups for water/electricity/sewer, 33
w/hookups for water/electricity, plus 55 tent units, reservation
information - (206)384-2622, showers, laundry, groceries, trailer
waste disposal, pond, game room, playfield, playground, $$$.
In Ferndale. I-5 to Ferndale exit #263, Portal Way north 1.0 mile.

FORKS (A-2)

BEAR CREEK RV PARK & MOTEL (Private)
18 trailer sites w/hookups for water/electricity/sewer, reservation information - (206)327-3558, showers, laundry, ice, restaurant, river, swimming, fishing, $$-$$$.
North of Forks. US 101 north 15.0 miles, located near milepost #206.

BOGACHIEL STATE PARK (Washington State Parks)
42 units, some trailers, community kitchen/shelter, trailer waste disposal, on Bogachiel River, good fishing, $-$$.
South of Forks. Highway 101 south 6.0 mile.

FORKS MOBILE HOME & RV PARK (Private)
7 trailer sites w/hookups for water/electricity/sewer, reservations - (206)374-5510, laundry, $$.
In Forks. US 101 to Calawah Way, east about 3 blocks to park.

HOH RIVER (Olympic National Park)
89 campsites, trailers to 21', trailer waste disposal, water, handicap access, river, fishing, hiking, elev. 578', $$.
South of Forks. US 101 south 14.0 miles, Hoh River Road east 19.0 miles.

HOH RIVER RESORT & RV PARK (Private)
24 sites, 20 w/hookups for water/electricity/sewer, plus 4 w/hookups for water/electricity, reservations - (206)374-5566, showers, laundry, satellite tv, groceries, propane, on Hoh River, fishing, $$$.
South of Forks. US 101 south 15.0 miles.

MORA CAMPGROUND (Olympic National Park)
94 campsites, trailers to 21', trailer waste disposal, water, handicap access, ocean access, on Quinault River, swimming, fishing, hiking, elev. sea level, $$.
West of Forks. US 101 north to La Push Road, southwest 15.0 miles.

SHORELINE RESORT & TRAILER COURT (Private)
61 trailer sites w/hookups for water/electricity/sewer, no tents, information - (206)374-6488, showers, laundry, propane, trailer waste disposal, ocean access, swimming, fishing, $$.
Southwest of Forks. US 101 north to La Push Road, southwest to La Push and resort.

THREE RIVERS RESORT (Private)
11 campsites, 5 w/hookups for water/electricity/sewer, 4 w/hookups for water/electricity, plus 2 w/out hookups, tents okay, reservations - (206)374-5300, showers, laundry, groceries, gasoline, propane, restaurant, $$.
West of Forks. US 101 north to La Push Road, southwest 8.0 miles.

FORT SPOKANE (F-2)

FORT SPOKANE (Coulee Dam Recreation Area)
Campsites, trailers okay - no hookups, group campsites, picnic area, drinking water, handicap access, trailer waste disposal, boat ramp & dock, swimming/lifeguard, summer amphitheater programs, elev. 1247', $$-$$$.
North of Fort Spokane. Campground is located just north of historic Fort Spokane on State 25.

PORCUPINE BAY (Coulee Dam Recreation Area)
Campsites, trailers okay - no hookups, picnic area, drinking water, trailer waste disposal, boat dock & ramp, swimming/lifeguard, elev. 1238', $$.
Southeast of Fort Spokane. State 25 southeast 8.1 miles, Porcupine Bay Road north 4.3 miles.

GLACIER (C-1)

DOUGLAS FIR (Mt. Baker-Snoqualmie National Forest)
30 units, trailers to 32', picnic area, community kitchen, water, on Nooksack River, fishing, hiking, elev. 1000', $-$$.
Northeast of Glacier. State 542 northeast 2.0 miles. Campground is located 8 miles north of trailhead to Mt. Baker.

SILVER FIR (Mt. Baker-Snoqualmie National Forest)
21 units, trailers to 32', picnic area, community kitchen, water, along Nooksack River, wheelchair access, fishing, elev. 2000', $-$$.
East of Glacier. State 542 east 12.5 miles. Campground is located 8 miles north of Heather Meadows Recreation Area.

GOLDENDALE (D-5)

BROOKS MEMORIAL STATE PARK (Washington State Parks)
47 units, 23 w/hookups for water/electricity, group sites - reservations advised (509)773-4611, community kitchen, nearby groceries, trailer waste disposal, fishing, hiking trails, winter sports, $$-$$$.
North of Goldendale. State 97 north 15.0 miles.

CROW BUTTE STATE PARK (Washington State Parks)
52 sites, 50 w/hookups for water/electricity/sewer, group sites - reservations advised (509)875-2644, picnic shelter, wheelchair access, trailer waste disposal, boat launch, fishing, water skiing, $$-$$$.
East of Goldendale. US 97 south 10.0 miles, State 14 east 49.0 miles.

HORSETHIEF LAKE STATE PARK (Washington State Parks)
14 units, some trailers - no hookups, trailer waste disposal, 2 boat launches - Columbia River & Horsethief Lake, scuba diving area, fishing, $$.
West of Goldendale. US 97 south 10.0 miles, State 14 west 18.0 miles.

MARYHILL STATE PARK (Washington State Parks)
53 sites, 50 w/hookups for water/electricity/sewer, community kitchen, wheelchair access, trailer waste disposal, on Columbia River, boat launch, fishing, swimming, wind surfing, water skiing, $$.
Southeast of Goldendale. US 97 south 10.0 miles, State 14 east 2.0 miles.

PEACH BEACH (Private)
50 units, 15 w/hookups for water/electricity/sewer, 35 w/out hookups, reservations - (509)773-4698, showers, picnic area, trailer waste disposal, fishing, swimming, hiking, river front sites, $$-$$$.
North of Goldendale. US 97 north to Park exit. Follow double yellow lines 1.0 mile to Peach Beach.

PINE SPRINGS RESORT (Private)
25 campsites, 3 RV sites, 10 w/hookups for water/electricity, plus 12 tent sites, reservations - (509)773-4434, picnic area, play area, trailer waste disposal, fishing, hiking, restaurant, store, propane, $$-$$$.
North of Goldendale. US 97 north 12.0 miles.

GRAND COULEE (F-2)

COULEE PLAYLAND RESORT & RV PARK (Private)
77 campsites, 46 w/hookups for water/electricity/sewer, 31 tent sites, reservation information - (509)633-2671, showers, laundry, groceries, snack bar, arcade, on Banks Lake, playground, trailer waste disposal, swimming, fishing, boat launch, boat rental, $$-$$$.
North of Grand Coulee. State 155 west 1.0 mile.

CURLY'S CAMPGROUND (Private)
22 campsites, 16 w/hookups for water/electricity/sewer, plus 6 tent units, information - (509)633-0750, showers, $$.
Northwest of Grand Coulee. State 174 northwest 2.0 miles.

LAKEVIEW TERRACE RV PARK (Private)
15 trailer sites w/hookups for water/electricity/sewer, reservation information - (509)633-2169, showers, laundry, playfield, playground, $$.
Southeast of Grand Coulee. State 174 southeast 3.0 miles.

SPRING CANYON (Coulee Dam Recreation Area)
Campsites, trailers okay - no hookups, group campsites, drinking water, picnic area, handicap access, groceries, trailer & boat waste disposal, boat dock & ramp, swimming/lifeguard, summer amphitheater programs, elev. 1234', $$-$$$.
Southeast of Grand Coulee. State 174 southeast approximately 5.0 miles to campground road, follow this 1.1 miles north to campground.

STEAMBOAT ROCK STATE PARK (Washington State Parks)
100 trailer sites w/hookups for water/electricity/sewer, wheelchair access, on Banks Lake, snackbar, boat launch, fishing, water skiing, scuba diving area, nearby horse trails, winter sports, $$.
South of Grand Coulee. State 155 southwest 7.2 miles, campground road will take you northwest.

GRANGER (E-5)

GRANGER RV PARK (Private)
45 campsites w/hookups for water/electricity/sewer, reservation information - (509)854-1300, showers, satellite tv, laundry, propane, ice, trailer waste disposal, $$$.
In Granger. From I-82 take State 223 south .3 mile.

GRANITE FALLS (C-1)

BEAVER CREEK (Mt. Baker-Snoqualmie National Forest)
4 group camping units, reservations - (206)436-1155, fishing, elev. 1600', $$$.
East of Granite Falls. CR 7 east 24.4 miles.

COAL CREEK BAR (Mt. Baker-Snoqualmie National Forest)
5 group sites, reservations - (206)436-1155, trailers to 18', fishing, elev. 1600', $$$.
East of Granite Falls. CR 7 east 23.5 miles.

GOLD BASIN (Mt. Baker-Snoqualmie National Forest)
93 units, trailers to 32', group sites, water, river, wheelchair access, fishing, elev. 1100', $-$$.
East of Granite Falls. CR 7 east 13.4 miles.

MARTEN CREEK (Mt. Baker-Snoqualmie National Forest)
4 units, trailers to 18', group site - reservations required (206)436-1155, fishing, elev. 1400', $-$$$.
East of Granite Falls. CR 7 east 20.6 miles.

TULALIP MILLSITE (Mt. Baker-Snoqualmie National Forest)
12 units, trailers to 32', group sites - reservations required (206)436-1155, elev. 1400', $$$.
East of Granite Falls. CR 7 east 18.6 miles.

TURLO (Mt. Baker-Snoqualmie National Forest)
19 units, trailers to 32', piped water, river, swimming, fishing, elev. 900', $-$$.
East of Granite Falls. CR 7 east 10.8 miles.

VERLOT (Mt. Baker-Snoqualmie National Forest)
26 units, trailers to 32', piped water, river, flush toilets, swimming, fishing, elev. 900', $-$$.
East of Granite Falls. CR 7 east 11.0 miles.

WILEY CREEK (Mt. Baker-Snoqualmie National Forest)
3 group sites, reservations required - (206)436-1155, no trailers, shelters, fishing, elev. 1200', $$$.
East of Granite Falls. CR 7 east 15.0 miles.

GRAYLAND (A-4)

GRAYLAND BEACH STATE PARK (Washington State Parks)
62 units, 60 w/hookups for water/electricity/sewer, wheelchair access, fishing, self-guided trail, beachcombing, kite flying, $$.
In Grayland. Located in Grayland on State 105.

KENANNA RV PARK (Private)
90 campsites w/hookups for water/electricity/sewer, reservation information - (206)267-3515, showers, laundry, cable tv, groceries, ice, propane, rec room, playfield, playground, trailer waste disposal, ocean access, sandy beach, surf fishing, $$$.
South of Grayland. State 105 south of town 2.0 miles.

OCEAN GATE RESORT (Private)
48 campsites, 24 w/hookups for water/electricity/sewer/cable tv, plus 24 tent units, reservation information - (206)267-1956, showers, laundry, picnic shelter, playground, trailer waste disposal, ocean access, surf fishing, $$-$$$.
In Grayland. Located on State 105, in Grayland.

TWIN SPRUCE RV PARK (Private)
49 campsites, 41 w/hookups for water/electricity/sewer, plus 8 w/hookups for water/electricity, reservation information - (206)267-1275, showers, laundry, ice, rec room, near beach, $$-$$$.
In Grayland. From State 105 take Schmid Road east .1 mile to park.

WESTERN SHORES MOTEL & TRAILER PARK (Private)
21 campsites w/hookups for water/electricity/sewer, tents okay, reservation information - (206)267-6115, coin showers, playground, $$.
In Grayland. Located on State 105 in Grayland.

HOODSPORT (B-3)

BIG CREEK (Olympic National Forest)
23 units, trailers to 30', swimming, fishing, hiking trail, elev 700', $.
West of Hoodsport. CR 9420 west 8.0 miles, FSR 24 south .1 mile, located just north of Lake Cushman.

GLEN AYR RV PARK (Private)
54 trailer sites w/hookups for water/electricity/sewer, no tents, reservation information - (206)877-9522, showers, laundry, propane, picnic shelter, therapy pool, rec room, lounge, ocean access, swimming, fishing, hiking, on Hood Canal, $$$.
North of Hoodsport. US 101 north 1.0 mile.

LAKE CUSHMAN RESORT (Private)
50 campsites, 10 w/hookups for water/electricity, tents okay, reservation information - (206)877-9630, showers, groceries, snack bar, lake, swimming, fishing, boat launch, boat rental, hiking, $-$$.
Northwest of Hoodsport. US 101 north to Lake Cushman Road, west 5.0 miles.

LAKE CUSHMAN STATE PARK (Washington State Parks)
85 units, 30 w/hookups for water/electricity/sewer, group sites - reservations advised (206)877-5491, community kitchen, wheelchair access, trailer waste disposal, boat launch, on Lake Cushman, fishing, hiking trails, $$-$$$.
Northwest of Hoodsport. US 101 north to Lake Cushman Road, campground is 7.0 miles west.

MINERVA BEACH (Private)
62 campsites, 40 w/hookups for water/electricity/sewer, 10 pull-thrus w/out hookups, plus 12 tent sites, reservation information - (206)877-5145, showers, laundry, heated swimming pool, on Hood Canal, scuba diving, fishing, crabbing & clamming, $$-$$$.
South of Hoodsport. US 101 south 3.2 miles.

POTLATCH STATE PARK (Washington State Parks)
37 units, 18 w/hookups for water/electricity/sewer, picnic shelter, trailer waste disposal, on Hood Canal, scuba diving area, fishing, crabbing & clamming, $$.
South of Hoodsport. US 101 south, past Potlatch to Potlatch State Park and campsites.

REST A WHILE RV PARK (Private)
92 campsites w/hookups for water/electricity/sewer, reservations - (206)877-9474, showers, laundry, groceries, cable tv, gas, propane, tackle shop, ocean access, swimming, fishing, boat launch, boat rental, $$$.
North of Hoodsport. US 101 north 2.5 miles.

STAIRCASE CAMPGROUND (Olympic National Park)
59 campsites, trailers to 21', on Elk Creek, near Lake Cushman, water, handicap access, swimming, fishing, hiking, elev. 765', $$.
Northwest of Hoodsport. US 101 north to Lake Cushman Road, west 16.0 miles.

HUMPTULIPS (A-3)

RIVERVIEW RV PARK (Private)
20 campsites, 6 w/hookups for water/electricity/sewer, 6 w/hookups for water/electricity, plus 8 w/out hookups, reservation information - (206)987-2216, showers, on Humptulips River, swimming, fishing, $$.
At Humptulips. West of US 101 about .3 mile.

HUNTERS (F-1)

GIFFORD (Coulee Dam Recreation Area)
Campsites, trailers okay - no hookups, picnic facilities, drinking water, trailer waste disposal, boat ramp & dock, elev. 1249', $.
North of Hunters. State 25 north, located just south of Gifford.

HUNTERS (Coulee Dam Recreation Area)
Campsites, trailers okay - no hookups, picnic facilities, drinking water, trailer waste disposal, swimming beach, boat ramp & dock, elev. 1233', $.
West of Hunters. Leave State 25 at Hunters and head west to campground and water.

ILWACO (A-5)

CHINOOK COUNTY PARK (Pacific County)
100 campsites, reservation information - (206)777-8442, showers, playground, river, fishing, $$.
Southeast of Ilwaco. US 101 southeast 5.0 miles to Chinook, park is located at east end of town.

COVE RV PARK (Private)
40 units w/hookups for water/electricity/sewer/cable tv, pets welcome, reservation information - (206)642-3689, showers, laundry, trailer waste disposal, ocean access, on Columbia River, fishing, $$.
In Ilwaco. Located at west end of port area.

CHRIS'S RV PARK & CAMPGROUND (Private)
80 campsites, 64 w/hookups for water/electricity, plus 16 w/out hookups, reservation information - (206)777-8475, showers, laundry, groceries, trailer waste disposal, picnic facilities, tackle shop, river, fishing, $$.
East of Ilwaco. US 101 southeast 10.0 miles, State 401 north 3.0 miles.

FORT CANBY STATE PARK (Washington State Parks)

254 units, 60 w/hookups for water/electricity/sewer, wheelchair access, groceries, trailer waste disposal, boat launch, fishing, interpretive center, ocean access, trails, $$-$$$.
Southwest of Ilwaco. Campground is 2.5 miles southwest of Ilwaco.

ILWACO KOA (Private)

200 campsites, 36 w/hookups for water/electricity/sewer, 90 w/hookups for electricity only, plus 74 tent units, reservations - (206)642-3292, showers, laundry, groceries, propane, playground, trailer waste disposal, playground, rec room, creek, ocean access, near Columbia River, fishing, $$$.
East of Ilwaco. US 101 southeast, located between Ilwaco and Chinook.

MAUCH'S SUNDOWN RV PARK (Private)

50 campsites, 42 w/hookups for water/electricity/sewer, plus 8 w/hookups for water/electricity, reservation information - (206)777-8713, showers, laundry, ice, trailer waste disposal, river, fishing, $$.
Southeast of Ilwaco. US 101 southeast 8.5 miles, located just west of Astoria Bridge.

NASALLE TRAILER COURT (Private)

24 trailer sites w/hookups for water/electricity/sewer, no tents, reservation information - (206)484-3351, showers, laundry, $$.
Northeast of Ilwaco. US 101 southeast 10.0 miles, State 401 north 12.0 miles, State 4 southeast 1.5 miles.

RIVER'S END CAMPGROUND (Private)

100 campsites, 20 w/hookups for water/electricity/sewer, 40 w/hookups for water/electricity, plus 40 tent sites, reservation information - (206)777-8317, showers, laundry, ice, rec room, playground, trailer waste disposal, river, fishing, $$.
Southeast of Ilwaco. US 101 east 4.3 miles, located this side of Chinook.

SOU'WESTER LODGE & TRAILER PARK (Private)

60 campsites w/hookups for water/electricity/sewer/cable tv, reservation information - (206)642-2542, showers, laundry, ocean access, fishing, $$$.
North of Ilwaco. US 101 north, just before Seaview take Seaview Beach Road west 1 block to park.

THE BEACON RV PARK (Private)
60 campsites, 40 w/hookups for water/electricity/sewer, plus 20 w/hookups for electricity only, reservation information - (206)642-2138, no tents, showers, ice, cable tv, river, fishing - salmon charters, close to shops & park, $$-$$$.
In Ilwaco. Located at east end of docks.

INDEX (C-2)

WALLACE FALLS STATE PARK (Washington State Parks)
6 tent units, no trailers, picnic shelter, wheelchair access, along Wallace River, series of waterfalls, $$.
Northwest of Index. US 2 west 6.0 miles to Gold Bar, campground is 2.0 miles northeast of Gold Bar.

IONE (G-1)

IONE MOTEL & RV PARK (Private)
14 campsites w/hookups for water/electricity/sewer, tents okay, reservations - (509)442-3213, showers, laundry, on Pend Oreille River, swimming, fishing, boat launch, water skiing, $$-$$$.
In Ione. Located at south end of town.

NOISY CREEK (Colville National Forest)
19 units, trailers to 32', piped water, boat launch, boating, swimming, fishing, water skiing, hiking trails, elev. 2600', $$.
Northeast of Ione. State 31 south 1.0 miles, CR 9345 northeast 9.0 miles.

KALAMA (B-5)

CAMP KALAMA RV PARK (Private)
100 campsites, 50 w/hookups for water/electricity/sewer, 20 w/hookups for water/electricity, plus 30 w/out hookups, tents okay, reservation information - (206)673-2456, showers, laundry, groceries, tackle shop, game room, playfield, playground, trailer waste disposal, on Kalama River, swimming, fishing, boat launch, $$-$$$.
In Kalama. From I-5 take exit #32, then follow Kalama River Road east .1 mile, south to park.

PORT OF KALAMA RV PARK (Port of Kalama)
22 trailer sites w/hookups for water/electricity/sewer, reservation information - (206)673-2325, showers, playfield, playground, trailer waste disposal, river, fishing, boat launch, $$.
In Kalama. Park is located 1 block west of I-5 exit #32.

RAINBOW PARK CAMPGROUND (Private)
46 campsites, 10 w/hookups for water/electricity/sewer, 34 w/hookups for water/electricity/ plus 2 w/hookups for water, reservation information - (206)673-4574, showers, groceries, playground, trailer waste disposal, river, swimming, fishing, $$-$$$.
In Kalama. From I-5 take exit #32, then follow Kalama River Road east 1.0 mile, head south across bridge to Modrow Road, campground is .3 mile.

KELSO (B-5)

MARV'S RV PARK (Private)
20 trailer sites w/hookups for water/electricity/sewer, reservation information - (206)795-3453, cable tv, showers, rec room, trailer waste disposal, propane, gas, camping supplies, fishing, $$$.
4West of Kelso. State 4 west 23.5 miles, located just this side of Cathlamet.

THE CEDARS RV PARK (Private)
25 campsites, 23 w/hookups for water/electricity, plus 2 w/out hookups, reservations - (206)274-7019, 2 pull-thrus, showers, cable tv, laundry, trailer waste disposal, lots of shade trees, $$.
North of Kelso. I-5 north to exit #46, Access Road .3 mile north to park.

KETTLE FALLS (F-1)

EVANS (Coulee Dam Recreation Area)
Campsites, trailers okay - no hookups, picnic area, drinking water, trailer waste disposal, summer amphitheater programs, boat ramp & dock, swimming/lifeguard, elev. 1285', $$.
North of Kettle Falls. State 25 approximately 9.0 miles north to campground.

KETTLE FALLS (Coulee Dam Recreation Area)
Campsites, trailers okay - no hookups, group campsites, drinking water, picnic area, wheelchair access, boat dock & ramp, swimming/lifeguard, summer amphitheater programs, elev. 1237', $$-$$$.
West of Kettle Falls. Leave Kettle Falls heading due west toward water and campground.

MARCUS ISLAND (Coulee Dam Recreation Area)
24 campsites, trailers okay, water, picnic area, boat dock & ramp, elev. 1281', $.
North of Kettle Falls. State 25 north approximately 5.0 miles.

WHISPERING PINES RV PARK (Private)
44 campsites w/hookups for water/electricity/sewer, reservation information - (509)738-2593, showers, laundry, store, game room, ice, playground, walk to river, lake, fishing, $-$$.
Northwest of Kettle Falls. US 395 north 6.5 miles, watch for signs.

LEAVENWORTH (D-3)

BLACKPINE CREEK HORSECAMP (Wenatchee Nat. Forest)
9 units, trailers to 22', well, horse ramp, elev. 3000', $.
West of Leavenworth. US 2 southwest .5 mile, Icicle Road #7600 southwest 19.2 miles.

BLUE SHASTIN TRAILER & RV PARK (Private)
60 campsites w/hookups for water/electricity/sewer, reservation information - (509)548-4184, showers, laundry, lounge, swimming pool, trailer waste disposal, river, fishing, hiking, $$$.
Southeast of Leavenworth. US 2 southeast 4.0 miles. US 97 south 7.0 miles.

BONANZA (Wenatchee National Forest)
5 units, trailers to 18', well, stream, hiking, elev. 3000', $$.
South of Leavenworth. US 2 southeast 4.5 miles, US 97 south 20.0 miles. Located near Blewett-Swauk Pass.

BRIDGE CREEK (Wenatchee National Forest)
6 units, trailers to 18', well, fishing, hiking, elev. 1900', $$.
Southwest of Leavenworth. US 2 southwest .5 mile, Icicle Road #7600 southwest 9.4 miles.

CHALET RV PARK (Private)
39 campsites, 15 w/hookups for water/electricity/sewer/cable tv, 16 w/hookups for water/electricity, plus 8 w/out hookups, reservations - (509)548-4578, showers, laundry, spa, horseshoes, fishing, shade, walking distance to town, $$-$$$.
East of Leavenworth. US 2 east .5 mile.

CHATTER CREEK (Wenatchee National Forest)
13 units, trailers to 22', group area, picnic area, well, fishing, hiking, elev. 2800', $$-$$$.
West of Leavenworth. US 2 southwest .5 mile, Icicle Road #7600 southwest 16.1 miles.

EIGHTMILE (Wenatchee National Forest)

44 units, trailers to 20', group site - reservations required (800)283-CAMP, handicap access, well, stream, fishing, hiking, elev. 1800', $$-$$$.

Southwest of Leavenworth. US 2 southwest .5 mile, Icicle Road #7600 southwest 8.0 miles.

GLACIER VIEW (Wenatchee National Forest)

20 tent units, picnic area, walk-in sites on lake shore, piped water, lake, boating, swimming, fishing, water skiing, elev. 1900', $$.

Northwest of Leavenworth. US 2 northwest 15.9 miles, State 207 northeast 3.4 miles, CR 290 west 3.9 miles, FSR 290 west 1.5 miles.

GOOSE CREEK (Wenatchee National Forest)

5 units, some trailers, fishing, elev. 2200', $.

North of Leavenworth. US 2 east .3 mile, State 209 north 17.5 miles, FSR 6100 north 3.2 miles.

ICICLE RIVER RANCH (Private)

80 campsites, 36 w/hookups for water/electricity/sewer, 6 w/hookups for water/electricity, plus 38 tent sites, reservation information - (509)548-5420, showers, river, swimming, fishing, $$-$$$.

Southwest of Leavenworth. US 2 southwest .5 mile, Icicle Road #7600 southwest 3.0 miles.

IDA CREEK (Wenatchee National Forest)

10 campsites, trailers to 20', well, handicap access, fishing, hiking, $$.

Southwest of Leavenworth. US 2 southwest .5 mile, Icicle Road #7600 southwest 14.2 miles.

JOHNNY CREEK (Wenatchee National Forest)

71 units, trailers to 20', well, handicap access, fishing, hiking, elev. 2300', $$.

Southwest of Leavenworth. US 2 southwest .5 mile, Icicle Road #7600 southwest 12.4 miles.

LAKE WENATCHEE RANGER STATION (Wenatchee National Forest)

8 tent units, piped water, boating, swimming, fishing, water skiing, Dirty Face Lookout Trailhead, elev. 1900', $.

Northwest of Leavenworth. US 2 northwest 15.9 miles, State 207 north 7.3 miles.

LAKE WENATCHEE STATE PARK (Washington State Parks)

199 units, some trailers - no hookups, group sites - reservations advised (509)763-3101, picnic shelter, wheelchair access, groceries, trailer waste disposal, summer interpretive programs, boat launch, boating, fishing, swimming, horse trails, horse rental, winter sports, $$-$$$.

Northwest of Leavenworth. US 2 northwest 16.0 miles to junction with State 207, campground is approximately 6.0 miles north via State 207.

NASON CREEK (Wenatchee National Forest)

76 units, 1 group site, trailers to 32', picnic area, piped water, flush toilets, river, fishing, Nason Ridge Trailhead, elev. 1800', $$.

Northwest of Leavenworth. US 2 northwest 16.0 miles, State 207 northeast 3.4 miles, CR 290 west .1 mile.

PINE VILLAGE KOA (Private)

112 campsites, 40 w/hookups for water/electricity/sewer, 24 w/hookups for water/electricity, plus 48 tent sites, reservations - (509)548-7709, showers, laundry, groceries, picnic shelter, playground, trailer waste disposal, swimming pool, hot tub, river, swimming, fishing, hiking, $$$.

East of Leavenworth. US 2 east .3 mile, River Bend Drive north .5 mile.

ROCK ISLAND (Wenatchee National Forest)

20 units, trailers to 22', well, stream, fishing, hiking, elev. 2900', $.

Southwest of Leavenworth. US 2 southwest .5 mile, Icicle Road #7600 southwest 17.7 miles.

TRONSEN (Wenatchee National Forest)

20 units, trailers to 20', well, stream, hiking, elev. 3200', $$.
South of Leavenworth. US 2 southeast 4.5 miles, US 97 south 25.0 miles, located near Blewett-Swauk Pass.

TUMWATER (Wenatchee National Forest)

81 units, group sites, trailers to 20', picnic area, handicap access, piped water, stream, flush toilets, fishing, hiking, elev. 2000', $$-$$$.
Northwest of Leavenworth. US 2 northwest 9.9 miles.

LONG BEACH (A-5)

ANDERSEN'S TRAILER COURT (Private)
56 campsites w/hookups for water/electricity/sewer, reservations - (206)642-2231, showers, cable tv, laundry, ice, trailer waste disposal, ocean access, fishing, playground, $$.
North of Long Beach. State 103 north 3.5 miles.

ANTHONY'S HOME COURT (Private)
21 campsites w/hookups for water/electricity/sewer, reservation information - (206)642-2802, showers, laundry, ice & pop, fish cleaning area, fish smoker, $$.
In Long Beach. State 103 north .6 mile, located at 1310 Pacific Highway North.

CRANBERRY TRAILER PARK (Private)
24 trailer sites w/hookups for water/electricity/sewer, no tents, adults only, reservations - (206)642-2027, showers, cable tv, ice, $$.
North of Long Beach. State 103 north 3.0 miles, Cranberry Road east .3 mile.

DRIFTWOOD RV TRAV-L-PARK (Private)
50 campsites w/hookups for water/electricity/sewer, reservations - (206)642-2711, showers, ice, cable tv, laundry, ocean access, near Columbia River, fishing, $$$.
In Long Beach. State 103 north .8 mile.

EVERGREEN COURT (Private)
27 campsites, 20 w/hookups for water/electricity/sewer/cable tv, plus 7 tent units, reservation information - (206)665-5100, showers, playground, trailer waste disposal, $-$$.
North of Long Beach. State 103 north 7.9 miles.

FOUR PINES RV COURT (Private)
34 campsites w/hookups for water/electricity/sewer. reservations - (206)642-3990, showers, $$-$$$.
North of Long Beach. State 103 north 1.0 mile.

OCEAN AIRE TRAILER PARK (Private)
10 trailer sites w/hookups for water/electricity/sewer/cable tv, no tents, trailers to 35', reservation information - (206)665-4027, showers, laundry, ice, $$.
North of Long Beach. State 103 north 9.0 miles to Ocean Park, 260th Street east .1 mile.

OCEAN PARK RESORT (Private)

100 campsites, 94 w/hookups for water/electricity/sewer, plus 6 w/hookups for water/electricity, reservation information - (206)665-4585, showers, cable tv, laundry, ice, propane, heated swimming pool, spa, playground, $$.
North of Long Beach. State 103 north 9.0 miles to Ocean Park, 259th Street east .1 mile.

PACIFIC PARK TRAILER PARK (Private)

50 trailer sites, 44 w/hookups for water/electricity/sewer/cable tv, plus 6 w/hookups for water/electricity, reservation information - (206)642-3253, showers, laundry, ocean access, $$.
North of Long Beach. State 103 north 2.0 miles.

PEGG'S OCEANSIDE RV PARK (Private)

30 campsites w/hookups for water/electricity/sewer, reservation information - (206)642-2451, showers, ice, ocean access, swimming, fishing, $$.
North of Long Beach. State 103 north 4.5 miles.

SAND CASTLE RV PARK (Private)

39 campsites, 29 w/hookups for water/electricity/sewer, no tents, reservations - (206)642-2174, showers, laundry, ice, ocean access, $$.
In Long Beach. State 103 north .5 mile.

SAND-LO MOTEL & TRAILER PARK (Private)

14 campsites w/hookups for water/electricity/sewer, reservations - (206)642-2600, showers, laundry, restaurant, groceries, fish cleaning area, $$.
North of Long Beach. State 103 north 1.0 mile.

WESTGATE RV PARK & MOTEL (Private)

36 sites w/hookups for water/electricity/sewer, no tents, reservation information - (206)665-4211, showers, ice, rec room, ocean access, fishing, fish cleaning room, $$.
North of Long Beach. State 103 north 7.0 miles; at Klipsan Beach.

WILDWOOD SENIOR RV PARK (Private)

50 campsites, 30 w/hookups for water/electricity/sewer, plus 20 w/out hookups, seniors only - over 50, reservation information - (206)642-2131, showers, trailer waste disposal, lake, fishing, $$.
Southeast of Long Beach. State 103 south to junction with US 101, US 101 east .5 mile, Sandridge Road north .8 mile.

LOOMIS (D-1)

IRON GATE (Okanogan National Forest)
1 tent unit, horse trails, corral, hitch rail & truck dock, trailhead to Pasayten Wilderness, elev. 6200', $.
West of Loomis. CR 9425 north 2.1 miles, CR 4066 north 1.0 mile, FSR 39 west 15.3 miles, FSR 39-500 (Daisy Creek Road) northwest 5.0 miles to trailhead camp.

THE STAGE STOP AT SULLY'S (Private)
18 campsites, w/hookups for water/electricity/sewer, reservations - (509)223-3275, groceries, ice, restaurant/tavern, $$.
In Loomis. Located at city center on Main Street.

LYNDEN (B-1)

HIDDEN VILLAGE RV PARK (Private)
63 campsites, 25 w/hookups for water/electricity/sewer, plus 38 w/hookups for water/electricity, tenting area, reservation information - (206)398-1041, showers, laundry, rec room, trailer waste disposal, pond, fishing, $$$.
Southwest of Lynden. State 539 south 3.0 miles.

LYNDEN KOA (Private)
100 campsites, 45 w/hookups for water/electricity/sewer, 25 w/hookups for water/electricity, plus 30 tent sites, reservations - (206)354-4772, showers, laundry, groceries, restaurant, propane, playfield, playground, swimming pool, trailer waste disposal, pond fishing, boat rental, miniature golf, $$$.
In Lynden. State 546 east 3.0 miles, Line Road south 1.5 miles to 8717 Line Road.

SUMAS RV PARK (Private)
39 campsites, 19 w/hookups for water/electricity/sewer/cable tv, 10 w/hookups for water/electricity, plus 10 w/out hookups, tenting area, reservation information - (206)988-8875, wheelchair access, showers, laundry, ice, rec room, trailer waste disposal, stream, fishing, $$-$$$.
Northeast of Lynden. State 546 east 5.0 miles, State 9 north to Sumas, Cherry Street .01 mile to campground.

WINDMILL INN & TRAILER COURT (Private)
6 trailer sites w/hookups for water/electricity/sewer, no tents, reservation information - (206)354-3424, showers, $$.
In Lynden. Located in Lynden on Front Street.

MARBLEMOUNT (C-1)

ALPINE PARK (Private)
48 campsites, 33 w/hookups for water/electricity/sewer, 15 tent units, reservation information - (206)873-4142, showers, laundry, river, fishing, $$.
East of Marblemount. State 20 east 1.8 miles.

COLONIAL CREEK (North Cascades National Park)
163 campsites, trailers to 22', information - (206)856-5700, wheelchair access, drinking water, flush toilets, picnic area, summer interpretive program, trailer waste disposal, at Diablo Lake, fishing, boat launch, hiking, $$.
East of Marblemount. State 20 east 24.0 miles.

GOODELL CREEK (North Cascades National Park)
22 campsites, trailers to 22', drinking water, on Skagit River, fishing, hiking, $-$$.
East of Marblemount. State 20 east 13.0 miles.

NEWHALEM CREEK (North Cascades National Park)
128 campsites, trailers to 22', drinking water, flush toilets, wheelchair access, trailer waste disposal, on Skagit River at Newhalem Creek, fishing, hiking, $$.
East of Marblemount. State 20 east 14.0 miles.

MARYS CORNER (B-4)

BARRIER DAM CAMPGROUND (Private)
40 campsites, 26 w/hookups for water/electricity, plus 14 tent units, reservation information - (206)985-2495, showers, groceries, rec room, trailer waste disposal, river, fishing, tackle store, fish guide service, $$.
East of Marys Corner. US 12 east 12.0 miles, Fuller Road south 1.0 mile.

HARMONY LAKESIDE RV PARK (Private)
65 campsites, 39 w/hookups for water/electricity/sewer, 21 w/hookups for water/electricity, plus 5 w/out hookups, no tents, reservation information - (206)983-3804, wheelchair access, showers, ice, playfield, trailer waste disposal, lake, fishing, boat launch, $$.
Northeast of Marys Corner. US 12 east 18.0 miles, Harmony Road north 2.5 miles.

IKE KINSWA STATE PARK (Washington State Parks)

103 units, 41 w/hookups for water/electricity/sewer, wheelchair access, snack bar, groceries, trailer waste disposal, boat launch, year-round fishing, swimming, horse trails, nearby fish hatcheries, $$.

East of Marys Corner. US 12 east 8.5 miles, follow signs leading north to park.

LAKE MAYFIELD RESORT/RV PARK & MARINA (Private)

90 campsites, 8 w/hookups for water/electricity/sewer, 42 w/hookups for waste/electricity, plus 40 tent units, reservation information - (206)985-2357, showers, satellite tv, groceries, restaurant, playfield, on Lake Mayfield, swimming, fishing, boat launch, boat rental, hiking, $$-$$$.

Southeast of Marys Corner. US 12 east 13.0 miles, Lake Bridge .3 mile, Winston Creek Road south 1.0 mile, Hadaller Road west .5 mile.

LEWIS & CLARK STATE PARK (Washington State Parks)

25 tent units, group sites - reservations advised (206)864-2643, community kitchen/shelter, interpretive center about Mt. St. Helens, nature trail, $$-$$$.

South of Marys Corner. From US 12, head south at Marys Corner to campground.

MAYFIELD LAKE COUNTY PARK (Lewis County)

54 campsites, group camp area, reservation information - (206)985-2364, wheelchair access, showers, picnic shelter, playground, trailer waste disposal, lake, swimming, fishing, boat launch, hiking, $$$.

East of Marys Corner. US 12 east 15.0 miles, west at Dam .3 mile to park.

MEDICAL LAKE (F-2)

CONNIES COVE (Private)

16 units, 2 w/hookups for water/electricity/sewer, 10 w/hookups for water/electricity, plus 4 w/hookups for electricity only, reservations - (509)299-3717, showers, picnic area, cafe, tackle shop, boat rental, boat launch & dock, fishing, lake swimming, $$.

South of Medical Lake. Take Clear Lake Road 3.0 miles to resort.

METALINE FALLS (G-1)

CRAWFORD STATE PARK (Washington State Parks)
10 primitive tent sites, wheelchair access, large limestone cave - guided tours during summer only, $.
Northwest of Metaline Falls. Take State 31 north approximately 9.0 miles and follow signs to Gardner Cave and Crawford State Park.

MILLPOND (Colville National Forest)
10 units, trailers to 22', well, stream, fishing, elev. 2400', $$.
East of Metaline Falls. State 31 east 1.5 miles, CR 9345 east 3.5 miles.

MT. LINTON RV PARK (Private)
26 campsites w/hookups for water/electricity/sewer, reservation information - (509)446-4553, showers, cable tv, laundry, playfield, river, fishing, $$-$$$.
South of Metaline Falls. State 31 south to Metaline; located at city center.

SULLIVAN LAKE (Colville National Forest)
35 units, trailers to 32', 1 group site - reservation required (509)446-2681, piped water, boating, fishing, water skiing, elev. 2600', $$-$$$.
East of Metaline Falls. State 31 east 1.5 miles, CR 9345 east 5.0 miles.

MONROE (C-2)

THUNDERBIRD PARK (Private)
120 campsites, 40 w/hookups for water/electricity/sewer, 30 w/hookups for water/electricity, plus 50 tent sites, reservation information - (206)794-8987, showers, laundry, trailer waste disposal, groceries, pavilion, rec room, swimming pool, river, playground, arcade, boat ramp, fishing, hiking, $$-$$$.
Southeast of Monroe. State 203 south 1.0 mile, Ben Howard Road east 5.0 miles to park.

MONTESANO (A-4)

COHO (Olympic National Forest)
46 units, trailers to 34', piped water, flush toilets, wheelchair access, paved nature trail, elev. 900', $$.
North of Montesano. CR 58 north 12.0 miles, FSR 22 north 20.0 miles, FSR 23 north 1.5 miles.

LAKE SYLVIA STATE PARK (Washington State Parks)

37 units, group sites - reservations advised (206)249-3621, community kitchen/shelter, wheelchair access, boat rental, snack bar, groceries, trailer waste disposal, boat launch, fishing, swimming, $$-$$$.
North of Montesano. Campground is just off State 12, north of Montesano.

SCHAFER STATE PARK (Washington State Parks)

55 units, 6 w/hookups for water/electricity, community kitchen/shelter, trailer waste disposal, beach access, fishing, on East Fork of Satsop River, $$.
Northeast of Montesano. State 12 east of Montesano just past Brady to Satsop River Road, follow this approximately 5.0 miles to campground.

MOSES LAKE (E-4)

BEST WESTERN HERITAGE INN & RV PARK (Private)

30 campsites w/hookups for water/electricity/sewer, reservation information - (509)659-1007, wheelchair access, showers, laundry, groceries, swimming pool, therapy pool, nearby golf, $$$.
East of Moses Lake. I-90 east to exit #221; located along frontage road.

BIG SUN RESORT & RV PARK (Private)

50 campsites w/hookups for water/electricity/sewer, reservation information - (509)765-8294, wheelchair access, showers, laundry, ice, playground, on Moses Lake, fishing, boat launch, boat rental, $$.
In Moses Lake. Leave I-90 at exit #176 and take Broadway north .5 mile, campground is west at 2300 W. Marina Drive.

COTTAGE RV PARK & MOTEL (Private)

19 campsites w/hookups for water/electricity/sewer, reservation information - (509)659-0721, showers, trailer waste disposal, $$.
East of Moses Lake. I-90 east to exit #220, located in Ritzville at city center.

MAR DON RESORT (Private)

350 campsites, 160 w/hookups for water/electricity/sewer, 55 w/hookups for water/electricity, 135 w/out hookups, plus beach tent area, information - (509)765-5061, flush toilets, showers, cafe/lounge, playground, large fish supply & grocery store, on

Potholes Reservoir, 800' marina, boat moorage, fishing dock, propane, gas, 2 boat launches, boat rental (no motors for rent), swimming beach, hiking, 60 lakes in area, $$-$$$.
Southwest of Moses Lake. State 17 southeast 10.0 miles, Potholes Reservoir Road west 8.0 miles.

OASIS PARK (Private)
69 campsites, 31 w/hookups for water/electricity/sewer, plus 38 w/hookups for electricity, reservation information - (509)754-5102, wheelchair access, showers, laundry, groceries, covered picnic area, chapel, swimming pool, mini golf, golf course, playfield, trailer waste disposal, pond, swimming, fishing, hiking, $$-$$$.
Northwest of Moses Lake. State 17 northwest 17.0 miles, State 282 northwest 5.0 miles, State 28 southwest 1.0 miles; in Ephrata.

ODESSA GOLF & RV PARK (Private)
12 campsites w/hookups for water/electricity, reservations - (509)982-0093, on Odessa Golf Course, golfers stay for free, $$.
Northeast of Moses Lake. I-90 east 27.0 miles, State 21 north 19.0 miles, State 28 to west end of Odessa and campground.

POTHOLES STATE PARK (Washington State Parks)
128 units, 60 w/hookups for water/electricity/sewer, trailer waste disposal, on Potholes Reservoir, boat launch, fishing, water skiing, $$.
Southwest of Moses Lake. State 17 southeast 10.0 miles, Potholes Reservoir Road west 13.0 miles.

SOAP LAKES SMOKIAM CAMPGROUND (City of Soap Lakes)
52 campsites w/hookups for water/electricity/sewer, information - (509)246-1211, showers, groceries, laundry, trailer waste disposal, playground, lake, swimming, fishing, Soap Lake mud baths, $$.
Northwest of Moses Lake. State 17 northwest 26.0 miles.

WILLOWS TRAILER VILLAGE (Private)
76 campsites, 35 w/hookups for water/electricity/sewer, 30 w/hookups for water/electricity, plus 11 tent units, reservation information - (509)765-7531, showers, laundry, groceries, fishing supplies, playfield, trailer waste disposal, $$-$$$.
South of Moses Lake. Leave I-90 at exit #179, State 17 south 2.0 miles, CR M southeast .3 mile.

NACHES (D-4)

BUMPING DAM (Wenatchee National Forest)
23 units, trailers to 22', well, nearby marina, fishing, elev. 3400', $$.
Northwest of Naches. US 12 west 4.3 miles, State 410 northwest 27.8 miles, FSR 1800 southwest to dam and campground.

BUMPING LAKE (Wenatchee National Forest)
45 units, trailers to 30', well, boat launch, boating, swimming, fishing, water skiing, elev. 3400', $$.
Northwest of Naches. US 12 west 4.3 miles, State 410 northwest 27.8 miles, FSR 1800 southwest 11.4 miles.

CEDAR SPRINGS (Wenatchee National Forest)
15 units, trailers to 22', well, fishing, on Bumping River, elev. 2800', $$.
Northwest of Naches. US 12 west 4.3 miles, State 410 northwest 27.8 miles, FSR 1800 southwest .5 miles.

CLEAR LAKE SOUTH (Wenatchee National Forest)
10 units, trailers to 22', well, boat launch, lake - speed limits, boating, fishing, elev. 3000', $.
Southwest of Naches. US 12 west 35.6 miles, State 43 south .9 mile, FSR 1312 south .5 mile.

COTTON WOOD (Wenatchee National Forest)
16 units, trailers to 22', well, on Naches River, fishing, elev. 2300', $.
Northwest of Naches. US 12 west 4.3 miles, State 410 northwest 17.7 miles.

COUGAR FLAT (Wenatchee National Forest)
12 units, trailers to 20', well, on Bumping River, fishing, elev. 3100', $.
Northwest of Naches. US 12 west 4.3 miles, State 410 northwest 27.8 miles, FSR 1800 southwest 6.0 miles.

HAUSE CREEK (Wenatchee National Forest)
42 units, trailers to 30', piped water, on Tieton River, flush toilets, wheelchair access, fishing, elev. 2500', $$.
Southwest of Naches. US 12 west 21.9 miles.

HELLS CROSSING (Wenatchee National Forest)
18 units, trailers to 20', picnic area, well, on American River, fishing, elev. 3200', $.
Northwest of Naches. US 12 west 4.3 miles, State 410 northwest 33.7 miles.

INDIAN CREEK (Wenatchee National Forest)

39 units, trailers to 30', piped water, near Rimrock & Clear Lakes, elev. 3000', $$.
Southwest of Naches. US 12 west 31.8 miles.

INDIAN FLAT (Wenatchee National Forest)

11 units, trailers to 20', well, on Bumping River, fishing, elev. 2600', $.
Northwest of Naches. US 12 west 4.3 miles, State 410 northwest 26.6 miles.

KANER FLAT (Wenatchee National Forest)

41 units, trailers to 30', picnic area, well, near Little Naches River, fishing, historic wagon train campsites along Old Naches Trail, elev. 2700', $.
Northwest of Naches. US 12 west 4.3 miles, State 410 northwest 24.9 miles, FSR 1900 northwest 2.5 miles.

LITTLE NACHES (Wenatchee National Forest)

21 units, trailers to 20', 3 group sites, well, on Little Naches River, fishing, elev. 2600', $$.
Northwest of Naches. US 12 west 4.3 miles, State 410 northwest 24.9 miles, FSR 1900 northwest .1 mile.

LODGEPOLE (Wenatchee National Forest)

34 units, trailers to 20', picnic area, well, river, fishing, elev. 3500', $$.
Northwest of Naches. US 12 west 4.3 miles, State 410 northwest 40.6 miles. Campground is located 8.3 miles from Chinook Pass & Mt. Rainier National Park.

RIVER BEND (Wenatchee National Forest)

6 units, trailers to 20', piped water, on Tieton River, fishing, elev. 2500', $.
Southwest of Naches. US 12 west 21.8 miles.

SAWMILL FLAT (Wenatchee National Forest)

26 units, trailers to 24', picnic area, well, on Naches River, wheelchair access, fishing, elev. 2500', $$.
Northwest of Naches. US 12 west 4.3 miles, State 410 northwest 23.7 miles.

SODA SPRINGS (Wenatchee National Forest)

26 units, trailers to 30', well, on Bumping River, fishing, natural mineral springs, elev. 3100', $.
Northwest of Naches. US 12 west 4.3 miles, State 410 northwest 27.8 miles, FSR 1800 southwest 4.8 miles.

SQUAW ROCK RESORT (Private)
64 campsites, 28 w/hookups for water/electricity/sewer, plus 36 w/hookups for water/electricity, reservations - (509)658-2926, showers, laundry, groceries, swimming pool, hot tub, restaurant, game room, playground, trailer waste disposal, on Naches River, fishing, hiking, $$$.
Northwest of Naches. US 12 west 4.3 miles, State 410 northwest 15.0 miles.

WILLOWS (Wenatchee National Forest)
16 units, trailers to 20', well, on Tieton River, fishing, elev. 2400', $.
West of Naches. US 12 west 20.0 miles.

WINDY POINT (Wenatchee National Forest)
15 units, trailers to 22', well, on Tieton River, fishing, elev. 2000', $.
West of Naches. US 12 west 12.7 miles.

NEAH BAY (A-1)

BAYVIEW RV PARK (Private)
39 trailer sites w/hookups for water/electricity/sewer, reservation information - (206)963-2542, showers, laundry, ocean access, fishing, $$$.
Southeast of Neah Bay. State 112 southeast 13.0 miles to Sekiu, Airport Road north .01 mile.

COHO RESORT (Private)
150 campsites, 44 w/hookups for water/electricity/sewer/cable tv, 50 w/hookups for water/electricity, plus 56 tent units, information - (206)963-2333, showers, laundry, ice, trailer waste disposal, boat gas, tackle shop, ocean access, fishing, boat launch, boat rental, $$.
Southeast of Neah Bay. State 112 southeast 13.0 miles to Sekiu, located at east end of town.

CURLEY'S RESORT (Private)
12 trailer sites w/hookups for water/electricity/sewer, trailers to 22', no tents, reservation information - (206)963-2281, showers, laundry, cable tv, boat moorage, ocean access, fishing, $$.
Southeast of Neah Bay. State 112 southeast 13.0 miles to Sekiu and resort.

NEAH BAY RESORT (Private)
50 campsites w/hookups for water/electricity/sewer, reservation information - (206)645-2288, showers, groceries, ocean access, fishing, boat launch, boat rental, $$$.
Southeast of Neah Bay. State 112 east 3.0 miles.

OLSON'S RESORT (Private)
250 campsites, 30 w/hookups for water/electricity/sewer, plus 220 w/out hookups, tents okay, reservation information - (206)963-2311, showers, groceries, ocean frontage, ocean access, fishing, boat launch, boat rental, fish charter boats, $$-$$$.
Southeast of Neah Bay. State 112 southeast 13.0 miles to Sekiu and resort.

PILLAR POINT (Clallam County)
36 primitive sites, pit toilets, boat launch, dock, fishing, $$.
East of Neah Bay. State 112 east 6.0 miles.

SAM'S TRAILER & RV PARK (Private)
26 campsites, 20 w/hookups for water/electricity/sewer, plus 6 w/out hookups, reservation information - (206)963-2402, showers, laundry, boat launch & moorage, ocean access, fishing, $$.
Southeast of Neah Bay. State 112 east 17.0 miles to Clallam Bay, located on east end of Clallam Bay.

SILVER SALMON RESORT (Private)
24 units w/hookups for water/electricity/sewer, tents okay, reservation information - (206)645-2388, showers, propane, boat launch, ocean fishing, close to shopping & food, $$-$$$.
In Neah Bay. On State 112 in city center.

THUNDERBIRD RESORT (Private)
40 campsite w/hookups for water/electricity/sewer, reservation information - (206)645-2450, showers, laundry, ice, trailer waste disposal, ocean access, fishing, boat launch, $$$.
In Neah Bay. Located in Neah Bay.

TRETTEVIKS TRAILER PARK (Private)
22 campsites, 10 w/hookups for water/electricity/sewer, plus 12 w/hookups for water/electricity, reservation information - (206)963-2688, laundry, ocean access, sandy beach, swimming, fishing, $$.
East of Neah Bay. State 112 east 6.0 miles.

TYEE MOTEL & RV PARK (Private)
20 trailer sites w/hookups for water/electricity/sewer, reservation information - (206)645-2223, showers, laundry, trailer waste disposal, ocean access, ocean fishing, $$$.
In Neah Bay. Located in Neah Bay.

VAN RIPER'S RESORT & RV PARK (Private)
42 trailer sites w/hookups for water/electricity, information - (206)963-2334, showers, ice, snacks, trailer waste disposal, ocean access, fishing, boat launch, boat rental, salmon charters, $$.
Southeast of Neah Bay. State 112 southeast to 13.0 miles to Sekiu and park.

WESTWIND RESORT (Private)
26 units w/hookups for water/electricity/sewer, reservation information - (206)645-2751, showers laundry, ice, ocean access, fishing, $$.
In Neah Bay. Located in Neah Bay.

NEWHALEM (D-1)

DEVIL'S PARK (Okanogan National Forest)
Tenting areas in Pasayten Wilderness, hike-in only, horse trails, meager grazing, scarce water in late summer, creek, $.
East of Newhalem. State 20 approximately 15.0 miles east to Devil's Park Trailhead #738 located on north side of highway, take trail 3.5 miles to campground.

DIABLO LAKE RESORT CAMPGROUND (Private)
15 campsites w/hookups for water, restrooms, groceries, fishing supplies, restaurant/lounge, game room, on Diablo Lake, marina, boat rentals, swimming, fishing, $$-$$$.
East of Newhalem. State 20 east 9.0 miles.

McMILLAN PARK (Okanogan National Forest)
Tenting areas in Pasayten Wilderness, hike-in only, horse trails, meager grazing, scarce water in late summer, creek, $.
East of Newhalem. State 20 approximately 15.0 miles east to Devil's Park Trailhead #738 located on north side of highway, take trail 2.0 miles to campground.

NEWPORT (G-1)

JERRY'S LANDING RV PARK (Private)
25 trailer sites, 16 w/hookups for water/electricity/sewer plus 9 w/hookups for water/electricity, trailers to 35', reservation information - (509)292-2337, showers, groceries, trailer waste disposal, lake, swimming, fishing, boat launch, boat rental, $$.
Southwest of Newport. US 2 southwest approximately 19.0 miles, Oregon Road west 1.0 mile to Eloika Lake.

PEND OREILLE PARK (Pend Oreille County)
40 campsites, reservations - (509)447-4821, drinking water, flush toilets, showers, old growth timber, hiker/horse trails, $$.
Southwest of Newport. US 2 southwest 16.0 miles.

PIONEER PARK (Colville National Forest)
13 units, 1 group site, trailers to 22', piped water, on Box Canyon Reservoir, wheelchair access, boat launch, boating, fishing, water skiing, elev. 2100', $$.
North of Newport. US 2 northeast .5 mile, CR Ch007 north 2.0 miles.

WATERS EDGE CAMPGROUND (Private)
40 campsites, 19 w/hookups for water/electricity/sewer/cable tv, 4 w/hookups for water/electricity, plus 17 tent units, reservation information - (509)292-2111, showers, laundry, ice, trailer waste disposal, tackle shop, swimming pool, lake, fishing, boat launch, boat rental, $$-$$$.
Southwest of Newport. US 2 southwest approximately 22.0 miles, Bridges Road west .5 mile.

NORTH BEND (C-3)

DENNY CREEK (Mt. Baker-Snoqualmie National Forest)
39 units, 3 group sites, trailers to 22', well, fishing, elev. 2200', $-$$.
Southeast of North Bend. Take I-90 southeast 17.0 miles, FSR 58 northeast 2.2 miles.

TINKHAM (Mt. Baker-Snoqualmie National Forest)
40 units, 7 group sites, trailers to 22', wheelchair access, well, river, waterfall, nature trail, fishing, elev. 1520', $-$$.
Southeast of North Bend. Take I-90 southeast 10.0 miles, FSR 55 southeast 1.5 miles.

OKANOGAN (E-1)

AMERICAN LEGION PARK (City of Okanogan)
49 campsites, information - (509)422-3600, drinking water, flush toilets, showers, picnic shelter, on Okanogan River, fishing, $.
In Okanogan. Located on State 215 at north edge of town.

CONCONULLY STATE PARK (Washington State Parks)
81 units, 10 w/hookups for water, community kitchen, trailer waste disposal, boat launch, fishing, swimming, nature trail, $$.
Northwest of Okanogan. US 97 north 2.4 miles, Conconully Road northwest 18.0 miles to campground.

COUNTY FAIRGROUNDS (Okanogan County)
88 campsites, 52 w/hookups for water/electricity/sewer, plus 36 w/hookups for water/electricity, tents okay, reservations - (509)422-1621, showers, on Okanogan River, fishing, $$.
North of Okanogan. Located on east side of Okanogan River; 1.0 mile north of town.

EAST SIDE PARK CAMPGROUND (City of Okanogan)
76 campsites, 36 w/hookups for water/electricity/sewer, plus 40 tent units, information - (509)826-1170, showers, wheelchair access, tennis, swimming pool, playfield, trail waste disposal, river, boat launch, $$.
Northeast of Okanogan. State 20 north 5.0 miles to Omak; located near Stampede Fairgrounds area.

OLYMPIA (B-3)

AMERICAN HERITAGE (Private)
105 campsites, 24 w/hookups for water/electricity/sewer, 52 w/hookups for water/electricity, plus 29 tent units, reservations - (206)943-8778, showers, laundry, groceries, propane, swimming pool, playfield, playground, trailer waste disposal, $$$.
South of Olympia. Take exit #99 off I-5 and go east .3 mile, turn south to 9610 Kimmie Street SW.

BLACK LAKE RV PARK (Private)
65 campsites, 32 w/hookups for water/electricity/sewer, 18 w/hookups for water/electricity, plus 15 w/out hookups, reservations - (206)357-6775, tents okay, showers, groceries, propane, trailer waste disposal, on Black Lake, swimming, fishing, boat launch, boat rental, $$.
Southwest of Olympia. I-5 to exit #104, US 101 west 2.0 miles, Black Lake Blvd. south 2.0 miles.

COACH POST MOTOR HOME & RV PARK (Private)
20 units w/hookups for water/electricity/sewer, no tents, reservation information - (206)754-7580, cable tv, showers, laundry, playfield, $$.
Southwest of Olympia. I-5 to exit #104, US 101 west 3.0 miles to Kaiser Road and campground.

COLUMBUS PARK (Private)
79 campsites, 48 w/hookups for water/electricity/sewer, plus 31 w/hookups for water/electricity, trailers to 35', reservations - (206)786-9460, wheelchair access, showers, laundry, picnic shelter, playground, playfield, trailer waste disposal, on Black Lake, stream, swimming, fishing, boat launch, paddle boat rental, $$.

Southwest of Olympia. I-5 to exit #104, US 101 west 2.0 miles to Black Lake Blvd., south 3.5 miles to campground.

DEEP LAKE RESORT (Private)
48 campsites, 13 w/hookups for water/electricity/sewer, 30 w/hookups for water/electricity, plus 5 tent units, trailers to 35', reservations - (206)352-7388, showers, laundry, groceries, mini golf, shuffleboard, playfield, playground, trailer waste disposal, lake, swimming, fishing, boat launch & rental, $$-$$$.
South of Olympia. I-5 to exit #95, Maytown Road east 2.5 miles, Tilley Road north .5 mile.

MARTIN WAY RV PARK (Private)
14 trailer sites, 10 w/hookups for water/electricity/sewer, plus 4 w/hookups for water/electricity, no tents, reservation information - (206)491-6840, showers, laundry, playfield, horseshoe pits, $$.
Northeast of Olympia. I-5 to exit #111, State 510 east .8 mile, Martin Way south .1 mile to park.

MILLERSYLVANIA STATE PARK (Washington State Parks)
191 units, 52 w/hookups for water/electricity, group sites - reservations advised (206)753-1519, community kitchen, wheelchair access, trailer waste disposal, boat launch, fishing, swimming, fitness trail, old-growth trees, $$-$$$.
South of Olympia. Take I-5 south of Olympia about 10.0 miles.

NISQUALLY PLAZA RV PARK (Private)
55 trailer sites, 27 w/hookups for water/electricity/sewer/cable tv, 21 w/hookups for water/electricity, plus 7 w/out hookups, no tents, reservation information - (206)491-3831, showers, laundry, groceries, swimming pool, playfield, playground, trailer waste disposal, gas, propane, river, fishing, boat launch, $$-$$$.
North of Olympia. I-5 north 7.0 miles to exit #114 and campground.

OLYMPIA CAMPGROUND (Private)
105 campsites, 28 w/hookups for water/electricity/sewer, 45 w/hookups for water/electricity/ plus 32 tent units, reservations - (206)352-2551, showers, tv hookup, laundry, groceries, propane, gas, picnic shelter, swimming pool, playground, trailer waste disposal, $$$.
South of Olympia. I-5 to exit #99, east .3 mile to Kimmie Road, north 1.0 mile to 83rd Avenue, proceed .3 mile to 1441 83rd Avenue SW.

PLEASANT ACRES RESORT (Private)

44 campsites, 25 w/hookups for water/electricity/sewer, plus 19 w/hookups for water/electricity only, tents okay, reservations - (206)491-3660, showers, laundry, groceries, tackle shop, picnic area, boat launch & dock, boat rental, $$-$$$.
North of Olympia. I-5 north 6.0 miles, located at 7225 14th Avenue SE.

SALMON SHORE RESORT (Private)

55 campsites, 30 w/hookups for water/electricity/sewer, 15 w/hookups for water/electricity, plus 10 w/hookups for electricity only, trailers to 40', reservation information - (206)357-8618, showers, laundry, groceries, picnic shelter, trailer waste disposal, lake, swimming, fishing, boat launch, boat rental, playfield, playground, $$.
Southwest of Olympia. I-5 to exit #104, US 101 west 2.0 miles to Black Lake Blvd., south 3.3 miles to resort.

PACIFIC BEACH (A-3)

BLUE PACIFIC MOTEL & TRAILER PARK (Private)

19 trailer sites, 13 w/hookups for water/electricity/sewer, plus 6 w/hookups for water/electricity, trailers to 30', no tents, reservation information - (206)289-2262, showers, ocean front sites, volleyball court, horseshoe pits, playfield, playground, $$$.
South of Pacific Beach. State 109 south 10.0 miles.

DRIFTWOOD ACRES OCEAN CAMPGROUND (Private)

50 campsites, 25 w/hookups for water/electricity/sewer, plus 25 w/hookups for water/electricity, tents okay, reservation information - (206)289-3484, showers, trailer waste disposal, ocean access, river, swimming, fishing, $$$.
South of Pacific Beach. State 109 south 7.0 miles, campground is located just north of Copalis Beach bridge.

LOOKOUT TRAILER COURT (Private)

20 trailer sites w/hookups for water/electricity/sewer, reservation information - (206)289-2220, showers, cable tv, $$$.
South of Pacific Beach. State 109 south 10.5 miles to Ocean City and court.

OCEAN CITY STATE PARK (Washington State Parks)

181 units, 29 w/hookups for water/electricity/sewer, group sites - reservations advised (206)289-3553, community kitchen, wheelchair access, trailer waste disposal, fishing, beach access, $$-$$$.
South of Pacific Beach. State 109 south 13.0 miles; located 2.0 miles north of Ocean Shores.

OCEAN SHORES RV & CHARTER & MARINA (Private)
99 campsites w/hookups for water/electricity/sewer, tenting
area, reservation information - (206)289-3393, showers, groceries, restaurant, boat ramp & dock, ocean fishing, kite flying,
$$-$$$.
South of Pacific Beach. State 109 south 15.0 miles to Ocean
Shores, Point Brown Avenue south 5.0 miles to park.

PACIFIC BEACH STATE PARK (Washington State Parks)
138 units, 20 w/hookups for water/electricity, trailer waste dis-
posal, fishing, beachcombing, clamming, $$.
At Pacific Beach. Campground is located off State 109 in Pacific
Beach.

RIVERSIDE TRAILER COURT (Private)
68 trailer sites, 53 w/hookups for water/electricity/sewer, plus
15 w/hookups for water/electricity, reservation information -
(206)289-2111, showers, rec room, trailer waste disposal, river,
fishing, beachcombing, $$$.
South of Pacific Beach. State 109 south 7.0 miles, campground
is located just north of Copalis Beach bridge.

ROD'S BEACH RESORT & RV PARK (Private)
80 trailer sites w/hookups for water/electricity/sewer, no tents,
reservation information - (206)289-2222, showers, cable tv, groceries, trailer waste disposal, heated swimming pool, ocean
access, fishing, rec room, playground, $$$.
South of Pacific Beach. State 109 south 7.5 miles, park is located
just south of Copalis Beach.

SHADES BY THE SEA (Private)
40 campsites, 2 w/hookups for water/electricity/sewer/cable tv,
33 w/hookups for water/electricity/cable tv, plus 6 w/out
hookups, reservation information - (206)289-2182, showers,
trailer waste disposal, $$$.
South of Pacific Beach. State 109 south 7.0 miles, campground
is located just north of Copalis Beach bridge.

STURGEON TRAILER HARBOR (Private)
70 trailer sites, 54 w/hookups for water/electricity/sewer, plus
16 w/hookups for water/electricity, no tents, reservation information - (206)289-2101, showers, rec room, space for horses,
$$$.
South of Pacific Beach. State 109 south 10.5 miles to Ocean City
and park.

SURF AND SAND RV PARK (Private)

44 campsites, 20 w/hookups for water/electricity/sewer/cable tv, 19 w/hookups for water/electricity/sewer, plus 5 w/hookups for water/electricity, reservation information - (206)289-2707, showers, restaurant, trailer waste disposal, ocean access, fishing, $$-$$$.
South of Pacific Beach. State 109 south 7.2 miles, park is located in Copalis Beach on beach access road.

TIDELANDS ON THE BEACH RV PARK (Private)

55 campsites, 16 w/hookups for water/electricity/sewer, plus 39 w/hookups for water/electricity, reservation information - (206)289-8963, showers, rec room, playfield & playground, trailer waste disposal, ocean access, swimming, fishing, $$-$$$.
South of Pacific Beach. State 109 south 8.1 mile.

PACKWOOD (C-4)

HATCHERY LOOP (Gifford Pinchot National Forest)

20 units, trailers to 22', piped water, wheelchair access, river, fishing, elev. 1400', $$.
Northeast of Packwood. US 12 northeast 7.1 miles, FSR 01272 west .8 mile to campground. Located 4 miles south of Mt. Rainier National Park.

LA WIS WIS (Gifford Pinchot National Forest)

100 units, trailers to 18', piped water, flush toilets, river, fishing, hiking, elev. 1400', $$.
Northeast of Packwood. US 12 northeast 2.1 miles, FSR 1272 west .6 mile. Located 4 miles south of Mt. Rainier National Park.

OHANAPECOSH (Mt. Rainier National Park)

232 campsites, trailers to 30', trailer waste disposal, on Ohanapecosh River, fishing, hiking, elev. 2000', $$.
Northeast of Packwood. US 12 northeast 8.0 miles, State 123 north; campground is located 1.5 miles south of Mt. Rainier National Park's Stevens Canyon Entrance.

PACKWOOD RV PARK (Private)

66 campsites w/hookups for water/electricity/sewer/cable tv, reservation information - (206)494-5145, showers, playfield, trailer waste disposal, $$-$$$.
In Packwood. Located at city center.

WALUPT LAKE (Gifford Pinchot National Forest)
44 units, trailers to 22', water, wheelchair access, lake - speed limits, boating, fishing, horse facilities, trail to Goat Rocks Wilderness, elev. 3900', $$.
Southeast of Packwood. US 12 southwest 2.7 miles, FSR 2100 southeast 16.4 miles, FSR 2160 east 4.5 miles.

POINT ROBERTS (B-1)

SUNNY POINT RESORT (Private)
60 campsites, 24 w/hookups for water/electricity/sewer, 4 w/hookups for water/electricity, plus 32 tent units, reservation information - (206)945-1986, showers, ice, $$$.
In Point Roberts. Resort is located at 1408 Gulf Road in Point Roberts.

WHALEN'S RV PARK (Private)
85 trailer sites w/hookups for water/electricity, reservation information - (206)945-2874, wheelchair access, showers, playfield, trailer waste disposal, ocean access, fishing, $$$.
In Point Roberts. Take Roosevelt Road east 1.0 mile.

POMEROY (F-4)

CENTRAL FERRY STATE PARK (Washington State Parks)
62 sites, 60 w/hookups for water/electricity/sewer, picnic shelter, wheelchair access, trailer waste disposal, on Snake River, boat launch, boating, fishing, water skiing, $$.
Northwest of Pomeroy. US 12 northwest 13.0 miles, State 127 north 9.0 miles.

CHIEF TIMOTHY STATE PARK (Washington State Parks)
68 units, 33 w/hookups for water/electricity/sewer, picnic shelter, wheelchair access, trailer waste disposal, boat launch, docks for boat campers, fishing, water sports, interpretive center on Lewis & Clark Expedition, groceries, $$.
East of Pomeroy. US 12 east 22.0 miles.

LYON'S FERRY MARINA & RV PARK (Private)
58 units, 38 w/hookups for water/electricity/sewer, 10 w/hookups for water/electricity, plus 10 w/hookups for electricity only, reservation information - (509)399-2387, showers, laundry, restaurant, store, ice, propane, river, swimming , fishing, boat dock & ramp, on Snake River, $$-$$$.
Northwest of Pomeroy. US 12 northwest 13.0 miles, State 261 northwest about 18.0 miles.

LYON'S FERRY STATE PARK (Washington State Parks)
52 units, some trailers - no hookups, picnic shelter, wheelchair access, trailer waste disposal, at confluence of Snake & Palouse Rivers, boat launch, fishing, swimming, $$.
Northwest of Pomeroy. US 12 northwest 13.0 miles, State 261 northwest about 18.0 miles.

PALOUSE FALLS STATE PARK (Washington State Parks)
10 primitive campsites, picnic shelter, 190' waterfall, $.
Northwest of Pomeroy. US 12 northwest 13.0 miles, State 261 northwest 21.0 miles, park entry road west 2.6 miles.

PORT ANGELES (A-1)

AL'S TRAVEL TRAILER PARK (Private)
33 trailer sites w/hookups for water/electricity/sewer, no tents, adults only, reservation - (206)457-6563, showers, laundry, salmon charter boats, $$.
East of Port Angeles. US 101 east 1.5 miles, Lee's Creek Road north .3 mile.

CAROL'S CRESCENT BEACH (Private)
60 trailer sites w/hookups for water/electricity/sewer, reservation information - (206)928-3344, showers, laundry, playfield, ocean access, swimming, fishing, $$$.
West of Port Angeles. US 101 west 5.0 miles, State 112 west 6.5 miles to Joyce, Crescent Beach Road north 3.0 miles.

CONESTOGA QUARTERS RV PARK (Private)
38 campsites, 34 w/hookups for water/electricity/sewer, plus 4 w/out hookups, reservation information - (206)452-4637, wheelchair access, showers, playground, trailer waste disposal, hiking, fishing charter boats, $$$.
East of Port Angeles. US 101 east 7.0 miles, Seibertt Creek Road 1.0 mile.

DUNGENESS RECREATION AREA (Clallam County)
65 campsites, information - (206)683-5847, wheelchair access, showers, trailer waste disposal, playground, ocean access, pond, swimming, fishing boat launch hiking, $$.
East of Port Angeles. US 101 east 10.0 miles, Kitchen Road north 4.0 miles.

ELMER'S TRAILER PARK (Private)
12 trailer sites w/hookups for water/electricity/sewer, reservations - (206)457-4392, showers, $$$.
East of Port Angeles. US 101 east 1.5 miles.

FAIRHOLM CAMPROUND (Olympic National Park)
87 campsites, trailers to 21', water, handicap access, groceries, trailer waste disposal, on Crescent Lake, swimming, fishing, boat launch, boat rental, hiking, elev. 580', $$.
West of Port Angeles. US 101 west/southwest 26.0 miles.

HEART O' THE HILLS (Olympic National Park)
105 campsites, trailers to 21', wheelchair access, water, hiking, elev. 1807', $$.
South of Port Angeles. US 101 to Race Street, south 6.0 miles to campground.

KLAHOWYA (Olympic National Forest)
54 units, trailers to 32', reservations - (800)283-CAMP, electrical sites, flush toilets, piped water, picnic area, wheelchair access, river, boat launch, interpretive service, boating, good fishing, hiking trails, elev. 800', $$.
West of Port Angeles. US 101 west 40.0 miles to milepost #212 and campground.

LINCOLN PARK (Port Angeles Parks)
35 primitive campsites, flush toilets, showers, picnic area, firepits, $.
West of Port Angeles. US 101 west 5.0 miles, State 112 just west of town.

LOG CABIN RESORT (Private)
40 campsites w/hookups for water/electricity/sewer, reservations - (206)928-3325, wheelchair access, showers, laundry, groceries, restaurant/lounge, trailer waste disposal, on Crescent Lake, swimming, fishing, boat launch, boat rental, hiking, $$$.
West of Port Angeles. US 101 west/southwest 16.0 miles to milepost #232, East Beach Road north 3.0 miles.

LYRE RIVER PARK (Private)
75 campsites, 55 w/hookups for water/electricity/sewer, plus 20 w/hookups for water/electricity, reservations - (206)928-3436, wheelchair access, showers, laundry, groceries, rec room, trailer waste disposal, ocean access, on Lyre River, swimming, fishing, small boat launch, hiking, $$$.
West of Port Angeles. US 101 west 5.0 miles, State 112 west 15.0 miles, West Lyre River Road north .5 mile.

PEABODY CREEK RV PARK (Private)
36 trailer sites w/hookups for water/electricity/sewer, trailers to 35', reservation information - (206)457-7092, showers, laundry, propane, creek, $$.
In Port Angeles. Located at 127 South Lincoln.

PORT ANGELES KOA (Private)
88 campsites, 18 w/hookups for water/electricity/sewer, plus 55 w/hookups for water/electricity, plus 15 tent units, reservations - (206)457-5916, showers, laundry, groceries, propane, swimming pool, playground, trailer waste disposal, $$$.
East of Port Angeles. US 101 east 5.0 miles.

SALT CREEK RECREATION AREA (Clallam County)
80 campsites, drinking water, flush toilets, showers, playground, trailer waste disposal, ocean access, stream, boat ramp, swimming, fishing, hiking, on old military base, $-$$.
Northwest of Port Angeles. US 101 west 5.0 miles, State 112 west 9.0 miles, Camp Hayden Road north 3.5 miles.

SHADY TREE RV PARK (Private)
33 campsites w/hookups for water/electricity/sewer, tents okay, reservation information - (206)452-7054, showers, pets okay, store, $$-$$$.
West of Port Angeles. US 101 west 5.0 mile, State 112 west .5 mile to park.

SILVER KING RESORT (Private)
175 campsites, 140 w/hookups for water/electricity, plus 35 w/out hookups, reservation information - (206)963-2800, showers, laundry, ice, groceries, propane, gas, tackle shop, trailer waste disposal, ocean access, fishing, boat launch, boat moorage, $$-$$$.
Northwest of Port Angeles. US 101 west 5.0 miles, State 112 west 30.0 miles to Jim Creek Recreation Area.

SOLEDUCK (Olympic National Park)
80 campsites, trailers to 21', water, handicap access, groceries, trailer waste disposal, on Soleduck River, swimming, fishing, hiking, elev. 1680', $$.
West of Port Angeles. US 101 west/southwest 28.0 miles, Soleduck River Road southeast 12.0 miles.

WELCOME INN TRAILER & RV PARK (Private)
75 trailer sites w/hookups for water/electricity/sewer, reservation information - (206)457-1553, showers, cable tv, laundry, trailer waste disposal, playfield, nearby restaurant & store, charter fishing, $$-$$$.
In Port Angeles. US 101 west 2.0 miles.

PORT TOWNSEND (B-2)

FORT FLAGLER STATE PARK (Washington State Parks)
118 units, group sites - reservations advised (206)385-1259, picnic shelter, wheelchair access, groceries, trailer waste disposal, boat launch, fishing, scuba diving area, clamming, crabbing, 1898 historical fort, Youth Hostel, $$-$$$.
Southeast of Port Townsend. Leave Port Townsend on State 20, after about 5.0 miles take the road marked Hadlock and Fort Flagler State Park.

FORT WORDEN STATE PARK (Washington State Parks)
53 units, 50 w/hookups for water/electricity/sewer, trailers okay, community kitchen, wheelchair access, snack bar, groceries, trailers waste disposal, boat launch, scuba diving area, fishing, full conference facilities & housing in historic building, Youth Hostel, $$.
In Port Townsend. Located at north end of town.

OLD FORT TOWNSEND STATE PARK (Washington State Parks)
43 units, some trailers, community kitchen, beach access, playfield, fishing, clamming beach, historic 1859 fort w/group facilities - reservations required (206)385-4730, $$-$$$.
South of Port Townsend. Campground is 3.0 miles east of town, east of State 20.

POINT HUDSON RV PARK (Private)
18 trailer sites w/hookups for water/electricity/sewer, no tents, information - (206)385-2828, showers, laundry, groceries, ocean access, fishing, boat launch, $$$.
In Port Townsend. Located at the docks; follow Water Street to end.

SMITTY'S ISLAND RETREAT (Private)
40 campsites w/hookups for water/electricity/sewer, reservation information - (206)385-2165, ocean access, fishing, $$.
Southeast of Port Townsend. Leave Port Townsend on State 20, after about 5.0 miles take the road marked Hadlock/Fort Flagler State Park; located 1.0 mile south of park.

PUYALLUP (B-3)

CAMP BENBOWS LAKE TANWAX RETREAT (Private)
150 campsites, 50 w/hookups for water/electricity/sewer, plus 100 w/hookups for water/electricity, reservations - (206)879-5426, showers, laundry, groceries, propane, fishing, picnic area, playfield, hiking, $$$.

South of Puyallup. State 161 south 20.0 miles, thru town of Graham, watch for signs about 4.5 miles south of Graham.

HENLEY'S SILVER LAKE RESORT (Private)
45 campsites, 12 w/hookups for water/electricity/sewer, 17 w/hookups for water/electricity, plus 16 tent units, reservation information - (206)832-3580, snacks, trailer waste disposal, lake, fishing, boat launch, boat rental, hiking, $$.
South of Puyallup. State 161 south 26.0 miles, State 7 northwest 4.0 miles.

MAJESTIC MOBILE MANOR & RV PARK (Private)
123 trailer sites w/hookups for water/electricity/sewer, reservation information - (206)845-3144, cable tv, showers, laundry, swimming pool, groceries, rec room, trailer waste disposal, stream, fishing, $$-$$$.
West of Puyallup. State 167 (River Road) west 3.0 miles.

NORTHWEST TREK WILDLIFE PARK (Private)
45 campsites, 30 RV sites - no hookups, plus 15 tent sites, trailers to 35', reservation information - (206)832-6116, wildlife park, wheelchair access, restrooms, restaurant, lounge, $$.
South of Puyallup. State 161 south 16.0 miles.

RAINBOW RESORT (Private)
52 trailer sites w/hookups for water/electricity/sewer, reservation information - (206)879-5115, showers, laundry, groceries, snacks, propane, tackle shop, rec room, playground, trailer waste disposal, lake, swimming, fishing, boat rental, $$-$$$.
South of Puyallup. State 161 south 15.0 miles, Tanwax Drive east .5 mile.

TANWAX RESORT (Private)
25 campsites, 16 w/hookups for water/electricity/sewer, plus 9 tent units, trailers to 32', reservation information - (206)879-5533, showers, trailer waste disposal, lake, fishing, boat rental, $$.
South of Puyallup. State 161 south 15.0 miles, Tanwax Drive east .5 mile.

T-J'S RV PARK (Private)
20 trailer sites w/hookups for water/electricity/sewer, adults only, no tents, reservation information - (206)847-7153, $$.
South of Puyallup. State 161 south 3.0 miles.

QUEETS (A-2)

KALALOCH (Olympic National Park)
177 campsites, trailers to 21', water, handicap access, trailer waste disposal, groceries, ocean access, swimming, fishing, hiking, elev. 50', $$.
North of Queets. US 101 north 6.0 miles.

QUILCENE (B-2)

FALLS VIEW CAMPGROUND (Olympic National Forest)
30 units, trailers to 32', picnic area, piped water, flush toilets, hiking trails, elev. 500', $$.
Southwest of Quilcene. US 101 southwest 3.5 miles. Campground is located 5.0 miles from Quilcene Bay.

RAINBOW (Olympic National Forest)
9 tent units, piped water, trail to Big Quilcene River, elev. 800', $.
Southwest of Quilcene. US 101 southwest 4.5 miles.

QUINAULT (A-3)

CAMPBELL TREE GROVE (Olympic National Forest)
11 units, trailers to 16', well, pit toilets, shelter, fishing, hiking trails, located in old-growth forest, on west fork of Humptulips River, $$.
Southeast of Quinault. US 101 south about 10.0 miles, FSR 2302 northeast an additional 15.0 miles to campground.

FALLS CREEK (Olympic National Forest)
21 units, trailers to 16', 10 tent sites, picnic area, piped water, flush toilets, community kitchen, wheelchair access, stream, hiking trails, on Lake Quinault, boat launch, boating, swimming, fishing, elev. 200', $$.
Northeast of Quinault. CR 5 northeast .2 mile.

GATTON CREEK (Olympic National Forest)
5 tent units, picnic area, pit toilets, stream, boating, swimming, fishing, on Lake Quinault, elev. 200', $$.
Northeast of Quinault. CR 5 northeast .5 mile.

RAIN FOREST RESORT VILLAGE & RV PARK (Private)
31 campsites, some w/hookups for water/electricity/sewer, information - (206)288-2535, showers, laundry, groceries, on Lake Quinault, swimming, fishing, canoe rental, restaurant, $$$.

East of Quinault. Leave US 101 on South Shore Road, resort is 3.5 miles east.

WILLABY (Olympic National Forest)
21 units, trailers to 16', picnic area, piped water, flush toilets, on Lake Quinault, stream, located near Quinault Rain Forest Nature Trail, boat launch, boating, swimming, fishing, hiking trails, elev. 200', $$
Northeast of Quinault. CR 5 northeast .5 mile.

RANDLE (C-4)

ADAMS FORK (Gifford Pinchot National Forest)
24 units, trailers to 22', well, swimming, fishing, on Cispus River, elev. 2600', $.
Southeast of Randle. County Road south 3.1 miles, FSR 23 southeast 15.7 miles, FSR 21 southeast 4.7 miles, FSR 56 east .2 mile to campground.

BLUE LAKE CREEK (Gifford Pinchot National Forest)
11 units, trailers to 32', well, fishing, hiking, on Cispus River, elev. 1900', $.
Southeast of Randle. County Road south 3.1 miles, FRS 23 southeast 13.2 miles.

IRON CREEK (Gifford Pinchot National Forest)
98 units, trailers to 32', piped water, fishing, hiking, on Lower Cispus River, old-growth forest, elev. 1200', $$.
Southeast of Randle. County Road south 3.1 miles, FSR 23 southeast 8.7 miles, FSR 1134 for 1.0 miles, FSR 25 west 6.0 miles.

MAPLE GROVE RESORT (Private)
70 campsites, 35 w/hookups for water/electricity, 28 w/hookups for water only, plus 7 w/out hookups, reservation information - (206)497-2741, wheelchair access, showers, laundry, groceries, snack bar, picnic shelter, playfield, playground, trailer waste disposal, river, fishing, hiking, nearby golf, $$-$$$.
In Randle. Leave US 12 on Cispus Road, resort is .3 mile south.

NORTH FORK (Gifford Pinchot National Forest)
33 units, trailers to 32', piped water, fishing, hiking, on North Fork Cispus River, bicycling, elev. 1500', $$.
Southeast of Randle. County Road south 3.1 miles, FSR 23 southeast 8.7 miles.

NORTH FORK GROUP (Gifford Pinchot National Forest)
3 group sites, reservations required - (206)497-7565, piped water, river, fishing, hiking, bicycling, elev. 1500', $$.
Southeast of Randle. County Road south 3.1 miles, FSR 23 southeast 8.7 miles.

TAKHLAKH (Gifford-Pinchot National Forest)
54 units, trailers to 22', piped water, lake - speed limits, fishing, boating, swimming, hiking trails, lava flow 1 mile east, view of Mt. Adams, elev. 4500', $$.
Southeast of Randle. County Road south 3.1 miles, FSR 23 southeast 28.9 miles, FSR 2329 north 1.6 miles.

TOWER ROCK (Gifford Pinchot National Forest)
22 units, trailers to 22', piped water, on Cispus River, fishing, elev. 1100', $$.
Southeast of Randle. County Road south 3.1 miles, FSR 23 southeast 6.8 miles, FSR 2306 west 1.8 miles.

RAYMOND (A-4)

BAYSHORE RV PARK (Private)
50 campsites, 44 w/hookups for water/electricity/sewer/cable tv, plus 6 w/hookups for water/electricity, reservation information - (206)267-2625, showers, laundry, rec room, trailer waste disposal, gas, ocean access, swimming, fishing, $$.
Northwest of Raymond. State 105 west 19.0 miles, park is located in Tokeland at 2941 Kindred.

BRUCEPORT PARK (City)
45 campsites, 9 w/hookups for water/electricity/sewer, 6 w/hookups for water/electricity, plus 30 tent sites, reservation information - (206)875-6025, showers, laundry, picnic shelter, groceries, playground, beach access, $.
Southwest of Raymond. US 101 south 11.0 miles.

GYPSY TRAIL RV & MOTOR HOME PARK (Private)
18 trailer sites w/hookups for water/electricity/sewer, no tents, reservation information - (206)875-5165, showers, laundry, trailer waste disposal, $$.
Southwest of Raymond. US 101 south 5.0 miles to South Bend; park is located on Central, about .1 mile off US 101.

HAPPY TRAILS KOA (Private)
43 campsites, 6 w/hookups for water/electricity/sewer, 26 w/hookups for water/electricity, plus 11 w/hookups for water only, reservations - (206)875-6344, showers, laundry, groceries, rec room, playground, sandy beach, trailer waste disposal, $$$.

Southwest of Raymond. US 101 southwest 15.5 miles, Bay Center Road west 3.0 miles.

TIMBERLAND RV PARK (Private)
24 campsites w/hookups for water/electricity/sewer, reservation information - (206)942-3325, showers, nearby fishing & golf, $$.
North of Raymond. US 101 north to junction with State 105, west .2 mile to Crescent Street; park is 2 blocks south.

REPUBLIC (E-1)

BLACK BEACH RESORT (Private)
60 sites w/hookups for water/electricity/sewer, reservations - (509)775-3989, laundry, groceries, playground, trailer waste disposal, Lake Curlew, swimming, fishing, boat launch, $$-$$$.
North of Republic. West Curlew Lake Road north 8.0 miles, Black Beach Road east 1.0 mile.

CURLEW LAKE STATE PARK (Washington State Parks)
87 units, 18 w/hookups for waste/electricity/sewer, wheelchair access, trailer waste disposal, boat launch, fishing, trails, gold mining district, winter sports, $$.
Northeast of Republic. State 21 northeast 10.0 miles.

FERRY LAKE (Colville National Forest)
9 units, trailers to 22', well, boat launch, boating, fishing, elev. 3300', $$.
Southwest of Republic. State 21 south 7.0 miles, FSR 53 southwest 6.0 miles, FSR 5330 north 1.0 mile, FSR 100 north .5 mile.

LONG LAKE (Colville National Forest)
12 units, trailers to 22', well, lake - no motors, boating, fly fishing, elev. 3200', $$.
Southwest of Republic. State 21 south 7.0 miles, FSR 53 southwest 8.0 miles, FSR 400 south 1.5 miles.

PINE POINT RESORT (Private)
32 campsites w/hookups for water/electricity/sewer, reservations - (509)775-3643, showers, laundry, groceries, trailer waste disposal, on Curlew Lake, swimming, fishing, boat launch, boat rental, playground, $$.
North of Republic. State 21 north 10.0 miles.

SWAN LAKE (Colville National Forest)
29 units, trailers to 32', community kitchen, well, boat launch, boating, swimming, fishing, hiking trails, elev. 3600', $$.
Southwest of Republic. State 21 south 7.0 miles, FSR 5300 southwest 8.0 miles.

TEN MILE (Colville National Forest)
9 units, trailers to 18', picnic area, piped water, stream, fishing, elev. 2200', $$.
South of Republic. State 21 south 10.0 miles.

TIFFANYS RESORT (Private)
22 campsites, 14 w/hookups for water/electricity/sewer, 2 w/hookups for water/electricity, plus 6 w/out hookups, tents okay, reservations - (509)775-3152, showers, laundry, groceries, playground, on Curlew Lake, swimming, fishing, boat launch, boat rental, $$$.
North of Republic. West Curlew Lake Road north 10.0 miles.

RICHLAND (E-5)

BEACH RV PARK (Private)
36 trailer sites w/hookups for water/electricity/sewer, reservation information - (509)588-5959, showers, laundry, ice, river, fishing, $$-$$$.
Northwest of Richland. I-82 west 11.0 miles to Benton City exit, located in Benton City on Abby Avenue.

CHARBONNEAU PARK (Corps)
55 campsites, 15 w/hookups for water/electricity/sewer, 24 w/hookups for electricity, 16 tent units, reservation information - (509)547-7781, showers, wheelchair access, rec room, playground, trailer waste disposal, lake, swimming, fishing, boat launch, $$.
Northeast of Richland. I-82 east 5.0 miles, State 14 northeast 4.0 miles to Pasco, US 12 south 3.0 miles, State 124 east 8.0 miles, Sun Harbor Drive north 2.0 miles.

COLUMBIA MOBILE VILLAGE (Private)
22 trailer sites w/hookups for water/electricity/sewer, reservation information - (509)783-3314, playfield, playground, $$.
Southeast of Richland. US 12 south 5.0 miles to Kennewick, State 14 to Clearwater Avenue, campground is 1.3 miles west.

COLUMBIA PARK (Benton County)
100 campsites, 18 w/hookups for water/electricity, plus 82 w/out hookups, reservations - (509)783-3711, showers, trailer waste disposal, nearby boat launch on Columbia River, bike/hike trails, $$.
Southeast of Richland. US 12 southeast to Columbia Center exit and follow signs.

DESERT GOLD TRAILER PARK & MOTEL (Private)
69 trailer sites w/hookups for water/electricity/sewer, plus 10 tent sites, reservations - (509)627-1000, showers, laundry, groceries, swimming pool, therapy pool, $$$.
Southeast of Richland. US 12 southeast to Columbia Drive SE and look for signs.

FISHHOOK PARK (Corps)
41 campsites, reservation information - (509)547-7781, wheelchair access, showers, playground, trailer waste disposal, lake, swimming, fishing, boat launch, elev. 4500', $$.
Northeast of Richland. I-82 east 5.0 miles, State 14 northeast 4.0 miles to Pasco, US 12 south 3.0 miles, State 124 east 15.0 miles, Page Road north 4.0 miles.

GREEN TREE RV PARK (Private)
70 trailer sites w/hookups for water/electricity/sewer, reservation information - (509)547-6220, showers, laundry, ice, $$$.
Northeast of Richland. I-82 east to exit #13, park is just north on 4th Avenue.

HOOD PARK (Corps)
69 trailer sites w/hookups for electricity, reservation information - (509)547-7781, wheelchair access, showers, playground, trailer waste disposal, lake, swimming, fishing, boat launch, elev. 3500', $$.
Northeast of Richland. I-82 east 5.0 miles, State 14 northeast 4.0 miles to Pasco, US 12 south 3.0 miles, located at junction with State 124.

PLYMOUTH PARK (Corps)
32 campsites, 17 w/hookups for water/electricity/sewer, plus 15 tent units, reservation information - (509)525-5632, wheelchair access, showers, trailer waste disposal, lake, river, swimming, fishing, boat launch, $$.
Southwest of Richland. I-82 south 29.0 miles to Plymouth, park is located 1.0 mile west of Umatilla Bridge.

SAN JUAN ISLANDS (B-1)

LOPEZ ISLAND/ODLIN COUNTY PARK (County)
30 campsites, no hookups, pit toilets, water, boat launch, low bank beach, $$-$$$.
On Lopez Island. This island is accessible via the Anacortes ferry, park is located 1.3 miles south of ferry landing.

LOPEZ ISLAND/SPENCER SPIT STATE PARK (Washington State Parks)

28 units, some trailers - no hookups, group sites - reservations advised (206)468-2251, picnic shelter, trailer waste disposal, fishing, beachcombing, clamming, $$-$$$.
On Lopez Island. This island is accessible via the Anacortes ferry, park is located on the northeast side of the island.

ORCAS ISLAND/CAPTAIN COOK RESORT (Private)

31 campsites, 18 RV sites w/hookups for water/electricity/sewer, reservations - (206)376-2242, showers, groceries, swimming pool, laundry, marina, restaurant & lounge, boat launch, fishing, crabbing & clamming, $$-$$$.
On Orcas Island. This island is accessible via the Anacortes ferry, resort is located 1.5 miles north of Eastsound.

ORCAS ISLAND/DOE BAY VILLAGE RESORT (Private)

8 RV sites w/hookups for water/electricity/sewer, tents okay, reservations - (206)376-2291, showers, hot tub, mineral baths, sauna, cafe, store, ocean & fresh water fishing, $$-$$$.
On Orcas Island. This is island is accessible via the Anacortes ferry, follow main road thru Eastsound to Moran State Park, this resort is an additional 12.0 miles.

ORCAS ISLAND/MORAN STATE PARK (Washington State Parks)

148 units, some trailers - no hookups, picnic shelter, wheelchair access, trailer waste disposal, boat rental, boat launch, fishing, located on top of Mt. Constitution, $$.
On Orcas Island. This island is accessible via the Anacortes ferry, campground is located on northeast side of island, past Eastsound.

ORCAS ISLAND/TOWN & COUNTRY (Private)

25 trailer sites w/hookups for water/electricity/sewer, reservation information - (206)378-4717, showers, laundry, playground, ocean access, lake, fishing, $$-$$$.
On Orcas Island. This island is accessible via the Anacortes ferry, campground is located northeast of harbor.

ORCAS ISLAND/WEST BEACH RESORT (Private)

62 campgrounds, 22 w/hookups for water/electricity/sewer, 15 w/hookups for water/electricity, plus 36 tent units, reservation information - (206)376-2240, showers, laundry, groceries, marina, gas, propane, scuba air, ocean access, swimming fishing, boat launch, boat rental, $$$.
On Orcas Island. This island is accessible via the Anacortes ferry, campground is located 3.5 miles west of Eastsound.

SAN JUAN ISLAND/LAKEDALE CAMPGROUND (Private)
110 campsites, 16 w/hookups for water/electricity, reservation information - (206)378-2350, showers, mini store, snacks, swimming in lake, fresh water & ocean fishing, small boat rental, tackle shop, $$$.
On San Juan Island. This island is accessible via the Anacortes ferry, take Roche Harbor Road 4.0 miles north of Friday Harbor.

SAN JUAN ISLAND/SAN JUAN MARINA RESORT (Private)
19 campsites, some w/hookups for waste/electricity, some beach front sites, reservations - (206)378-2992, water, flush toilets, boat ramp, $$-$$$.
On San Juan Island. This island is accessible via the Anacortes ferry, take Westside Road north 6.0 miles.

SAN JUAN ISLAND/SNUG HARBOR MARINA RESORT (Private)
16 units, 4 bay front sites w/hookups for water/electricity, plus 12 forested sites w/out hookups, reservations - (206)378-4762, showers, flush toilets, picnic area, groceries, gas & diesel, bait & tackle shop, propane, boat launch, boat rentals, fishing, moorage for boats, $$$.
On San Juan Island. This island is accessible via the Anacortes ferry, take Beaverton Valley Road 8.0 miles west of Friday Harbor.

SHAW ISLAND/SOUTH BEACH COUNTY PARK (County)
12 campsites, overflow area for tents, pit toilets, drinking, water, beach, small boat launch, nearby groceries & gas, $-$$.
On Shaw Island. This island is accessible via the Anacortes ferry, take main road to first left, turn onto paved road, park is .5 mile.

STUART ISLAND STATE PARK (Washington State Parks)
19 primitive sites, boat-in only, buoys & floats, nearby fishing, $.
On Stuart Island. Stuart Island is located northwest of San Juan Island.

SUCIA ISLAND STATE PARK (Washington State Parks)
51 primitive sites, boat-in only, buoys & floats, picnic shelter scuba diving area, crabbing, clamming, geological formations, $.
On Sucia Island. Sucia Island is approximately 2.5 miles north of Orcas Island.

TURN ISLAND STATE PARK (Washington State Parks)
10 primitive site, boat-in only, bouys, fishing, no drinking water, beaches, trails, $.
On Turn Island. Turn Island is east of San Juan Island's Friday Harbor.

AQUA BARN RANCH (Private)
195 campsites, 105 w/hookups for water/electricity/sewer, 65 w/hookups for water/electricity, plus 25 tent units, reservation information - (206)255-4618, wheelchair access, showers, laundry, ice, restaurant, swimming pool, therapy pool, playground, trailer waste disposal, river, fishing, $$$.
Southeast of Seattle. I-5 south to I-405 eastbound, exit #4A to State 169, east 3.5 miles.

BLAKE ISLAND STATE PARK (Washington State Parks)
41 units, boat-in only, floats & bouys, group sites - reservations advised (206)947-0905, picnic shelter, wheelchair access, scuba diving area, fishing, nature trail, hiking, $-$$$.
West of Seattle. On Blake Island in Puget Sound, located 3.0 miles west of Seattle.

RIVER BEND RV PARK (Private)
42 trailer sites w/hookups for water/electricity/sewer, adults only, no tents, reservation information - (206)255-2613, showers, laundry, rec room, trailer waste disposal, $$$.
Southeast of Seattle. I-5 south to I-405 eastbound, exit #4A to State 169, east 4.5 miles.

SEATTLE SOUTH KOA (Private)
152 campsites, 133 w/hookups for water/electricity/sewer, plus 18 w/hookups for water/electricity, tents okay, reservations - (206)872-8652, wheelchair access, showers, laundry, groceries, propane, heated swimming pool, lounge, playground, rec room, horseshoe pits, nearby golf, $$$.
Southeast of Seattle. I-5 south to exit #152, east on Orillia Road.

TRAILER INNS RV PARK (Private)
100 trailer sites w/hookups for water/electricity/sewer, no tents, reservation information - (206)747-9181, showers, laundry, ice, swimming pool, therapy pool, sauna, rec room, playground, $$$.
East of Seattle. I-90 east to Bellevue exit #11A, follow signs.

TWIN CEDARS RV PARK (Private)
70 trailer sites w/hookups for water/electricity/sewer, reservation information - (206)742-5540, showers, laundry, ice, trailer waste disposal, stream, lounge, wheelchair access, $$$.
North of Seattle. I-5 north to Lynnwood exit #183, 164th Street 1.3 miles west to State 99, south to 17826 Highway 99N.

WILLOW VISTA MOBILE/RV PARK (Private)
25 campsites w/hookups for water/electricity/sewer, information
- (206)872-8264, showers, laundry, swimming pool, trailer waste
disposal, rec room, $$-$$$.
Southeast of Seattle. I-5 south to I-405, east to State 167, south
to 84th Avenue; located to the north at 21740 84th Avenue.

SEQUIM (A-2)

DIAMOND POINT RV PARK & CAMPGROUND (Private)
43 campsites, 31 w/hookups for water/electricity/sewer, plus 12
w/hookups for water/electricity, tents okay, reservation information - (206)683-2284, showers, laundry, ice, trailer waste
disposal, restaurant, ocean access, fishing, boat launch, $$-$$$.
East of Sequim, US 101 east 10.0 miles, Diamond Point Road
north 3.3 miles.

DUNGENESS FORKS (Olympic National Forest)
10 campsites, stream, fishing, hiking elev. 1000', $.
South of Sequim. US 101 southeast 4.0 miles, FSR 28 to FSR
2880 southwest 7.5 miles.

EAST CROSSING (Olympic National Forest)
10 campsites, stream, fishing, hiking, elev. 1200', $.
South of Sequim. US 101 southeast 4.0, FSR 28 to FSR 2860
southwest 9.0.

RAINBOW'S END RV PARK (Private)
52 campsites, 37 w/hookups for water/electricity/sewer/cable
tv, plus 15 tent sites, reservation information - (206)683-3863,
wheelchair access, showers, laundry, trailer waste disposal,
propane, gas, trout pond, stream, fishing, $$$.
West of Sequim. US 101 west 1.5 miles.

SEQUIM BAY RESORT (Private)
43 campsites w/hookups for water/electricity/sewer, reserva-
tions - (206)681-3853, showers, laundry, trailer waste disposal,
fishing, $$$.
Northwest of Sequim. Take West Sequim Bay Road northwest 2.5
miles.

SEQUIM BAY STATE PARK (Washington State Parks)
89 units, 26 w/hookups for water/electricity/sewer, wheelchair
access, community kitchen/shelter, trailer waste disposal, boat
launch, fishing, scuba diving area, moorage camping, $-$$.
East of Sequim. Take US 101 east 4.0 miles.

SEQUIM WEST RV PARK & MOTEL (Private)
29 trailer sites w/hookups for water/electricity/sewer, no tents, reservations - (206)683-4144, showers, laundry, ice, cable tv, restaurant, $$$.
In Sequim. Located at 740 West Washington (US 101).

SOUTH SEQUIM BAY RV PARK (Private)
30 campsites, 24 w/hookups for water/electricity/sewer, plus 6 w/hookups for water only, reservations - (206)683-7194, showers, playfield, trailer waste disposal, pond, $$-$$$.
East of Sequim. US 101 east 5.0 miles, Old Blyn Highway northeast .3 mile.

SUNSHINE MOBILE HOME/RV PARK (Private)
57 campsites, 49 w/hookups for water/electricity/sewer, plus 8 w/out hookups, reservation information - (206)683-4769, showers, laundry, stream, nearby golf & fishing, $$-$$$.
West of Sequim. US 101 west 4.0 miles.

SHELTON (A-3)

BROWN CREEK (Olympic National Forest)
19 units, trailers to 20', well, swimming, fishing, hiking trails, elev. 600', $.
Northwest of Shelton. US 101 north 7.5 miles, CR 242 northwest 5.3 miles, FSR 23 north 8.7 miles, FSR 2353 east .5 mile.

JARRELL'S COVE MARINA (Private)
10 campsites, trailers to 27', reservations - (206)426-8823, showers, laundry, groceries, marina w/gasoline & diesel, playground, ocean access, swimming, fishing, hiking, $$.
Northeast of Shelton. State 3 north 8.0 miles, Spencer Lake Road east 4.0 miles, North Island Drive 3.0 miles north, Haskell Hill Road west 1.0 mile.

SQUAXIN ISLAND STATE PARK (Washington State Parks)
20 tent sites, primitive, picnic shelter, boat-in only, bouys & floats, large lawn area, beautiful scenery, $.
East of Shelton. Squaxin Island is between Harstene Island and Shelton.

SKYKOMISH (C-2)

BECKLER RIVER (Mt. Baker-Snoqualmie National Forest)
25 units, trailers to 22', picnic area, well, fishing, swimming, on site caretaker, elev. 900', $-$$.
Northeast of Skykomish. US 2 east 1.0, FSR 65 north 2.0 mile.

FOSS RIVER (Mt. Baker-Snoqualmie National Forest)
5 units, some trailers, fishing, hiking, elev. 1400', $.
Southeast of Skykomish. US 2 east 2.0 miles, FSR 2622 south
4.5 miles. Campground is located 2.0 miles north of Alpine Lakes
Wilderness Boundary.

MILLER RIVER (Mt. Baker-Snoqualmie National Forest)
24 group sites, reservations required - (206)677-2414, trailers to
22', well, swimming, fishing, elev. 1000', $$$.
Southwest of Skykomish. US 2 west 2.5 miles, FSR 64 southeast
1.0 mile, FSR 6410 south 1.0 miles. Campground is 6.0 miles
north of Alpine Lakes Wilderness Boundary.

MONEY CREEK (Mt. Baker-Snoqualmie National Forest)
17 units, trailers to 22', group sites, picnic area, well, swimming,
fishing, on site caretaker, elev. 900', $$.
West of Skykomish. US 2 west 2.5 miles, FSR 6400 southeast .1
mile.

TYE CANYON (Mt. Baker-Snoqualmie National Forest)
2 tent units, no trailers, stream, fishing, hiking, elev. 2200', $.
East of Skykomish. US 2 east 10.0 miles.

WEST FORK MILLER RIVER (Mt. Baker-Snoqualmie National Forest)
4 tent units, no trailers, fishing, elev. 1700', $.
South of Skykomish. Miller River Road #2516 south 8.0 miles
staying right when road forks.

SNOHOMISH (B-2)

FERGUSON PARK (City of Snohomish)
11 trailer sites w/hookups for water/electricity, trailers to 34',
reservation information - (206)568-3115, wheelchair access,
showers, laundry, rec room, playground, trailer waste disposal,
lake, swimming, fishing, boat launch, $$$.
In Snohomish. Located near junction of US 2 and State 9.

FLOWING LAKE COUNTY PARK (Snohomish County)
30 RV sites w/hookups for water/electricity/sewer, plus 10 tent
units, flush toilets, picnic area & shelters, boat launch, swim-
ming, fishing, $$-$$$.
In Snohomish. US 2 to milepost #10, turn left and travel 5.0
miles to 48th Avenue, take right and proceed to end of road and
county park.

SPOKANE (G-2)

BARBARS RESORT (Private)
25 campsites, 20 w/hookups for water/electricity, plus 5 w/hookups for electricity, trailers to 35', reservation information - (509)299-3830, showers, playground, trailer waste disposal, lake, swimming, fishing, boat launch, boat rental, $$.
Southwest of Spokane. I-90 southwest to exit #264, Salnaive Road north 2.0 miles.

BERNIE'S LAST RESORT (Private)
40 campsites, 8 w/hookups for water/electricity/sewer, 12 w/hookups for water/electricity/ plus 20 tent units, reservation information - (509)299-7273, showers, laundry, rec room, ice, trailer waste disposal, lake, swimming, fishing, boat rental, $$-$$$.
Southwest of Spokane. I-90 southwest 7.0 miles to exit #270, south .02 mile to Medical Lake turnoff, take this 3.2 miles northwest to Medical Lake, Four Lakes Road will lead you to the resort.

FISHTRAP LAKE RESORT (Private)
20 trailer sites w/hookups for water/electricity, tents okay, reservation information - (509)235-2284, groceries, ice, trailer waste disposal, lake, swimming, fishing, boat launch, boat rental, $$.
Southwest of Spokane. I-90 southwest to exit #254, Fishtrap Road southeast 3.5 miles to resort.

KOA OF SPOKANE (Private)
200 campsites, 180 w/hookups for water/electricity/sewer, plus 20 tent units, reservations - (509)924-4722, showers, tv hookup, pull-thrus, laundry, groceries, swimming pool, game room, playground, trailer waste disposal, $$$.
East of Spokane. I-90 east to exit #293, Barker Road north 1.3 miles.

LAST ROUNDUP MOTEL/RV PARK & CAMPGROUND (Private)
23 campsites, 13 w/hookups for water/electricity/sewer, plus 10 tent units, information - (509)257-2583, showers, laundry, ice, playfield, $$.
Southwest of Spokane. I-90 southwest to Sprague exit #245, campground is east .5 mile.

LIBERTY LAKE PARK (Spokane County)
21 trailer sites w/hookups for water/electricity, trailers to 35', no pets, information - (509)456-4730, wheelchair access, playground, trailer waste disposal, lake, swimming, fishing, hiking, $-$$.

East of Spokane. I-90 east to exit #296, Liberty Lake Road south approximately 4.0 miles to park.

MOUNT SPOKANE STATE PARK (Washington State Parks)
14 units, some trailers - no hookups, picnic shelter, wheelchair access, hiking, horse trails, winter sports, $$.
Northeast of Spokane. US 2 northeast 10.0 miles, State 206 northeast 19.0 miles.

OVERLAND STATION (Private)
32 trailer sites w/hookups for water/electricity/sewer, reservation information - (509)747-1703, showers, laundry, groceries, playground, $$-$$$.
In Spokane. I-90 to exit #272 and campground.

PARKLAND MOTEL & RV PARK (Private)
15 trailer sites w/hookups for water/electricity/sewer, no tents, reservation information - (800)533-1626, ice, play area, $$$.
In Spokane. I-90 east to exit #283-B, travel .8 mile to Havana Street then north .03 mile to Sprague Avenue. Park is located to the east at 4412 Sprague Avenue.

PICNIC PINES ON SILVER LAKE (Private)
42 campsites, 30 w/hookups for water/electricity/sewer, plus 12 tent units, reservation information - (509)299-3223, ice, rec room, playground, on Silver Lake, swimming, fishing, boat launch, boat rental, restaurant/lounge, $$.
Southwest of Spokane. I-90 southwest 7.0 miles to exit #270, south .02 mile to Medical Lake turnoff, then 3.5 miles northwest to Medical Lake and Silver Lake Road which leads to campground.

RIVERSIDE STATE PARK (Washington State Parks)
103 units, some trailers - no hookups, group sites - reservations advised (509)456-3964, community kitchen/shelter, Spokane House Interpretive Center, boat launch, fishing, horse trails & rental, ORV area, $$-$$$.
Northwest of Spokane. Located 6.0 miles northwest of Spokane.

SHADOWS RV PARK & CAMPGROUND (Private)
60 campsites, 20 w/hookups for water/electricity/sewer, plus 40 w/hookups for water/electricity, trailers to 40', reservations - (509)467-6951, showers, laundry, trailer waste disposal, $$$.
North of Spokane. US 395 north of city center 5.0 miles to junction with US 2, Division Street exit to campground.

SMOKEY TRAIL RV CAMPSITE (Private)
70 campsites, 20 w/hookups for water/electricity/sewer, 10 w/hookups for water/electricity, 10 w/hookups for electricity only, plus 30 tent units, reservation information - (509)747-9415, showers, laundry, groceries, playground, trailer waste disposal, hiking, nearby golf $$-$$$.
Southwest of Spokane. I-90 southwest to exit #272, Hallet Road east 1.0 mile, Mallon Road south .5 mile.

SPRAGUE LAKE RESORT (Private)
60 campsites, 30 w/hookups for water/electricity/sewer, plus 30 tent units, reservation information - (509)257-2864, showers, laundry, ice, playground, trailer waste disposal, lake, swimming, fishing, boat launch, boat rental, $$.
Southwest of Spokane. I-90 southwest to Sprague exit #245, go through Sprague city center and head west 2.0 miles to lake and resort.

TRAILER INNS RV PARK (Private)
158 trailer sites w/hookups for water/electricity/sewer, no tents, pets okay, reservation information - (509)535-1811, showers, laundry, ice, swimming pool, therapy pool, sauna, lounge, game room, playground, $$$.
In Spokane. I-90 east to exit #285, follow signs to park at 6021 East Fourth Avenue.

STANWOOD (B-1)

CAMANO ISLAND STATE PARK (Washington State Parks)
89 units, some trailers - no hookups, group sites - reservations advised (206)387-3031, community kitchen/shelter, trailer waste disposal, boat launch, year-round saltwater fishing, clamming, scuba diving area, 5 mile nature trail, $$-$$$.
West of Stanwood. State 532 west 5.0 miles to Camano Island, southwest 6.0 miles to campground.

WENBERG STATE PARK (Washington State Parks)
78 units, 10 w/hookups for water/electricity, picnic shelter, groceries, trailer waste disposal, on Lake Goodwin, boat launch, fishing, swimming, $$.
Southeast of Stanwood. From Stanwood head south 6.0 miles and take road to Lake Goodwin east 3.2 miles to campground.

TACOMA (B-3)

DASH POINT STATE PARK (Washington State Parks)
138 units, 28 w/hookups for water/electricity, group sites - reservations advised (206)593-2206, picnic shelter, trailer waste disposal, fishing, $$-$$$.
Northeast of Tacoma. State 509 northeast 5.0 miles.

FIR ACRES MOTOR HOME/RV PARK (Private)
14 trailer sites w/hookups for water/electricity/sewer, reservation information - (206)588-7894, showers, laundry, $$$.
South of Tacoma. I-5 south to exit #125, east .1 mile on Bridgeport Way SW.

GIG HARBOR CAMPGROUND (Private)
137 campsites, 52 w/hookups for water/electricity/sewer, 41 w/hookups for water/electricity, plus 44 tent units, reservation information - (206)858-8138, showers, cable tv hookup, laundry, groceries, heated swimming pool, rec room, playground, trailer waste disposal, propane, fishing, nearby boat launch.
Northwest of Tacoma. I-5 to Gig Harbor exit #132, State 16 to 6.0 miles beyond Narrows Bridge, Burnham Drive north 1.0 mile.

KARWAN VILLAGE MOBILE HOME/RV PARK (Private)
10 trailer sites w/hookups for water/electricity/sewer, no tents, no pets, adults only, reservations - (206)588-2501, showers, laundry, $$$.
South of Tacoma. I-5 south to exit #129; northbound take exit #128. Park is west on 84th Street.

KOPACHUCK STATE PARK (Washington State Parks)
43 units, some trailers - no hookups, group sites - reservations advised (206)265-3606, picnic shelter, wheelchair access, trailer waste disposal, on Henderson Bay in Puget Sound, boat fishing, nearby boat launch, clamming, $$-$$$.
Northwest of Tacoma. State 16 northwest 11.0 miles, take road west then follow south to park.

SALTWATER STATE PARK (Washington State Parks)
52 sites, some trailers - no hookups, group sites - reservations advised (206)764-4128, community kitchen/shelter, wheelchair access, trailer waste disposal, on Puget Sound, scuba diving area, hiking, $$-$$$.
Northeast of Tacoma. I-5 north 16.0 miles, State 516 west 2.0 miles, State 509 south 2.0 miles.

TONASKET (E-1)

BEAVER LAKE (Okanogan National Forest)
12 units, trailers to 22', hand pumped water, boat launch, boating, swimming, fishing, hiking trails, elev. 3000', $.
Northeast of Tonasket. State 20 east 20.1 miles, CR 4953 north 5.0 miles, FSR 32 northeast 6.5 miles.

BONAPARTE LAKE (Okanogan National Forest)
26 units, trailers to 32', picnic area, piped water, flush toilets, boat launch, boating, swimming, fishing, hiking trails, elev. 3600', $$.
Northeast of Tonasket. State 20 east 20.1 miles, CR 4953 north 4.0 miles, FSR 32 north .6 mile. Located .3 mile south from Bonapart Lake Resort.

BONAPARTE LAKE RESORT (Private)
32 campsites w/hookups for water/electricity/sewer, tents okay, reservation information - (509)486-2828, showers, laundry, cafe, groceries, ice, propane, playground, trailer waste disposal, lake, swimming, fishing, boat launch, boat rental, elev. 3500', $$.
East of Tonasket. State 20 east 20.1 miles, Bonaparte Road north 6.0 miles.

MACK'S LAKESHORE BORDER RV PARK (Private)
41 campsites, 11 w/hookups for water/electricity/sewer, plus 30 w/hookups for water/electricity, reservation information - (509)476-3114, showers, laundry, trailer waste disposal, lake, swimming, fishing, boat launch, $$-$$$.
North of Tonasket. US 97 north 25.0 miles; located at US/Canada border.

OSOYOOS LAKE STATE PARK (Washington State Parks)
86 units, some trailers - no hookups, picnic shelter, snackbar, trailer waste disposal, boat launch, fishing, swimming, water skiing, winter nesting area for Canada Geese, $$.
North of Tonasket. State 97 north 18.5 miles, located north of Oroville.

RAINBOW RESORT (Private)
40 campsites, 26 w/hookups for water/electricity/sewer, plus 14 w/hookups for water/electricity, reservations - (509)223-3700, showers, ice, on Spectacle Lake, swimming, fishing, boat launch, boat rental, fishing supplies, snacks, $$$.
Northwest of Tonasket. US 97 north approximately 7.0 miles to Loomis Road, west 6.0 miles to resort.

SPECTACLE FALLS RESORT (Private)
30 campsites, 20 w/hookups for water/electricity/sewer, plus 10 w/hookups for water/electricity, reservations - (509)223-4141, ice, trailer waste disposal, on Spectacle Lake, swimming, fishing, boat launch, boat rental, boat gas, $$.
Northwest of Tonasket. US 97 north approximately 7.0 miles to Loomis Road, west 8.0 miles to resort.

SPECTACLE LAKE RESORT (Private)
40 campsites, 34 w/hookups for water/electricity/sewer, plus 6 tent units, reservations - (509)223-3433, laundry, ice, swimming pool, playfield, playground, on Spectacle Lake, swimming, fishing, boat launch, boat rental, $$$.
Northwest of Tonasket. US 97 north approximately 7.0 miles to Loomis Road, west 5.0 miles to resort.

SUN COVE RESORT (Private)
48 units w/hookups for water/electricity/sewer, plus tenting area, reservation information - (509)476-2223, pull-thrus, showers, trailer waste disposal, laundry, store, RV supplies, gas, ice, rec room, arcade, tavern, heated pool, lake swimming, boating, canoeing, boat ramp, horse rentals, fishing, hiking, $$-$$$.
Northwest of Tonasket. US 97 north 16.0 miles to Oroville, Wannacut Lake Road west 10.0 miles, resort road north 1.0 mile.

UPPER BEAVER LAKE (Okanogan National Forest)
5 tent units, well, hiking, elev. 3000', $.
Northeast of Tonasket. State 20 east 20.1 miles, FSR 3245 northeast 3.3 mile.

WEST FORK SAN POIL (Okanogan National Forest)
8 units, trailers to 32', stream, fishing, elev. 2300', $.
Southeast of Tonasket. State 30 east 12.6 miles, CR 9455 southeast 25.6 miles, FSR 359 southeast 3.2 miles.

TROUT LAKE (D-5)

CULTUS CREEK (Gifford Pinchot National Forest)
51 units, trailers to 32', piped water, stream, wheelchair access, trailhead to Indian Heaven Backcountry, berry picking, elev. 4000', $-$$.
Northwest of Trout Lake. State 141 southwest 5.5 miles, FSR 24 northwest 12.6 miles.

PETERSON GROUP CAMP (Gifford Pinchot National Forest)
1 group unit, trailers to 22', reservations required - (509)395-2501, piped water, wheelchair access, hiking, elev. 2800', $$$.

Southwest of Trout Lake. State 141 southwest 5.5 miles, FSR 24 west 2.5 miles.

PETERSON PRAIRIE (Gifford Pinchot National Forest)
30 units, trailers to 32', piped water, wheelchair access, hiking, berry picking, elev. 2800', $-$$.
Southwest of Trout Lake. State 141 southwest 5.5 miles, FSR 24 west 2.5 miles.

TWISP (E-1)

BLACK PINE LAKE (Okanogan National Forest)
21 units, trailers to 22', picnic area, piped water, lake - electric motors only, wheelchair access, boat launch, boating, fishing, hiking trails, elev. 4200', $$.
Southwest of Twisp. CR 9114 west 11.0 miles, FSR 43 south 8.0 miles.

J R (Okanogan National Forest)
6 units, trailers to 18', piped water, stream, wheelchair access, bicycling, elev. 3900', $.
East of Twisp. State 20 east 12.1 miles.

LOUP LOUP (Okanogan National Forest)
20 units, trailers to 22', piped water, stream, bicycling, elev. 4200', $.
East of Twisp. State 20 east 13.0 miles, FSR 42 north .6 mile.

PARADISE VALLEY RV RESORT (Private)
96 campsites, 28 w/hookups for water/electricity/sewer, 18 w/hookups for water/electricity, plus 50 w/out hookups, reservations - (509)997-4572, wheelchair access, showers, laundry, groceries, picnic shelter, playground, trailer waste disposal, river, swimming, fishing, paddle boat rental, playfield, hiking, 5-hole putting green, $$.
West of Twisp. Twisp River Road west 1.5 miles, Poorman Creek Road southwest 1.0 miles.

POPLAR FLAT (Okanogan National Forest)
15 units, trailers to 22', picnic area, piped water, river, wheelchair access, fishing, hiking trails, elev. 2900', $.
West of Twisp. CR 9114 west 10.8 miles, FSR 44 northwest 9.4 miles.

RIVER BEND RV PARK (Private)
110 campsites, 56 w/hookups for water/electricity/sewer, 24 w/hookups for water/electricity, plus 30 tent sites, reservation information - (509)997-3500, showers, laundry, groceries, rec hall, playfield, playground, trailer waste disposal, river, fishing, $$-$$$.
Southeast of Twisp. State 20 southeast 6.0 miles.

WAR CREEK (Okanogan National Forest)
11 units, trailers to 22', well, fishing, hiking trails, elev. 2400', $.
West of Twisp. CR 9114 west 10.8 miles, FSR 44 west 3.3 miles.

USK (G-1)

BLUESLIDE RESORT (Private)
60 campsites, 31 w/hookups for water/electricity/sewer, 20 w/hookups for electricity only, plus 9 w/out hookups, group sites, reservations - (509)445-1327, wheelchair access, showers, laundry, groceries, heated pool, playground, trailer waste disposal, on Pend Oreille River, swimming, fishing, boat launch, boat rental, hiking, gas, propane, tackle shop, $$.
North of Usk. State 20 north 21.0 miles.

BROWNS LAKE (Colville National Forest)
17 units, trailers to 22', piped water, lake - no motors, boat launch, boating, fishing, elev. 3400', $$.
Northeast of Usk. FSR 50 northeast 6.5 miles, FSR 5030 north 3.0 miles.

SOUTH SKOOKUM LAKE (Colville National Forest)
15 units, trailers to 22', picnic area, well, lake - speed limits, boat launch, boating, fishing, hiking, elev. 3600', $$.
Northeast of Usk. FSR 50 northeast 7.5 miles.

VANCOUVER (B-6)

BATTLE GROUND LAKE STATE PARK (Washington State Parks)
50 units, includes 15 primitive horse camp sites, group sites - reservations advised (206)687-4621, community kitchen, wheelchair access, snack bar, trailer waste disposal, boat launch, scuba diving area, fishing, swimming, horse trails, $-$$$.
Northeast of Vancouver. At Vancouver, take the Battle Ground exit off I-5 heading east, follow this road 21.0 miles to Battle Ground Lake State Park.

BEACON ROCK STATE PARK (Washington State Parks)
35 units, group sites - reservations advised (206)427-8265, community kitchen/picnic shelter, wheelchair access, trailer waste facility, on Columbia River, boat launch, fishing, trail to top of Beacon Rock, $$-$$$.
East of Vancouver. State 14 east 35.0 miles to Beacon Rock and campground.

BIG FIR CAMPGROUND (Private)
80 campsites, 19 w/hookups for water/electricity/sewer, 26 w/hookups for water/electricity, plus 42 tent units, reservation information - (206)887-8970, some pull-thrus for 70' trailer combo, showers, ice, RV supplies, groceries, video games, trailer waste disposal, stream, fishing, rec area, $$$.
Northeast of Vancouver. I-5 to exit #14, east 4.0 miles to campground.

LEWIS RIVER RV PARK (Private)
85 campsites, 25 w/hookups for water/electricity/sewer, 45 w/hookups for water/electricity, plus 15 tent units, trailers to 60', reservations - (206)225-9556, wheelchair access, showers, laundry, groceries, swimming, pool, trailer waste disposal, gas, deli, river, fishing, golf, $$$.
Northeast of Vancouver. I-5 north 20.0 miles to exit #21, State 503 east 5.0 miles.

99 MOBILE LODGE & RV PARK (Private)
60 trailer sites w/hookups for water/electricity/sewer, no tents, reservation information - (206)573-0351, showers, laundry, trailer waste disposal, $$.
North of Vancouver. I-5 north to 134th Street exit, located on State 99 at 129th Street.

PARADISE POINT STATE PARK (Washington State Parks)
79 units, trailer waste disposal, beach access, East Fork Lewis River access, boat launch, fishing, hiking trail, $.
North of Vancouver. I-5 north 15.0 miles.

REED ISLAND STATE PARK (Washington State Parks)
5 primitive campsites, boat-in only, picnic facilities, on Columbia River, no water, water skiing, fishing, $-$$.
East of Vancouver. State 14 east 16.0 miles to Camas/Washougal Marina, boat to campground.

VOLCANO VIEW CAMPGROUND (Private)
75 campsites, 23 w/hookups for water/electricity/sewer, 25 w/hookups for water/electricity/ plus 27 tent units, reservation information - (206)231-4329, showers, hot tub, groceries, rec room, playfield, trailer waste disposal, $$-$$$.

Northeast of Vancouver. I-5 north to State 503 exit #21, State 503 for 24.0 mile to Amboy, south 1.0 mile.

VANTAGE (D-4)

GINKGO/WANAPUM STATE PARK (Washington State Parks)
54 sites w/hookups for water/electricity/sewer, Ginkgo Petrified Forest Interpretive Center, boat launch, fishing, beach access, trail, $$.
North of Vantage. I-90 east 1.0 miles to park exit.

VANTAGE KOA (Private)
150 campsites, 100 w/hookups for water/electricity/sewer, plus 50 tent units, reservation information - (509)856-2230, showers, laundry, groceries, rec room, playground, swimming pool, therapy pool, trailer waste disposal, lake, swimming, fishing, $$$.
In Vantage. Located 2 blocks north of I-90 exit #136.

WALLA WALLA (F-5)

FORT PARK/WALLA WALLA CAMPGROUND (City of Walla Walla)
76 campsites, 21 w/hookups for water/electricity, plus 55 tent units, reservation information - (509)527-4527, wheelchair access, coin showers, playfield, playground, trailer waste disposal, stream, hiking, museum in park, $$.
Southwest of Walla Walla. State 125 southwest 4.0 miles, Dalles Military Road west .5 mile.

WAUCONDA (E-1)

BETH LAKE (Okanogan National Forest)
14 units, trailers to 32', picnic area, piped water, lake - speed limits, boat launch, boating, swimming, fishing, hiking trails, elev. 2900', $$.
North of Wauconda. State 20 west 2.0 miles, CR 4953 north 5.0 miles, FSR 32 north 6.0 miles, FSR 3245 northwest 3.3 miles.

LOST LAKE (Okanogan National Forest)
18 units, 3 group sites, trailers to 32', piped water, picnic area, flush toilets, boat launch, interpretive services, boating, swimming, fishing, hiking trails, elev. 3800', $$.
North of Wauconda. State 20 west 2.0 miles, CR 4953 northeast 5.0 miles, FSR 32 approximately 2.0 miles northeast, FSR 33 northwest 3.5 miles, FSR 50 south .5 mile.

SWEAT CREEK (Okanogan National Forest)
8 units, trailers to 18', picnic area, well, elev. 3500', $.
Southeast of Wauconda. State 20 southeast 8.5 miles.

WENATCHEE (D-3)

BEEHIVE SPRINGS (Wenatchee National Forest)
4 tent units, no trailers, picnic area, piped water, elev. 4100', $.
Southwest of Wenatchee. Leave US 2 on Squilchuck Road #2107,
follow this 10.0 miles to campground.

LINCOLN ROCK STATE PARK (Washington State Parks)
94 units, 67 w/hookups for water/sewer/electricity, 27 w/out
hookups, wheelchair access, picnic shelter, trailer waste dis-
posal, boat launch, fishing, boating, water skiing, $$.
North of Wenatchee. State 28 and US 2 north 6.0 miles.
Campground is adjacent to Rocky Reach Hydro Electric Dam.

SQUILCHUCK STATE PARK (Washington State Parks)
Group camping only - reservations required (509)844-3044, win-
ter recreation area, $$$.
Southwest of Wenatchee. Leave Wenatchee heading southwest on
Squilchuck Road, campground is 9.0 miles.

WENATCHEE RIVER COUNTY PARK (Chelan County)
105 campsites, 40 w/hookups for water/electricity/sewer, 24
w/hookups for water/electricity, plus 41 tent sites, information -
(509)662-2525, showers, playground, trailer waste disposal, on
Wenatchee River, fishing, $$-$$$.
Northwest of Wenatchee. State 28 north 4.0 miles, US 2/97 west
5.0 miles.

WESTPORT (A-4)

COHO RV PARK (Private)
76 campsites w/hookups for water/electricity/sewer/cable tv,
reservations - (206)268-0111, showers, wheelchair access, laundry, ice, large meeting room w/kitchen, ocean access, fishing,
fish charter, BBQ, crabpot & fish cleaning room, $$$.
In Westport. Located in dock area.

G & M TRAILER PARK & BOAT MOORAGE (Private)
30 campsites w/hookups for water/electricity/sewer/cable tv,
reservations - (206)268-0265, showers, ice, on harbor, harbor &
surf fishing, $$.
In Westport. Located in dock area on north side of boat basin.

HAMMOND TRAILER PARK (Private)
16 sites w/hookups for water/electricity/sewer, plus tenting area, reservation information - (206)268-9645, showers, laundry, RV supplies, nearby stores and restaurants, nearby fishing, $$-$$$.
In Westport. From city center take Montesano Street south 1.0 mile to Roberts Road; park is at 1845 Roberts Road.

HOLAND CENTER RV PARK (Private)
80 trailer sites w/hookups for water/electricity/sewer, reservation information - (206)268-9582, showers, cable tv, $$.
In Westport. Located 2 blocks off docks on State 105.

ISLANDER RV PARK (Private)
65 trailer sites w/hookups for water/electricity/sewer, no tents, reservations - (206)268-9166, wheelchair access, showers, laundry, ice, swimming pool, coffee shop, lounge, ocean access, fishing, fish charter, fish cleaning area, $$-$$$.
In Westport. Located on Revetment Drive at northwest end of boat basin.

PACIFIC MOTEL & TRAILER PARK (Private)
80 campsites w/hookups for water/electricity/sewer, some tent units, reservations - (206)268-9325, showers, heated swimming pool, $$-$$$.
South of Westport. State 105 just south of town.

TOTEM RV PARK (Private)
75 campsites, 44 w/hookups for water/electricity/sewer/cable tv, 24 w/hookups for water/electricity, plus 7 w/out hookups, tents okay, reservations - (206)268-0025, showers, laundry, groceries, drive-in restaurant, picnic shelter, trailer waste disposal, ocean access, fishing, $$-$$$.
In Westport. Located in dock area.

TWIN HARBORS STATE PARK (Washington State Parks)
326 units, 49 w/hookups for water/electricity/sewer, group sites - reservations advised (206)268-6502, wheelchair access, trailer waste disposal, fishing, beachcombing, nature trail, $$-$$$.
South of Westport. State 105 south 3.0 miles to campground.

WESTPORT CITY PARK (City)
40 campsites, restrooms, tennis, playground, $$.
In Westport. Located in city center; on Washington Avenue, one block west of Montesano.

WILBUR (F-2)

BELLS TRAILER PARK (Private)
30 trailer sites w/hookups for water/electricity/sewer, reservations - (509)647-5888, showers, laundry, ice, picnic area, groceries enarby, $$$.
In Wilbur. Located at eastern edge of town; one block off US 2.

HAWK CREEK (Coulee Dam Recreation Area)
Campsites, trailers okay - no hookups, reservation information - (509)622-0881, drinking water, lake, fishing, boat launch, boat dock, elev. 1277', $$.
Northeast of Wilbur. US 2 east to Creston, Fort Spokane Highway north 17.0 miles.

KELLER FERRY (Coulee Dam Recreation Area)
Campsites, trailers okay - no hookups, drinking water, picnic area, amphitheater, trailer & boat waste disposal, boat ramp & dock, boat fuel, swimming/lifeguard, elev. 1229', $$-$$$.
North of Wilbur. State 21 approximately 14.0 miles to Keller Ferry Landing and campground.

THE RIVER RUE RV PARK (Private)
22 trailer sites, 19 w/hookups for water/electricity/sewer, plus 3 w/hookups for water/electricity, reservations - (509)647-2647, wheelchair access, showers, groceries, tackle shop, deli/snack bar, propane, playfield, playground, trailer waste disposal, near Lake Roosevelt & fishing, $$.
North of Wilbur. State 21 north 14.0 miles.

WINSLOW (B-2)

FAY BAINBRIDGE STATE PARK (Washington State Parks)
36 campsites, 26 w/hookups for water, picnic shelter, wheelchair access, trailer waste disposal, on Puget Sound. boat launch, scuba diving area, fishing, $$.
Northwest of Winslow. State 305 northwest 5.0 miles to campground road.

FORBES LANDING (Private)
22 trailer sites w/hookups for water/electricity/sewer, reservation information - (206)638-2257, showers, groceries, restaurant, ocean access, fishing, boat rental, $$-$$$.
North of Winslow. State 305 northwest 13.0 miles, State 3 north 7.0 miles, State 104 southeast 7.0 miles, Hansville Road north 7.0 miles.

KITSAP MEMORIAL STATE PARK (Washington State Parks)
48 units, some trailers - no hookups, group sites, reservations advised - (206)779-3205, community kitchen/shelter, trailer waste disposal, fishing, clamming, playfields, horseshoe pits, beach, $$-$$$.
Northwest of Winslow. State 305 northwest 13.0 miles, State 3 north 4.0 miles.

POINT-NO-POINT RESORT (Private)
38 campsites w/hookups for water/electricity/sewer, trailers to 32', reservation information - (206)638-2233, showers, laundry, ice, ocean access, fishing, boat rental, $$-$$$.
North of Winslow. State 305 northwest 13.0 miles, State 3 north 7.0 miles, State 104 southeast 7.0 miles, Hansville Road north 7.0 miles.

SCENIC BEACH STATE PARK (Washington State Parks)
52 units, some trailers - no hookups, community kitchen, wheelchair access, trailer waste disposal, on Hood Canal, fishing, $$.
Northwest of Winslow. State 305 northwest 13.0 miles, State 3 south 8.0 miles, take road west to Scenic Beach State Park.

WINTHROP (D-1)

BIG TWIN LAKE CAMPGROUND (Private)
82 units, 42 w/hookups for water/electricity/sewer, 40 w/out hookups, tenting area, reservation information - (509)996-2650, pull-thrus, showers, laundry, trailer waste disposal, ice, playground, lake swimming, boat rentals, fishing, $$-$$$.
Southwest of Winthrop. From Riverside, take State 20 south 3.0 miles, Twin Lake Road west 2.3 miles.

BUCK LAKE (Okanogan National Forest)
9 units, trailers to 18', piped water, boating, fishing, elev. 3200', $.
North of Winthrop. CR 1213 north 6.6 miles, FSR 51 north 2.8 miles, FSR 5130 northwest .6 mile, FSR 100 northwest 2.3 miles.

DERRY'S RESORT ON PEARRYGIN LAKE (Private)
154 campsites, 64 w/hookups for water/electricity/sewer, plus 90 tent units, reservations - (509)996-2322, showers, laundry, groceries, ice, playfield, playground, trailer waste disposal, on Pearrygin Lake, swimming, fishing, boat launch, $$-$$$.
Northeast of Winthrop. Riverside north .5 mile, Bluff Street east 2.0 miles, Pearrygin Lake Road east 1.0 mile to campground.

EARLY WINTERS (Okanogan National Forest)
13 units, trailers to 18', piped water, river, wheelchair access, fishing, elev. 2400', $$.
Northwest of Winthrop. State 20 northwest 16.0 miles.

FALLS CREEK (Okanogan National Forest)
8 units, trailers to 18', well, waterfall, fishing, elev. 2300', $.
North of Winthrop. CR 1213 north 6.6 miles, FSR 5160 north 5.3 miles.

FLAT (Okanogan National Forest)
12 units, trailers to 18', well, stream, wheelchair access, fishing, elev. 2600', $.
North of Winthrop. CR 1213 north 6.6 miles, FSR 51 north 2.8 miles, FSR 5130 northwest 2.0 miles.

KLIPCHUCK (Okanogan National Forest)
46 units, trailers to 32", piped water, stream, flush toilets, wheelchair access, fishing, hiking trails, elev. 3000', $$.
Northwest of Winthrop. State 20 northwest 17.2 miles, FSR 300 northwest 1.2 miles.

LONE FIR (Okanogan National Forest)
27 units, trailers to 22', piped water, river, wheelchair access, fishing, hiking trails, provides access to Silver Star Glacier, elev. 3800', $$.
Northwest of Winthrop. State 20 northwest 26.8 miles.

METHOW RIVER/WINTHROP KOA (Private)
100 campsites, 16 w/hookups for water/electricity/sewer, 56 w/hookups for water/electricity, plus 23 tent units, reservations - (509)996-2258, showers, laundry, groceries, trailer waste disposal, heated swimming pool, river, fishing, playground, $$$.
Southeast of Winthrop. State 20 south 1.0 mile.

PEARRYGIN LAKE STATE PARK (Washington State Parks)
86 units, 57 w/hookups for water/electricity/sewer, 27 trailer sites w/hookups for water only, wheelchair access, trailer waste disposal, boat launch, fishing, winter sports, $$.
Northeast of Winthrop. Riverside north .5 mile, Bluff Street east 2.0 miles, Pearrygin Lake Road to campground.

PINE-NEAR TRAILER PARK (Private)
28 campsites w/hookups for water/electricity/sewer, plus tenting area, reservations - (509)996-2391, showers, laundry, trailer waste disposal, $$-$$$.
At Winthrop. Riverside north .5 mile, Bluff Street east .1 mile, park is on Castle, right across from Shaffer Museum.

RIVER BEND (Okanogan National Forest)
5 units, trailers to 22', well, river, fishing, elev. 2700', $.
Northwest of Winthrop. State 20 northwest 13.2 miles, CR 1163 northwest 6.9 miles, FSR 5400 northwest 2.5 miles, FSR 60 west .5 mile.

YACOLT (B-5)

SUNSET (Gifford Pinchot National Forest)
16 units, trailers to 22', picnic area, well, stream, wheelchair access - includes trail, fishing, hiking, berry & mushroom picking, elev. 1000', $.
East of Yacolt. CR 16 southeast 3.0 miles, CR 12 east 8.0 miles, FSR 42 to campground.

YAKIMA (D-4)

CIRCLE H RV RANCH (Private)
36 campsites w/hookups for water/electricity/sewer, reservation information - (509)457-3683, wheelchair access, showers, laundry, swimming pool, spa, therapy pool, lounge, playground, $$$.
In Yakima. I-82 to exit #34, 18th Street north .3 mile to park.

TRAILER INNS RV PARK (Private)
101 trailer sites w/hookups for water/electricity/sewer, no tents, pets okay, reservation information - (509)452-9561, wheelchair access, showers, laundry, trailer waste disposal, swimming pool, therapy pool, sauna, lounge, playground, $$$.
In Yakima. I-82 to exit #31; located at 1610 N. First Street.

YAKIMA KOA (Private)
117 campsites, 37 w/hookups for water/electricity/sewer, 37 w/hookups for water/electricity, 6 w/hookups for electricity, plus 37 tent units, reservations - (509)248-5882, showers, laundry, groceries, playground, trailer waste disposal, river, fishing, boat rental, $$$.
In Yakima. I-82 to exit #34, State 24 east 1.0 mile, Keyes Road north .3 mile.

YAKIMA SPORTSMAN STATE PARK (Washington State Parks)
66 units, 36 w/hookups for water/electricity/sewer, community kitchen/shelter, trailer waste disposal, stocked children's fishing pond, river fishing for adults, $$.
East of Yakima. Campground is located east 1.0 mile.

CAMPGROUND INDEX

BAYWOOD PARK - 137
BEACH RV PARK - 203
BEACHSIDE - 126
BEACON ROCK STATE PARK - 219
BEAR CREEK RV PARK & MOTEL - 160
BEAR SPRINGS - 94
BEAVER - 141
BEAVER BAY CAMP - 153
BEAVER CREEK - 164
BEAVER LAKE - 215
BEAVER LODGE RV PARK - 149
BEAVER SULFER - 81
BEAVERTAIL - 123
BECKLER RIVER - 209
BEDROCK - 92
BEEHIVE SPRINGS - 221
BELFAIR STATE PARK - 135
BELKNAP WOODS R- 95
BELLACRES MOBILE ESTATE - 76
BELLS TRAILER PARK - 223
BEND KOA - 36
BEND O' THE RIVER CAMPGROUND - 73
BERNIE'S LAST RESORT - 211
BESTWESTERN HERITAGE INN & RV PARK - 180
BETH LAKE - 220
BEVERLY BEACH - 97
BIAK BY THE SEA MOTOR HOME PARK - 68
BIG CREEK - 135
BIG CREEK - 165
BIG EDDY - 125
BIG ELK - 58
BIG FIR CAMPGROUND - 219
BIG LAKE - 115
BIG PINE - 74
BIG POOL - 93
BIG SLIDE LAKE - 59
BIG SPRUCE TRAILER PARK - 121
BIG SUN RESORT & RV PARK - 180
BIG TWIN LAKE CAMPGROUND - 224
BIRCH BAY STATE PARK - 137
BLACK BEACH RESORT - 202
BLACK BUTTE MOTEL & RV PARK - 42
BLACK CANYON - 99
BLACK LAKE RV PARK - 188
BLACK PINE LAKE - 217
BLACKBERRY - 120
BLACKHORSE - 82
BLACKPINE CREEK HORSECAMP - 171
BLAKE ISLAND STATE PARK - 207
BLUE BAY - 115
BLUE JAY CAMPGROUND - 35
BLUE LAKE CREEK - 200
BLUE LAKE RESORT - 115
BLUE LAKE RESORT - 154
BLUE PACIFIC MOTEL & TRAILER PARK - 190
BLUE POOL - 99
BLUE SHASTIN TRAILER & RV PARK - 171
BLUEBILL LAKE - 98

DOSEWALLIPS STATE PARK - 139
DOUGLAS FIR - 161
DRIFT CREEK LANDING - 126
DRIFTWOOD ACRES OCEAN CAMPGROUND - 190
DRIFTWOOD II - 63
DRIFTWOOD RV PARK - 39
DRIFTWOOD RV PARK - 50
DRIFTWOOD RV TRAV-L-PARK - 174
DRIFTWOOD SHORES RV PARK - 35
DUFUR CITY PARK - 58
DUNE LAKE - 64
DUNGENESS FORKS - 208
DUNGENESS RECREATION AREA - 194
EAGLE CREEK - 46
EAGLE ROCK - 80
EAGLE VALLEY RV & MOBILE HOME PARK - 112
EARLY WINTERS - 225
EAST CROSSING - 208
EAST DAVIS LAKE - 52
EAST LAKE - 89
EAST LAKE RESORT & RV PARK - 89
EAST SHORE RECREATION SITE - 109
EAST SIDE PARK CAMPGROUND - 188
ECONOLODGE & RV PARK - 62
EIGHTMILE - 172
ELK LAKE - 36
ELK RIVER RV CAMPGROUND - 104
ELKHORN - 139
ELKHORN VALLEY - 113
ELKTON RV PARK - 58
ELLENSBURG KOA - 157
ELMER'S TRAILER PARK - 194
EMIGRANT - 41
EMIGRANT CAMPGROUND - 32
EMIGRANT SPRINGS - 103
ENTIAT CITY PARK - 157
EUGENE KOA - 62
EUGENE MOBILE VILLAGE - 62
EVANS - 170
EVERGREEN COURT - 174
EVERGREEN MANOR & RV PARK - 137
EVERGREEN PARK - 105
FAIRHOLM CAMPROUND - 195
FALLS - 41
FALLS CREEK - 199
FALLS CREEK - 225
FALLS VIEW CAMPGROUND - 199
FAR-E-NUF TRAILER PARK - 89
FAREWELL BEND - 79
FAREWELL BEND - 108
FAY BAINBRIDGE STATE PARK - 223
FERGUSON PARK - 210
FERN HILL CAMPGROUND & RV PARK - 135
FERN RIDGE SHORES - 62
FERNDALE CAMPGROUND - 159
FERNVIEW - 118
FERRY LAKE - 202
FIR ACRES MOTOR HOME/RV PARK - 214

FISH CREEK - 59
FISH LAKE - 67
FISH LAKE - 130
FISH LAKE RESORT - 130
FISH MILL LODGES - 64
FISHERMEN'S BEND - 96
FISHERY - COVERTS LANDING - 58
FISHHOOK PARK - 204
FISHIN' HOLE PARK & MARINA - 126
FISHTRAP LAKE RESORT - 211
FLAT - 225
FLEMING'S HAVEN RESORT - 150
FLOWING LAKE COUNTY PARK - 210
FLUMET FLAT - 81
FLYING "M" RANCH - 131
FOGARTY CREEK RV PARK - 55
FORBES LANDING - 223
FOREST GLEN - 113
FORKS MOBILE HOME & RV PARK - 160
FORT CANBY STATE PARK - 168
FORT CASEY STATE PARK - 155
FORT CREEK RESORT - 67
FORT EBEY STATE PARK - 156
FORT FLAGLER STATE PARK - 197
FORT KLAMATH LODGE & RV PARK - 67
FORT PARK/WALLA WALLA CAMPGROUND - 220
FORT SPOKANE - 161
FORT STEVENS - 34
FORT WORDEN STATE PARK - 197
FORTYNINER CAMPGROUND & MOTEL - 146
FOSS RIVER - 210
FOSSIL MOTEL & TRAILER PARK - 67
FOSTER'S COLD SPRINGS RESORT - 42
FOUR PINES RV COURT - 174
FOUR SEASONS RV RESORT - 70
FOURBIT FORD - 41
FOURMILE LAKE - 84
FOX CREEK - 157
FRENCH GULCH CAMP & TRAILHEAD - 82
FRENCH PETE - 37
FRISSELL CROSSING - 37
FROG LAKE - 72
FROST ROAD TRAILER PARK - 142
G & M TRAILER PARK & BOAT MOORAGE - 221
GATES TRAILER RANCH - 69
GATTON CREEK - 199
GERBER RESERVOIR - 38
GIFFORD - 167
GIG HARBOR CAMPGROUND - 214
GILLETTE - 150
GINKGO/WANAPUM STATE PARK - 220
GLACIER VIEW - 172
GLEN AYR RV PARK - 165
GLENYAN KOA - 32
GOLD BASIN - 164
GOLD LAKE - 99
GOLD'N ROGUE KOA - 71
GONE CREEK - 72

HOOD VIEW - 72
HOOVER - 56
HOOVER GROUP CAMP - 56
HORSE CREEK - 38
HORSEFALL BEACH - 98
HORSEFALL STAGING - 98
HORSESHOE BEND - 80
HORSESHOE COVE - 152
HORSETHIEF LAKE STATE PARK - 162
HOT LAKE RV RESORT - 86
HOT SPRINGS - 89
HOUSE ROCK - 118
HOWARD MILLER STEELHEAD PARK - 152
HOWARD PRAIRIE LAKE RESORT - 32
HUCKLEBERRY HILL MOBILE HOME PARK - 48
HUDSON/PARCHER PARK - 109
HUMBUG - 56
HUMBUG MOUNTAIN - 105
HUNT PARK/WASCO COUNTY FAIRGROUNDS - 123
HUNTER CREEK RV PARK - 70
HUNTER'S RV - 87
HUNTERS - 167
HYATT LAKE - 32
HYATT LAKE RESORT - 33
ICE CAP CREEK - 95
ICICLE RIVER RANCH - 172
IDA CREEK - 172
IDAVILLE TRAILER COURT - 121
IDLE WHEELS - 100
IKE KINSWA STATE PARK - 177
ILLAHEE STATE PARK - 136
ILWACO KOA - 168
INDIAN CREEK - 183
INDIAN CREEK RECREATION PARK - 70
INDIAN CROSSING - 82
INDIAN FLAT - 183
INDIAN FORD - 116
INDIAN HENRY - 60
INDIAN MARY PARK - 74
IONE MOTEL & RV PARK - 169
IPSUT CREEK - 158
IRON CREEK - 200
IRON GATE - 176
ISEBERG PARK RV - 34
ISLAND PARK - 101
ISLANDER RV PARK - 222
ISLET - 99
J R - 217
JACK'S RV PARK - 151
JACKMAN PARK - 68
JACKSON F. KIMBALL - 48
JACKSON HOT SPRING - 33
JANTZEN BEACH RV PARK - 105
JARRELL COVE STATE PARK - 136
JARRELL'S COVE MARINA - 209
JERRY'S LANDING RV PARK - 186
JESSIE M. HONEYMAN - 64
JETTY FISHERY - 122

JIM MARION'S LAKE MARTHA RV PARK - 140
JOE GRAHAM HORSE CAMP - 72
JOHN NEAL MEMORIAL PARK - 96
JOHN P. AMACHER PARK - 112
JOHN'S RV PARK - 37
JOHNNY CREEK - 172
JOSEPH P. STEWART - 130
JUBILEE LAKE - 123
JUNIPERS RESERVOIR RV RESORT - 87
KACHESS - 147
KAH-NEE-TA - 128
KALALOCH - 199
KAMPERS WEST KAMPGROUND RV PARK - 34
KANASKAT/PALMER STATE PARK - 158
KANE'S HIDEAWAY MARINA - 56
KANER FLAT - 183
KARWAN VILLAGE MOBILE HOME/RV PARK - 214
KAYAK POINT COUNTY PARK - 140
KELLER FERRY - 223
KELLEY'S RV PARK - 50
KENANNA RV PARK - 165
KENO CAMP - 83
KERBY TRAILER PARK - 47
KETTLE FALLS - 170
KIAHANIE - 129
KILCHIS RIVER PARK - 122
KIMBALL CREEK BEND RV RESORT - 70
KING SILVER TRAILER PARK - 127
KINGFISHER - 60
KINGSLEY - 78
KITSAP MEMORIAL STATE PARK - 224
KLAHOWYA - 195
KLAMATH FALLS KOA - 84
KLIPCHUCK - 225
KOA OF SPOKANE - 211
KOA SALEM, INC. - 113
KOPACHUCK STATE PARK - 214
KOZY CABINS & RV PARK - 151
KOZY KOVE MARINA & RV PARK - 127
LA WIS WIS - 192
LADD CREEK - 55
LAGOON (SILTCOOS) - 64
LAKE CHELAN STATE PARK - 145
LAKE CREEK - 158
LAKE CUSHMAN RESORT - 166
LAKE CUSHMAN STATE PARK - 166
LAKE EASTON STATE PARK - 147
LAKE FORK - 77
LAKE GOODWIN RESORT - 140
LAKE IN THE WOODS - 69
LAKE LEO - 150
LAKE MAYFIELD RESORT/RV PARK & MARINA - 178
LAKE McMURRAY RESORT - 140
LAKE OF THE WOODS - 84
LAKE OF THE WOODS RESORT - 85
LAKE OWYHEE - 124
LAKE OWYHEE RESORT - 125
LAKE PLEASANT RV PARK - 138

LAKE SYLVIA STATE PARK - 180
LAKE THOMAS - 150
LAKE VIEW PARK - 64
LAKE WENATCHEE RANGER STATION - 172
LAKE WENATCHEE STATE PARK - 173
LAKE'S EDGE RV PARK - 65
LAKESHORE MOTOR PARK - 107
LAKESHORE TRAVEL PARK - 65
LAKEVIEW TERRACE RV PARK - 163
LANE COUNTY HARBOR VISTA - 65
LANGLOIS TRAVEL PARK - 88
LAPINE - 90
LARIAT MOTEL & RV PARK - 34
LARRABEE STATE PARK - 140
LAST ROUNDUP MOTEL/RV PARK & CAMPGROUND - 211
LAURENTS SUN VILLAGE RESORT - 154
LAVA LAKE - 90
LAVA LAKE RV CAMPGROUND - 90
LAVERNE PARK - 50
LAZY ACRES MOTEL & RV PARK - 72
LAZY BEND - 60
LAZY DAZE MOTOR HOME PARK - 38
LEPAGE PARK - 120
LES CLARE RV PARK & CAMPGROUND - 74
LEWIS & CLARK CAMPGROUND/RV PARK - 142
LEWIS & CLARK STATE PARK - 178
LEWIS & CLARK TRAIL STATE PARK - 156
LEWIS RIVER RV PARK - 219
LIARS COVE RESORT - 151
LIBERTY LAKE PARK - 211
LICK CREEK - 83
LILO'S HACIENDA RV PARK - 130
LILY GLEN CAMPGROUND - 33
LINCOLN CITY KOA - 92
LINCOLN PARK - 195
LINCOLN ROCK STATE PARK - 221
LINK CREEK - 116
LITTLE CRATER - 73
LITTLE CRATER - 90
LITTLE FAWN - 36
LITTLE NACHES - 183
LITTLE REDWOOD - 39
LOCKABY - 60
LODGEPOLE - 183
LOEB - 39
LOG CABIN RESORT - 195
LONE FIR - 225
LONE FIR RESORT - 154
LONE PINE RV PARK - 120
LONG LAKE - 202
LOOKOUT TRAILER COURT - 190
LOON LAKE - 110
LOON LAKE LODGE RESORT - 110
LOPEZ ISLAND/ODLIN COUNTY PARK - 204
LOPEZ ISLAND/SPENCER SPIT STATE PARK - 205
LOST CREEK - 52
LOST LAKE - 68
LOST LAKE - 102

MOUNTAIN VIEW MOBILE PARK - 79
MOUNTAIN VIEW TRAILER PARK - 140
MT. HOME MOBILE VILLAGE - 108
MT. HOOD RV VILLAGE - 129
MT. LINTON RV PARK - 179
MT. VIEW PARK RV & CAMPING - 57
MT. VIEW RV PARK - 85
MUD LAKE - 77
MULKEY RV PARK - 96
MUTINY BAY RESORT - 156
NASALLE TRAILER COURT - 168
NASON CREEK - 173
NEAH BAY RESORT - 185
NEBO TRAILER PARK - 112
NEHALEM BAY - 44
NEHALEM BAY TRAILER PARK - 44
NEHALEM SHORES RV PARK - 44
NEPTUNE PARK RESORT - 49
NESIKA BEACH RV PARK CAMPGROUND - 71
NEWHALEM CREEK - 177
NISQUALLY PLAZA RV PARK - 189
NOISY CREEK - 169
NORSELAND MOBILE ESTATES & RV PARK - 136
NORTH DAVIS CREEK - 90
NORTH EEL CREEK - 110
NORTH FORK - 158
NORTH FORK - 200
NORTH FORK GROUP - 201
NORTH HILLS MOBILEHOME PARK - 85
NORTH LAKE RESORT & MARINA - 87
NORTH WALDO - 99
NORTHWEST TREK WILDLIFE PARK - 198
OAK FORK - 73
OAK HARBOR CITY BEACH - 156
OAKLAND'S FISH CAMP - 127
OASIS CAFE/MOTEL/RV PARK - 83
OASIS PARK - 181
OCEAN AIRE TRAILER PARK - 174
OCEAN CITY STATE PARK - 190
OCEAN GATE RESORT - 165
OCEAN PARK RESORT - 175
OCEAN SHORES RV & CHARTER & MARINA - 191
OCEANSIDE RV CAMP - 71
OCHOCO DIVIDE- 107
OCHOCO LAKE - 107
ODELL CREEK - 53
ODESSA GOLF & RV PARK - 181
OFFUT LAKE RESORT & RV PARK - 143
OHANAPECOSH - 192
OKLAHOMA - 153
OLALLIE - 95
OLD FORT TOWNSEND STATE PARK - 197
OLLOKOT - 83
OLSON'S RESORT - 185
OLYMPIA CAMPGROUND - 189
ORCAS ISLAND/CAPTAIN COOK RESORT - 205
ORCAS ISLAND/DOE BAY VILLAGE RESORT - 205
ORCAS ISLAND/MORAN STATE PARK - 205

PLAINVIEW TRAILER PARK - 50
PLAZA RV & MOBILE HOME PARK - 137
PLEASANT ACRES RESORT - 190
PLYMOUTH PARK - 204
POINT - 37
POINT HUDSON RV PARK - 197
POINT-NO-POINT RESORT - 224
POLALLIE - 102
POLK COUNTY FAIRGROUNDS - 112
POOLE CREEK - 81
POPLAR FLAT - 217
PORCUPINE BAY - 161
PORT ANGELES KOA - 196
PORT OF BROOKINGS BEACH FRONT RV - 39
PORT OF KALAMA RV PARK - 169
PORT ORFORD RV TRAILER VILLAGE - 105
PORT SIUSLAW RV PARK & MARINA - 65
PORTLAND - FAIRVIEW RV PARK - 105
PORTSIDE RV PARK - 40
POTHOLES STATE PARK - 181
POTLATCH STATE PARK - 166
POWERS COUNTY PARK - 106
PRAIRIE - 90
PRAIRIE GROUP AREA - 91
PRINCESS CREEK - 53
PRINEVILLE RESERVOIR - 107
PRINEVILLE RESERVOIR RESORT - 108
PROMONTORY - 61
PROSPECTOR TRAVEL TRAILER PARK - 125
PUMA - 93
QUINN MEADOW HORSE CAMP - 37
QUINN RIVER - 91
QUINNAT CHARTER & RV PARK - 77
QUOSATANA - 71
RAIN FOREST RESORT VILLAGE & RV PARK - 199
RAINBOW - 61
RAINBOW - 199
RAINBOW FALLS STATE PARK - 144
RAINBOW PARK CAMPGROUND - 170
RAINBOW RESORT - 198
RAINBOW RESORT - 215
RAINBOW'S END RV PARK - 208
RAINES RESORT - 101
REED ISLAND STATE PARK - 219
REEDER BEACH RV PARK - 114
REMOTE CAMPGROUND & CABINS - 111
REST A WHILE RV PARK - 166
RHODODENDRON TRAILER PARK - 65
RILEY - 129
RIPPLEBROOK - 61
RIVER BEND - 183
RIVER BEND - 226
RIVER BEND PARK - 40
RIVER BEND RV PARK - 207
RIVER BEND RV PARK - 218
RIVER OAKS RV PARK - 143
RIVER'S END CAMPGROUND - 168
RIVERBEND PARK - 141

RIVEREDGE - 121
RIVERFRONT RV TRAILER PARK - 75
RIVERSIDE - 61
RIVERSIDE - 80
RIVERSIDE LAKE RESORT - 44
RIVERSIDE STATE PARK - 212
RIVERSIDE TRAILER COURT - 191
RIVERVIEW LODGE CAMPGROUND - 101
RIVERVIEW RV PARK - 167
ROARING RIVER - 61
ROBIN HOOD VILLAGE - 136
ROBINHOOD - 102
ROCK CREEK - 81
ROCK CREEK - 91
ROCK CREEK - 131
ROCK CREEK RESERVOIR - 128
ROCK GARDEN RV PARK - 138
ROCK ISLAND - 173
ROCKPORT STATE PARK - 152
ROCKY POINT RESORT & MARINA - 85
ROD'S BEACH RESORT & RV PARK - 191
ROGUE ELK CAMPGROUND - 130
ROGUE VALLEY OVERNIGHTERS - 75
ROLLING HILLS MOBILE TERRACE - 76
ROSLAND - 91
ROUNDUP TRAVEL TRAILER PARK - 91
ROUTSON PARK - 78
RV PARK - 104
RV RESORT AT CANNON BEACH - 44
RV TOWN INC. - 148
SADDLE MOUNTAIN - 44
SALBASGEON MOTEL & RV PARK - 110
SALMON CREEK FALLS - 100
SALMON LA SAC - 148
SALMON MEADOWS - 151
SALMON RIVER EVERGREEN PARK - 92
SALMON SHORE RESORT - 190
SALT CREEK RECREATION AREA - 196
SALTWATER STATE PARK - 214
SAM'S TRAILER & RV PARK - 185
SAN JUAN ISLAND/LAKEDALE CAMPGROUND - 206
SAN JUAN ISLAND/SAN JUAN MARINA RESORT - 206
SAN JUAN ISLAND/SNUG HARBOR MARINA RESORT - 206
SAND BAR MOBILE & RV PARK - 50
SAND BEACH - 101
SAND BEACH PARKING - 101
SAND CASTLE RV PARK - 175
SAND PRAIRIE - 100
SAND-LO MOTEL & TRAILER PARK - 175
SANDS TRAILER PARK - 41
SAWMILL FLAT - 183
SCENIC BEACH STATE PARK - 224
SCHAFER STATE PARK - 180
SCHROEDER - 75
SCHWARZ PARK/DORENA LAKE - 51
SCOTTS FRUIT STAND & RV PARK - 143
SCOUT LAKE - 116
SEA & SAND RV PARK - 55

SEA BIRD RV PARK - 40
SEA PERCH RV PARK & CAMPGROUND - 131
SEA PORT RV PARK - 48
SEA RANCH RESORT - 45
SEADRIFT MOTEL & CAMPGROUND - 87
SEAL ROCK - 139
SEAL ROCKS TRAILER COVE - 127
SEAQUEST STATE PARK - 143
SEATTLE SOUTH KOA - 207
SELMAC LAKE - 75
SEQUIM BAY RESORT - 208
SEQUIM BAY STATE PARK - 208
SEQUIM WEST RV PARK & MOTEL - 209
SHADES BY THE SEA - 191
SHADOW BAY - 100
SHADOWS RV PARK & CAMPGROUND - 212
SHADY ACRES RV PARK - 47
SHADY DELL - 100
SHADY PINES RESORT - 151
SHADY REST RV PARK - 124
SHADY TRAILS - 131
SHADY TREE RV PARK - 196
SHAMROCK MOBILE HOME VILLAGE - 62
SHAW ISLAND/SOUTH BEACH COUNTY PARK - 206
SHEEP SPRINGS HORSE CAMP - 43
SHELTON - 67
SHERON ESTATES MOBILE PARK - 113
SHERWOOD - 102
SHERWOOD FOREST KOA - 54
SHERWOOD HILLS ADULT RV PARK - 136
SHORE ACRES RESORT - 146
SHORELINE RESORT & TRAILER COURT - 160
SHOREWOOD TRAVEL TRAILER VILLAGE - 122
SILTCOOS LAKE RESORT - 65
SILVER BEACH RESORT - 146
SILVER FALLS - 114
SILVER FALLS - 158
SILVER FIR - 161
SILVER KING RESORT - 196
SILVER LAKE MOTEL & RESORT - 143
SILVER SALMON RESORT - 185
SILVER SHORES RV PARK - 159
SILVER SPRINGS - 158
SIMAX GROUP CAMP - 52
SISTERS KOA - 116
SKOOKUM LAKE - 61
SLEEPY HOLLOW RV PARK - 111
SLIDE - 120
SLIDE CREEK - 38
SMILING RIVER - 43
SMITTY'S ISLAND RETREAT - 197
SMOKEY POINT RV PARK - 159
SMOKEY TRAIL RV CAMPSITE - 213
SNOQUALMIE RIVER CAMPGROUND - 159
SNUG HARBOR - 40
SOAP LAKES SMOKIAM CAMPGROUND - 181
SODA SPRINGS - 183
SOLEDUCK - 196

TRASK RIVER MOTOR HOME PARK - 122
TRETTEVIKS TRAILER PARK - 185
TRILLIUM LAKE - 73
TRONSEN - 173
TROUT CREEK - 119
TUCKER PARK - 79
TULALIP MILLSITE - 164
TUMALO - 37
TUMWATER - 173
TURLO - 164
TURN ISLAND STATE PARK - 206
TWANOH STATE PARK - 137
TWENTYFIVE MILE CREEK RESORT - 145
TWENTYFIVE MILE CREEK STATE PARK - 145
TWIN CEDARS RV PARK - 207
TWIN HARBORS STATE PARK - 222
TWIN LAKES RESORT - 117
TWIN RIVERS VACATION PARK - 113
TWIN SPRUCE RV PARK - 165
TYE CANYON - 210
TYEE - 66
TYEE - 118
TYEE MOTEL & RV PARK - 185
UKIAH-DALE FOREST - 123
UMPQUA BEACH RESORT - 110
UMPQUA LIGHTHOUSE - 111
UNION CREEK - 108
UNION CREEK CAMPGROUND - 35
UNITY LAKE - 124
UNITY MOTEL & TRAILER PARK - 124
UPPER BEAVER LAKE - 216
VALLEY FALLS STORE & CAMPGROUND - 88
VALLEY OF THE ROGUE - 75
VAN RIPER'S RESORT & RV PARK - 186
VANTAGE KOA - 220
VENICE RV PARK - 45
VENICE RV PARK - 114
VERLOT - 164
VIENTO - 79
VILLADOM MOBILE HOME PARK - 129
VILLAGE TRAILER PARK - 41
VOLCANO VIEW CAMPGROUND - 219
WAHTUM LAKE - 103
WALLACE FALLS STATE PARK - 169
WALLOWA LAKE - 83
WALT'S COZY CAMP - 49
WALTON LAKE - 108
WALUPT LAKE - 193
WAR CREEK - 218
WASHINGTON PARK - 135
WATER WHEEL CAMPGROUND - 49
WATERFRONT MARINA - 138
WATERS EDGE CAMPGROUND - 187
WAXMYRTLE (SILTCOOS) - 66
WAYSIDE RV & MOBILE PARK - 66
WEBB PARK - 102
WELCOME INN TRAILER & RV PARK - 196
WENATCHEE RIVER COUNTY PARK - 221

246

WENBERG STATE PARK - 213
WEST DAVIS LAKE - 52
WEST FORK MILLER RIVER - 210
WEST FORK SAN POIL - 216
WEST SOUTH TWIN - 91
WESTERN SHORES MOTEL & TRAILER PARK - 165
WESTERNER MOTOR HOME PARK - 125
WESTGATE RV PARK & MOTEL - 175
WESTPORT CITY PARK - 222
WESTWIND RESORT - 186
WHALEN'S RV PARK - 193
WHALESHEAD RV PARK - 40
WHISKEY SPRINGS - 41
WHISPERING FALLS - 80
WHISPERING PINES RV PARK - 171
WHISTLER'S BEND - 113
WHITCOMB CREEK - 119
WHITE HORSE - 76
WHITE RIVER CAMPGROUND - 159
WHITEFISH HORSE CAMP - 53
WHITTAKER CREEK - 94
WILD MARE HORSE CAMP - 99
WILDCAT - 108
WILDERNESS VILLAGE - 153
WILDERNESS WEST RESORT - 150
WILDWOOD RESORT - 141
WILDWOOD SENIOR RV PARK - 175
WILEY CREEK - 164
WILLABY - 200
WILLIAM M. TUGMAN - 111
WILLIAMS LAKE RESORT - 146
WILLIAMSON RIVER - 49
WILLIAMSON RIVER TRAILER PARK - 49
WILLOW LAKE RESORT - 42
WILLOW POINT CAMPGROUND - 33
WILLOW PRAIRIE HORSE CAMP - 42
WILLOW VISTA MOBILE/RV PARK - 208
WILLOWS - 184
WILLOWS TRAILER VILLAGE - 181
WILSON'S COTTAGES & CAMP - 67
WINBERRY CREEK - 93
WINCHUCK - 40
WINDMILL INN & TRAILER COURT - 176
WINDY COVE COUNTY PARK - 111
WISEMAN'S MOBILE COURT - 86
WISH POOSH - 149
WOAHINK LAKE RV RESORT - 66
WOLF CREEK - 69
WOLF CREEK - 103
WOOD PARK - 102
WOODBURN I-5 RV PARK - 131
WOODLAND ECHOES FAMILY RESORT - 47
WOODWARD - 129
WYETH - 46
YAKIMA KOA - 226
YAKIMA SPORTSMAN STATE PARK - 226
YELLOWBOTTOM - 119
YUKWAH - 119

LOOKING FOR A REAL BACK TO NATURE
EXPERIENCE?

FREE CAMPGROUNDS OF WASHINGTON &
OREGON by KiKi Canniff details the region's
hundreds of unimproved campgrounds. These
campgrounds will appeal most to people who
camp to escape civilization. Most cost free
sites don't offer showers, hookups or other
civilized luxuries, just the bare necessities
and a chance to commune with nature.

GENERAL INDEX

41, 42, 44, 46, 48, 49, 50, 51, 52,
53, 54, 56, 57, 59, 60, 61, 63, 64,
65, 66, 67, 68, 69, 72, 73, 75, 76,
77, 78, 81, 82, 83, 84, 85, 86, 97,
88, 89, 90, 91, 92, 93, 95, 98, 99,
100, 102, 103, 104, 106, 107, 108,
110, 111, 113, 115, 116, 117, 119,
123, 124, 125, 128, 130, 136, 138,
139, 140, 141, 143, 144, 145, 146,
147, 148, 149, 150, 151, 152, 154,
155, 157, 159, 162, 163, 165, 166,
171, 172, 173, 175, 177, 178, 179,
180, 181, 182, 186, 187, 188, 189,
190, 193, 195, 197, 199, 200, 201,
202, 203, 204, 205, 206, 210, 211,
212, 213, 215, 216, 217, 218, 220,
223, 224, 225.

Lake (no motors) - 60, 61, 63, 64,
69, 72, 73, 76, 77, 82, 91, 95, 99,
102, 106, 108, 116, 123, 128, 202,
218.

Laundry facilities - 31, 32, 33,
34, 35, 36, 37, 38, 39, 40, 41, 42,
43, 44, 45, 47, 48, 49, 50, 51, 54,
55, 57, 62, 63, 64, 65, 66, 67, 68,
69, 70, 71, 73, 74, 75, 76,78, 81,
84, 85, 86, 87, 88, 89, 90, 91, 92,
93, 95, 96, 97, 98, 100, 101, 103,
104, 105, 106, 107, 108, 109, 110,
111, 112, 113, 114, 115, 116, 117,
118, 119, 120, 121, 122, 124, 125,
126, 127, 128, 129, 130, 131, 135,
136, 137, 138, 139, 140, 141, 142,
143, 145, 146, 147, 148, 149, 150,
151, 152, 153, 154, 155, 157,
159,. 160, 161, 163, 165, 166,
167, 168, 169, 170, 171, 173, 174,
175, 176, 177, 179, 180, 181, 184,
185, 186, 187, 188, 189, 190, 193,
194, 195, 196, 197, 198, 199, 200,
201, 202, 203, 204, 205, 207, 208,
209, 210, 211, 212, 213, 214, 215,
216, 217, 218, 219, 220, 221, 222,
223, 224, 225, 226.

Ocean access - 34, 35, 39, 40, 43,
44, 45, 47, 48, 50, 55, 63, 64, 65,
66, 68, 70, 71, 97, 98, 101, 102,
104, 105, 110, 111, 121, 122, 126,
127, 131, 135, 136, 137, 138, 156,
160, 165, 166, 167, 158, 174, 175,
184, 185, 186, 190, 191, 192, 193,
194, 195, 196, 197, 199, 201, 205,
208, 209, 221, 222, 223, 224.

Off-road vehicles - 63, 64, 66, 98,

99, 101, 148, 150, 212.

Oregon cities - 30-131.
    Adel - 31
    Albany - 31
    Arlington - 31
    Ashland - 32
    Astoria - 33
    Aurora - 34
    Azalea - 34
    Baker City - 34
    Bandon - 35
    Beaver - 36
    Bend - 36
    Blue River - 37
    Bly - 38
    Brookings - 38
    Burns - 40
    Butte Falls - 41
    Camp Sherman - 42
    Cannon Beach - 43
    Canyonville - 45
    Cascade Locks - 45
    Cascade Summit - 46
    Cave Junction - 46
    Charleston - 47
    Chemult - 48
    Chiloquin - 48
    Condon - 49
    Coos Bay - 50
    Coquille - 50
    Corbett - 51
    Cottage Grove - 51
    Crater Lake Ntl. Park - 52
    Crescent - 52
    Crescent Lake - 52
    Creswell - 54
    Culver - 54
    Dale - 54
    Dallas - 54
    Dee - 55
    Depoe Bay - 55
    Detroit - 55
    Diamond Lake - 57
    Dodson - 58
    Drain - 58
    Dufur - 58
    Eddyville - 58
    Elgin - 58
    Elsie - 59
    Enterprise - 59
    Estacada - 59
    Eugene - 62
    Florence - 63
    Fort Klamath - 66
    Fossil - 67
    Fox - 67
    Frenchglen - 67

BOOKS ABOUT OREGON & WASHINGTON
by KiKi Canniff

THE BEST FREE HISTORIC ATTRACTIONS IN OREGON & WASHINGTON. Includes the region's best ghost towns, covered bridges, aging lighthouses, museums, pioneer wagon trails, historic towns, archaeological digs, Indian artifact collections, railroad memorabilia, pioneer homes and more! *"KiKi Canniff is an expert on freebies"* **Woman's World Magazine.** ($10.95)

FREE CAMPGROUNDS OF WASHINGTON & OREGON; Third Edition. This lightweight guide details the region's 700 free campgrounds. A terrific book for folks who enjoy camping close to nature. *"...very well done, easy to read and to understand ... the cost of this book is saved with the first campground used!"* **This Week Magazine.** ($8.95)

A CAMPER'S GUIDE TO OREGON & WASHINGTON; A guide to the region's pay campgrounds. Perfect for campers who want showers, hookups or other civilized facilities. Opening material introduces the region's variety of terrains, climates, scenery and elevations. Each of the 1500 campground listings has complete details on facilities available plus easy to follow directions. *This handy guide belongs on every Northwest camper's 'must have' list."* **The Chronicle.** ($12.95)

THE NORTHWEST GOLFER; A guide to the public golf courses in Washington & Oregon. Details the region's 252 public courses. Includes number of holes each course offers, total yardage, par, costs, rental information, what the terrain is like, type of hazards, facilities offered, directions, reservation information, and schedule. *"A HOLE IN ONE ... The whole information package about Northwest golf."* **The Oregonian.** ($9.95)

ABOUT THE AUTHOR

KiKi Canniff is a Portland writer who specializes in recreational attractions found in Oregon & Washington. She is an avid camper who enjoys hiking, golf, nature, history and exploring.

COMING SOON:

**THE BEST FREE PLACES TO TAKE KIDS
IN OREGON & WASHINGTON**

**THE BEST FREE COASTAL ATTRACTIONS
IN OREGON & WASHINGTON**

**THE BEST FREE NATURAL & SCENIC
ATTRACTIONS IN OREGON & WASHINGTON**

To receive advance information on these and other books by Kiki Canniff send your name and address to Ki² Books, P.O. Box 13322, Portland, Oregon 97213.

ORDER COUPON

Please send:

___CAMPER'S GUIDE TO OR/WA @ $12.95 ea.　　　　_____

___FREE CAMPGROUNDS OF WA /OR @ $8.95 ea. _____

___ Camper's special - both guides $18.00/set　　_____

___BEST FREE HISTORIC ATTRACTIONS IN OR/WA;
　　Favorite Freebies Vol. 1 @ $10.95 ea.　　　_____

___THE NORTHWEST GOLFER @ $9.95 ea.　　　　_____

Shipping ___2.00___

TOTAL ENCLOSED _____

Name _____

Address _____

City/State/Zip Code _____

Send this order coupon to Ki² Enterprises, P.O. Box 13322,
Portland, Oregon 97213

✄---✄

Please send:

___CAMPER'S GUIDE TO OR/WA @ $12.95 ea.　　　_____

___FREE CAMPGROUNDS OF WA /OR @ $8.95 ea. _____

_____Camper's special - both guides $18.00/set　　_____

___BEST FREE HISTORIC ATTRACTIONS IN OR/WA;
　　Favorite Freebies Vol. 1 @ $10.95 ea.　　　_____

___THE NORTHWEST GOLFER @ $9.95 ea.　　　　_____

Shipping ___2.00___

TOTAL ENCLOSED _____

Name _____

Address _____

City/State/Zip Code _____

Send this order coupon to Ki² Enterprises, P.O. Box 13322,
Portland, Oregon 97213